The Post-Confessionals

The Post-Confessionals

Conversations with American Poets
of the Eighties

EDITED BY
Earl G. Ingersoll
Judith Kitchen
Stan Sanvel Rubin

Rutherford ● Madison ● Teaneck
Fairleigh Dickinson University Press
London and Toronto: Associated University Presses

Associated University Presses
440 Forsgate Drive
Cranbury, NJ 08512

Associated University Presses
25 Sicilian Avenue
London WC1A 2QH, England

Associated University Presses
P.O. Box 488, Port Credit
Mississauga, Ontario
Canada L5G 4M2

The paper used in this publication meets the requirements
of the American National Standard for Permanence of Paper
for Printed Library Materials Z39.48–1984

Library of Congress Cataloging-in-Publication Data

The Post-confessionals.

Bibliography: p.
1. American poetry—20th century—History and criticism. 2. Poets, American—20th century—Interviews. 3. Poetry—Authorship. I. Ingersoll, Earl G., 1938– . II. Kitchen, Judith.
III. Rubin, Stan Sanvel.
PS325.P6   1989   811'.54'09   87-46424
ISBN 0-8386-3330-7 (alk. paper)

PRINTED IN THE UNITED STATES OF AMERICA

Contents

6   CONTENTS

Preface

In a large, collaborative project such as this, we have many individuals and organizations that deserve at least a small expression of our gratitude for their assistance and contributions.

First, we owe the largest and most obvious debt to the poets themselves whose responses to questions put to them by a variety of interviewers are clearly the heart of this book. In all cases, they found time in their busy schedules to assist us with the complex task of devising a print equivalent for their videotaped remarks. In a similar vein, we wish to thank the interviewers who also helped us with the editing of the conversations in which they participated: Gregory Fitz Gerald, William Heyen, and A. Poulin, Jr.

Second, we wish to acknowledge our gratitude to those journals in which a number of these conversations first appeared.

In addition, we owe a debt of gratitude to the State University of New York for its generous support of the Brockport Writers Forum and Videotape Library. Established in 1967 under the leadership of Philip L. Gerber, the chairman of the English Department at the time, and Gregory Fitz Gerald, its founding director, the "Forum" has become an internationally renowned institution, attracting literary luminaries such as Nobel laureate Isaac Bashevis Singer and promising luminaries of the twenty-first century. The Forum Library now contains well over two hundred videotaped interviews with a wide-ranging group of poets, fiction writers, dramatists, and literary critics, providing a valuable resource for contemporary and future scholars. Its holdings have been catalogued by Professors Joseph McElrath in *Resources for American Literary Study* (1976) and David Hale in *Bulletin of Bibliography* (1985).

Finally, we wish to thank all those who have encouraged and assisted us in this project, a list too long to include here. We would be remiss, however, if we omitted the names of several colleagues. A special debt of gratitude is owed to Robert J. Gemmett, Dean of Letters and Sciences, for his unstinting support of the Writers Forum. We wish to thank also Frank Filardo, Director of Television Services, for his invaluable technical expertise. And to our families, we offer a special thanks for yet unacknowledged support for this project, which at times seemed to have no end.

The Post-Confessionals

Introduction

Beyond the "War Zone"

This collection of lively "discussions of craft" with poets from the Brockport Writers Forum Videotape Library makes no claim to being all-inclusive. Yet the collective voices of the poets recorded here—voices sometimes meditative, sometimes passionate, often surprisingly personal—add up to more than any single voice, and, together, they tell us much about the state of American poetry and poetics today. Diverse though they are in subject matter, style, and personality, the poets represented in this collection have much in common, besides the fact that they have all been recent guests of the nationally known Writers Forum program at the SUNY College at Brockport, now in its twenty-second season. All are important contemporaries, who have achieved significant recognition, including honors such as the Guggenheim Fellowship, the Lamont Prize, the National Critics Circle Prize, and the American Book Award. All have published at least one major book (most several), and all are still actively writing and publishing poems in the major journals; many have new books just released or announced for the near future. Among them are the poets who will shape—who are shaping—what will be known as the poetry of this period. Though the age range here is from the later fifties to the early thirties, most may be considered "younger" poets in the acceptable sense of that perhaps overused term. Many of them are included in Dave Smith and David Bottoms's *The Morrow Anthology of Younger Poets* (1985) and in William Heyen's *Contemporary American Poets: The Generation of 2000* (1985). (Still others of the poets here missed the January 1940 cutoff birthdate of the Morrow anthology by a matter of a few months.)

When poets such as Robert Frost, Wallace Stevens, and William Stafford all published their first books after the age of forty, it is clear that age alone cannot be the determining factor in assessing the influence, let alone the accomplishment, of a poet. What is perhaps more significant is that the poets in this collection share a common inheritance; this may be the bond that, more than anything else, truly marks a "generation" of writers. Looked at in this way, the writers gathered here, despite some disparity in age, can all be seen to belong to what James E. B. Breslin, in his essay "Poetry and Criticism in the Early Eighties," has called the "fourth generation—born around 1940 and beginning to write around 1960"; they are writers who "seem to have grown up fascinated by the generation of innovators who preceded them" (1984, 253). Breslin resorts to metaphor to describe what he sees as distinguishing the current "scene" from its immediate predecessors:

> If American poetry in the middle fifties resembled a peaceful public park on a pleasant Sunday afternoon, and if by the early sixties it had been transformed into a war zone, the air heavy with manifestos, then by the early eighties the atmosphere has lightened and the scene more resembles a small affluent town in Northern California. Anxiety about the economy or nuclear war occasionally darkens the mood, but the citizens are generally healthy, fit, stable and productive. No one seems moved by overweening ambition or any ambition to unsettle the way things are. Yet if there is a lack of risk-taking, there is plenty of life. (1984, 250).

If this reads rather more like a *Time* magazine encapsulation of post–World War II social history than it does an accurate summary of the contemporary poetry scene, it is only fair to point out that Breslin's book deals with the years 1945 to 1965, the period of transformation (as his title has it) from "Modern to Contemporary." The figures that concern him most recently include Ammons, Ashbery, Ginsberg, Lowell, Merrill, Snyder, Rich, and (James) Wright, among others; in other words, the "contemporary poets" who have become institutionalized, if not canonized. If it seems a bit odd that he makes no distinction, in this list (his own) of "established" poets, between poets living and dead, it is clear that he is not much interested in the poetry actually being written today; he accuses our younger poets of generalized blandness, a kind of heterogeneous security of place which precludes the kind of risk-taking that may lead to discovery:

> Beginning poets nowadays have a seductive variety of modes to choose from, as if in my imaginary small California town there were so many jobs, shops, restaurants, and recreative areas that one never had to leave it. (1984, 254)

Part of the legacy of the great twentieth-century modernist poets was a new sense of the poem as artifact, a triumph of self-reflexive form. In turn, the seeming explosion of poets in the sixties—the poets who immediately precede those featured in this collection—with their social-political-psychological programs (Snyder, Ginsberg, Bly), their forceful personalities, their passionate commitment to the individual life (Wright, Roethke), their probing of that life for its reservoirs of intensity which seemed like ultimate truth (Lowell, Berryman, Plath, Sexton), poses a special challenge for those who succeed them. A multitude of aesthetics competed for attention during that decade—some rooted in figures themselves established in the previous decade, the way those termed "the confessionals" seemed to have sprung from Lowell, and Ginsberg of the fifties became Ginsberg of "The Sixties"; others, like those of Bly and Snyder, seeming to promise some future renewal of consciousness for us all, nothing less than a new way of life. The poets who worked and flourished in the sixties form a composite figure of almost frightening energy and accomplishment for anyone coming after them. At the same time, the poets in this collection are necessarily aware both of the failure to transform public awareness and of the personal disasters that overtook some of their most famous predecessors. Theirs is a more guarded vision.

In his subtle and provocative study, *Self and Sensibility in Contemporary American Poetry,* Charles Altieri identifies what he sees as the "dominant poetic mode of the late seventies" and laments what he considers its shortcomings:

> The central aim of the art is not to interpret experience but to extend language to its limits in order to establish poignant awareness of what lies beyond words. There is virtually never any sustained act of formal, dialectical thinking or any elaborate, artificial construction that cannot be imagined as taking place in, or at least extending from, settings in naturalistically conceived scenes. (1984, 11)

These poems, he contends, "must clearly illustrate the controlling hand of the craftsman, but the craft must remain subtle and unobtrusive." Craft, Altieri argues, valued in and of itself, serves only to shut off all but preformulated notions of self and experience; most of all, it serves to close off thought and experimentation which might lead to new discoveries. Like Breslin, he accuses contemporary poets of not taking risks:

> By insisting on specific issues and by placing authority within the qualities of personal experience, they risk very little, probably too little, that invites the de-mystifying spirit. (1984, 14)

This is not the place to deal with Altieri's challenging and wide-ranging argument, other than to commend it to readers. It is fair to say, however, that, along with Breslin, Altieri subscribes to what might be termed a "burn-out theory," explaining what he sees as a current poetic malaise in terms of the social inheritance of the sixties:

> Ours is an age that must come to terms with failed expectations and, worse, the guilt of recognizing why we held such ambitious dreams. So it is not

simply the case that we reject ideas that poetry can help transform the self or the world because these ideals are anachronistic delusions. It was we, not others, who held these illusions. (1984, 37)

To claim that the legacy of the sixties is an arena in which all of what have seemed the meaningful questions about poetry—its relationship to society, its value as truth—have been, if not answered, at least asked so brilliantly that it hardly seems possible, so soon, to ask them again with any power, is to agree with such critics as Breslin and Altieri. Yet another legacy of the sixties may be that, precisely by throwing open to question all the received dogmas concerning poetry, the ferment of this period restored to us the very act of questioning as a poetic act; not only the questioning of society and values, but the questioning of poetry itself as an activity of the human mind and will.

Certainly, the stance of critics in our time is one of suspicion; it may not be too much to say that the poets who followed hard on the sixties, who came to their own poetic maturity under the influence—or against the pull—of those dynamic voices, have been first of all suspicious both of themselves and of their chosen art. Have poets ever been, as a whole, better educated, more aware of critical and linguistic theories, more prepared to view the adoption (or creation) of a style as an ethical act? More ready to judge themselves harshly for the limitations of the personal style as well as the subject matter they have chosen? Have poets, to put it simply, ever written more about the poetic act and its ramifications? (Pick up any leading poetry journal and weigh the space devoted to essays, reviews, and letters against that which seems to contain fresh and com-pelling poetry.)

The loud and public "poetry wars" of the sixties seem to have turned inward, in our time, rather than to have disappeared. There may be much more tolerance for a wide range of poetic projects, but poets today are as likely to berate one another for the use of a pronoun as for a political stance—or rather, they will do both with equal tentativeness or vehemence. They will also, some of them, write many pages of prose in defense of the poetic stance they have chosen and those they admire.

If all of this seems rather eclectic, disorganized, and muted compared to the brilliantly focussed chaos of the sixties, it is not necessarily a sign of enervation or disarray in the ongoing venture. Rather, the current intro-spection of American poetry—which manifests itself not so much in the themes and subject matter of that poetry as in the way poets think, write, and talk about it—reflects a condition not of torpor, but of searching, an attitude not of complacency, but of a new assumption of responsibility for the future of poetry. The conversations in this book, at any rate, reflect an honesty and intensity of commitment which suggest that the calling of poet is, in our nonapocalyptic decade, as serious a business as it ever has been. The voices in this book—which are the voices "behind" as well as "within" some of the finest poems being written today—do not only call us to listen closely to strong individual talents; taken together, they point us toward the future of an art that may be in a profound state of transition.

"Representative Voices": The Post-Confessionals

The year 1970 marks the first appearance of book-length collections by several of the "senior" figures in this collection: Charles Wright's *The Grave of the Right Hand*, Michael Harper's *Dear John, Dear Coltrane*, William Matthews's *Ruining the New Road*, and Stanley Plumly's *In the Outer Dark*. Lisel Mueller's first book, *Dependencies*, appeared in 1965; her second, *The Private Life*, was awarded the 1976 Lamont Prize. They are all poets—along with Linda Pastan, Nancy Willard (who won the Devins Award in 1967), and Carl Dennis—who came to critical attention during the seventies. Poets such as Jonathan Holden, Stephen Dunn, and Gregory Orr published books in the seventies but have come to prominence in the eighties. Still others, including Rita Dove, Katha Pollitt, and Edward Hirsch, published their first books during the eighties and have rather quickly attracted critical attention and major awards. Two of the more idiosyncratic poets represented here—Philip Schultz and Paul Zimmer—have achieved prominence in contrasting ways. Zimmer's career (which actually began in 1962) depended on a series of small-press publications throughout the seventies, during which his reputation grew to a near legend among his fellow poets; in the eighties, he has achieved both university-press publication and major recognition, in 1985, from the Academy of American Poets. Schultz's first book, *Like Wings* (1978), the product of years of labor, was nominated for a National Book Award and the Pulitzer Prize in 1978 and won the American Academy and Institute of Arts and Letters award. His second, *Deep within the Ravine* (1984), received the Lamont prize. All of these poets' careers, whatever the routes taken, have come to be recognized as among the most significant of the eighties.

If this collection represents what might be termed the "mainstream" of American poetry during the seventies and eighties, then it is a mainstream no longer almost entirely white and male in description and New Critical in disposition. This reflects the healthy change in the poetry "establishment" that began in the sixties and continued as perhaps the single most significant fact of the poetry of the seventies. This alone should serve to alert us that the poetry of the present day is part of a continuing revolution, albeit now a quiet one, the same "postmodern" expansion of the canon (and questioning of whether there can be a canon) that has overtaken, one by one, all the arts. The reader of the present volume will find ample evidence, too, that, contrary to some who still insist on cavilling against "academic" poetry, the academy today harbors poets of diverse impulses and influences. Indeed, this collection should contribute to breaking down what remains of the always largely fanciful and essentially Romantic distinction between "academic" and "nonacademic" poetry, as if there were two clearly identifiable, constantly warring monoliths. The "language poets" and "performance poets" of today maintain their own versions of a myth of separation, but partisans of both must inevitably justify the activities of their favored ones in what are recognizable as the most "academic" of polemics. (Barrett Watten's 1985 *Total Syntax*, for example, published as part of a university press series entitled "Poetics of the New," begins with a highly informed survey of the Russian Formalists and ends with a discussion of Wittgenstein, Duchamps, and the Surrealists, among others. The concept of "literary criticism" which the book attacks is one at least a generation out of date among literary critics.)

What is most clear is that poets of the current period do not lack for ideas—but not the visionary, "there-is-an-answer" ideas of some of their predecessors. What these poets lack in fervor (and there is fervor among them) they more than make up for in intellectual honesty, perhaps their identifying characteristic as a group. The reader will be struck by the moments of honest confusion as well as by the frequent lucidity of these discussions. These are poets who, by and large, at least want to know where they're going, and that there's a reason for going there. They are not afraid of always learning—not just in terms of self-revelation, but in terms of the history and possibilities of their art. Yet they don't want that art to become needlessly severed from the realities of history and the claims of daily experience.

What, then, concerns them? This question, best answered by the discussions themselves, suggests three broadly related areas that are given concrete shape and individual nuance by each poet. Each is an area of concern that establishes a significant distance from Modernist tenets and tells us what these poets have made, and are making, of the inheritance of the sixties. Together, they define a mode we can term "post-confessional."

1. PERSONAL EXPERIENCE AND AUTHENTICITY.

More than anything else, the question that preoccupies these poets, and that identifies them as "post-confessional," is the question of *sin-*

cerity. The "I" is cast into suspicion. Altieri attributes what he takes to be the crisis of authenticity in contemporary poetry to the "heritage of failed prophetic ambitions" of the sixties as well as to "basic emotional problems inescapable within a narcissistic society" (1984, 210). Poets themselves—including two in this book, Stanley Plumly and Jonathan Holden—have cited this as a major issue. As Holden puts it:

> The more personal a poem is—the more a poem purports to be about the self of the author—the more the question of how sincere the poem sounds will be a factor in our judgment of it. (1980, 10).

The great terrain of subjectivity and autobiography whose opening was signaled by Robert Lowell's *Life Studies* (1959) seems, a quarter of a century later, to be something of an abandoned battlefield strewn with unexploded mines. While it is often highly personal experience that first prompts these poets to poetry—Lisel Mueller, for example, speaks of beginning to write at age twenty-nine in order to express her grief at her mother's death—the general thrust is nearly always away from the personal and toward something sensed to be larger. Mueller's emblematically titled second book, *The Private Life,* published in 1976, has, she tells us, "two main springs . . . the domestic, the experience of family, my husband, my two daughters" *and* "the Vietnam War." While this mix of personal and public may not sound so far from the spirit of Lowell, the poets in this collection share a modesty about the position of the self, a tentativeness about the self as the source of ultimate discovery, which is as far from *Life Studies* and the work of Berryman, Sexton, and Plath as it is from the prophetic voices of Ginsberg and Bly. As Michael Harper puts it with characteristic directness: "I think all poets are being self-indulgent when they write too much about their own lives." Stephen Dunn, widely praised in recent years for his distinctive synthesis of the intimate and the communal, agrees:

> The closer you attempt to get to your own experience, the more the dangers are clear—solipsism, self-congratulation, all the perils of the "I" voice. So whenever I can deal with the personal somewhat directly and make it available in larger terms for others, the personal being overheard, rather than that kind of private impulse of the personal, then I'm pleased.

Some of the most powerful and surprising poets in this collection may seem to be exceptions. When Philip Schultz says, "I am a prisoner of my own private mythology," he doesn't, nevertheless, mean that he's engaged solely in an autobiographical exercise; the highly personal archetypes he creates move us as if they *were* the life, a form of risk-taking akin to, but not be identified with, "confessional" self-revelation. Even though he is a self-conscious practitioner of the lyric poet's impulse to seek "the origin of self in past moments," Gregory Orr understands the lyric poet's stance as itself a representative one, expressing "the very human longing for the unconditional." At what might be thought of as opposite extremes in this collection, Charles Wright's work is highly personal and introspective in a manner suggestive of traditional meditative poetry, while Paul Zimmer invents vivid personae—and reinvents himself *as* persona—in order to explore what are at times highly personal events and subjective states in the guise of a playful impersonality. ("If it's personal," Nancy Willard says, "I would probably transform it into story or persona, to get distance.")

In their own ways, all of these poets are attempting to respond to a condition in which the self seems as much a danger as a promise. While this notion would not be alien to poets of another time—Robert Frost, to name one—it is a new combination of self-consciousness and self-restraint that marks the poets in this volume. The risk they take—and their dilemma—is perhaps best expressed by Stanley Plumly in nearly paradoxical terms:

> I would like to think that my poems are preoccupied with the self and the I, and yet are not egocentric. I place myself at the center, but I also see myself as a kind of invisible presence in the poem. I'm not really in the way of the material.

2. AUDIENCE AND HISTORY.

"The modern poet has lost confidence in his readers," John Berryman could write in 1960, "but so far from causing him to reduce his demands therefore, this loss of confidence has led to an *increase* in his demands. Good poetry has never been easy to read with advanced understanding, but it has seldom been made so deliberately difficult" (1976, 271–72). Nothing could be farther from the attitude of the poets represented here. The urge to inclusiveness distinguishes their approach to audience. As Paul Zimmer notes, "I don't believe people who say that they write for themselves. When you write, it's implicit in the act that you want to share." One of the reasons he writes, according to Stephen Dunn, is "to make those connections between people, to have people at least *believe* what I say."

The commitment to audience is nearly the equivalent of an ethical commitment. Edward Hirsch, one of the youngest poets here, expresses it well:

I love the breakthroughs of confessionalism, the emotional risks, the way poets like Lowell and Berryman and Plath began writing about their own experiences. I don't think we should underestimate the importance of that and I want to keep some of the risk and largeness and passion and the way they brought into poetry subjects that had previously been excluded. At the same time, I became uncomfortable with the fact that there weren't enough other people in that poetry, and there were ways in which poets were prizing their own experience over other people's experience.

Hirsch goes on to express perfectly what we have termed the "post-confessional" impulse:

> . . . we live as multiple selves, and we want to bring these things into poetry. I love poetry that has a personal risk, poetry where there is a lot at stake; but I dislike the activity of centering your own suffering above the suffering of all others. We do have to speak about our deeper, inner lives; at the same time, I think we want to be representative voices and speak about our place and our culture. That means that in writing post-confessional poetry we can learn from confessional poetry the subjects that have been circumscribed and ways to write about them so that we can write about our deeper and darker selves without being grounded or limited to that material.

These words express the attitude of many of the poets here. There seems to be a common desire to amplify the positive (and very traditional) function of poetry as a salutary force for the spirit. A studiedly "impersonal" poet such as Carl Dennis puts it in terms of an old word which has fallen out of the vocabulary of contemporary critics:

> That's the kind of progression I like to see; poets taking on the challenge of feeling empathy for those who would ordinarily be difficult to empathize with.

What is interesting is the distinctively political edge in the notion of an "expansive" empathy that can connect the reader to lives unlike his/her own. There is, throughout this volume, a sense of urgency to this task. As Lisel Mueller notes, "There's no way anymore for the individual to escape from History, the public life we all share." And Michael Harper warns us:

> . . . to be careful of making too much of what we think to be our own importance. This is an *American* phenomenon, by the way, and it goes along with the innocence we as a people have. . . . which is one of the reasons why we're always surprised.

The awareness of the political dimension is pervasive among these poets, but it is not typically a polemical or ideological matter. Rather, the political insights of these poets are diffused throughout their work, at once quieter and more thoughtful than the often heated confrontations of an earlier period. If it may seem to lack the passion of particular causes, it is nevertheless a poetry which characteristically accepts the essentially political ramifications of any public utterance of language in our time. There is skepticism about the overtly political—Charles Wright, speaking of Vietnam, comments, "I think poetry can change your life; but it can't change a war, or it couldn't change that one"—but there is also a sense of responsibility. Just as history is seen as inescapable, the very act of addressing an audience is recognized by most of these poets as having an implicitly political dimension. Nowhere, perhaps, is this nonpolemical commitment better expressed than by Katha Pollitt:

> There's politics and politics. I doubt that I'd sit down and write a poem against nuclear war or in favor of the ERA, because there isn't much to say on those subjects that can't be said in a magazine article. But politics is more than newspaper headlines. It's how you see the human condition in our time, your view of life.

And Nancy Willard, who in some ways offers a contrast to Pollitt in subject matter and style (for example, the two differ sharply on Jung), says that her own poems are:

> . . . political in the broad sense. I like the epigram, "To the fish, all lines are political." I can't really separate life and politics.

3. LANGUAGE AND FORM.

The sense of responsibility outlined above—the general awareness of what Carl Dennis terms "the social function of the imagination"—might seem to call for an unadventurous use of language. The poet, after all, is no longer innocent concerning the relationship of language to history. These poets share Rita Dove's insight that "history is the way we perceive it, and we do perceive it through words." It is heartening, therefore, to realize how fully committed these poets are to exploring all the formal resources of their art—form being, perhaps, the area in which the true "freedom" of the poet is manifest. Dove's fascination with "the way language enters into history . . . a word that determines whether you live or die," as her own rich music testifies, points to a new sense of the *possibilities* of poetry to give imaginative voice to what is most urgent in communal as well as individual psychic life. The urge toward expression is tempered here by a strong sense of the need for communication. As

Michael Waters says, "If language is a tool for communication, poetry becomes an extremely precise tool."

The desire to discover forms that will embody more "objective" truths than organicist notions allow for is exemplified by Jonathan Holden in his recent book, *Style and Authenticity in Postmodern Poetry:*

> When "form" is conceived and applied as a category in conjunction with the word "content," "content" must likewise be redefined so as to include more than some mysterious "feeling" revealed by "form." It must refer also to a category of subject matter. (1986, 16)

Holden takes issue with Robert Pinsky's *The Situation of Poetry*, which argues for a more discursive, rather than imagistic, poetic style. Pinsky's advocacy of "the prose virtues"—Clarity, Flexibility, Efficiency, Cohesiveness—nevertheless displays a similar concern that the poet not stray from shared experience of the world: "when poetry gets too far from prose, it may be in danger of choking itself on a thick, rich handful of words." (1976, 162)

Assumptions about form—its nature and function—help to define a generation. There is no area in which it is clearer that the art of poetry is in transition. The contemporary French theorist Lyotard has argued that the distinction between "the modern" and "the postmodern" lies precisely in what is asked of form; for both, the subject matter is "the unpresentable," but in the modern, "the form, because of its recognizable consistency, continues to offer to the reader or viewer matter for solace and pleasure." The postmodern, on the other hand, "is that which denies itself the solace of good forms" (1984, 81). According to this distinction, the "post-confessionals" stand somewhere between the two, dedicated to giving meaningful shape to language, but wary of too easy a celebration of the creative powers of the poet.

As described here, the poetic act, like the word "form," is double-sided. William Matthews speaks of "the private game of form as opposed to the public aspect of form that the reader gets." It is the former, he says, "which helps the poet write the poem." Again and again, form as the process of discovery *is* celebrated here. It is the arena of excitement, evoking some of the most vivid portions of these discussions, at the same time revealing its problematic nature:

> . . . it is almost sexual. It's almost a kind of pursuit, with the smell of the hunt. I'm fascinated by the shape that this poem is going to take, its form rather than its content. Of course, I'm very interested in what I'm going to reveal to myself . . . but the poet in me is very curious about the final shape of the poem. (Philip Schultz)

It's that mysterious rush of images and metaphors that I always have the fear will stop. (Linda Pastan)

If you were *in* chaos, you couldn't write it; it'd be pure turbulence. Poets are people who can get close enough to chaos to feel the rush of energy, that primordial power of the imagination, but they can control it within a form. (Robert Morgan)

Since I truly believe that considerations of form are at the heart of poetry, all considerations of poetry are considerations of form—I don't mean forms, but *form*—then one should try as hard as possible to generate forms that are one's own. (Charles Wright)

There has clearly been a renewal of interest in traditional forms, but this is by no means a "conservative" tendency; as poet and co-editor Judith Kitchen notes, "Mine is the first generation for whom form is an experiment." The poets here have the opposite of a programmatic approach; they are not a "movement." They want, most of all, to preserve what was gained by "free verse" while rediscovering the shaping power inherent in craft—the poet as *maker*:

You start with a draft which is a big mess with lots of stray strings that have to be snipped off. . . . That's where technique comes in—making a verbal pattern that is very tight. Then the poem stands up by itself like a little Christmas package with no strings left over. (Katha Pollitt)

I'm at the point in my life when I trust my craft enough to know that if I get a certain amount of raw material on the page I can make it into a poem. (Linda Pastan)

These poets seem to trust the poem; they don't want to restrain the poetic impulse by imposing *a priori* limits. Bruce Bennett, who is especially adept at finding a contemporary voice for traditional forms, understands what he's doing as an exhilarating sort of "freedom":

I've found that writing is an adventure; it's very exciting to sit down and not know what you're going to do. . . . I think that there is something in not sitting down to write a particular kind of poem that allows for that kind of freedom.

And Jonathan Holden, who as critic has written so much about poems, cautions:

I find that if one thinks too self-consciously about genre or *what* is a poem, one is apt to stop writing poems altogether. The best thing to do is to get into action and rely upon your sense of all the poems you've read for a sense of what a poem is.

Such faith in process finally may define the most important "risk" these poets of our cautious culture take.

The reader will discover many other points of correspondence and contrast here. Wright's belief that poems tend "toward the condition of circularity" points to a different conception of language from the claims of narrativity asserted, for example, by Stanley Plumly ("The English language is a narrative instrument"). There is a running "debate" between the narrative and lyric impulses (the latter forms the basis of an eloquent discussion by Gregory Orr). There are fascinating, sometimes unexpected, revelations of poetic influence, such as Katha Pollitt's acknowledgment of Tennyson, Robert Morgan's debt to Sandburg, Linda Pastan's early interest in Eliot, and Paul Zimmer's homage to Dickinson (who seems an even more important influence than Whitman on the poets here). In a way, this volume is an extended conversation with many common themes—the nature of a poetic education and the meaning of a poetic life, the experience of workshops and readings, the teaching of poetry, the aesthetics of the book, the keeping of journals, methods of revision, and many other matters both practical and theoretical that offer, for specialist and nonspecialist alike, a penetrating view of American poetry in the making.

Stan Sanvel Rubin
Director
The Writers Forum and Videotape Library
SUNY Brockport

Works Cited

Altieri, Charles. 1984. *Self and Sensibility in Contemporary American Poetry.* Cambridge: Cambridge University Press.

Berryman, John. 1976. *The Freedom of the Poet.* New York: Farrar, Straus, and Giroux.

Breslin, James E. B. 1984. *From Modern to Contemporary: American Poetry, 1945–1965.* Chicago: University of Chicago Press.

Holden, Jonathan. 1980. *The Rhetoric of the Contemporary Lyric.* Bloomington: Indiana University Press.

———. 1986. *Style and Authenticity in Postmodern Poetry.* Columbia: University of Missouri Press.

Lyotard, Jean-François. 1984. *The Postmodern Condition: A Report on*

Knowledge. Translated by Geoff Bennington and Brian Massumi. Minneapolis: University of Minnesota Press.

Pinsky, Robert. 1976. *The Situation of Poetry: Contemporary Poetry and Its Traditions.* Princeton: Princeton University Press.

Watten, Barrett. *Total Syntax.* 1985. Carbondale: University of Southern Illinois Press.

"Metaphysics of the Quotidian"
A CONVERSATION WITH CHARLES WRIGHT

Charles Wright

Charles Wright was born in Pickwick Dam, Tennessee, and educated at Davidson College, the University of Iowa, and the University of Rome, where he was a Fulbright Fellow. His eight books include *The Grave of the Right Hand* (1970), *China Trace* (1977), *The Southern Cross* (1981), *The Other Side of the River* (1984), and, most recently, *Zone Journals* (1988). *Country Music: Selected Early Poems* (Wesleyan) received the 1983 American Book Award for poetry. In addition, he has translated the work of Eugenio Montale and Dino Campana.

Mr. Wright's many awards include the 1976 Edgar Allan Poe Award from the Academy of American Poets, fellowships from the National Endowment for the Arts, the Guggenheim Foundation, the Ingram Merrill Foundation, and the P.E.N. Translation Prize. Helen Vendler has said of his work that "by its visionary language it assumes the priority of insight, solitude, and abstraction, while remaining beset by a mysterious loss of something that can be absorbed and reconstituted only in death."

Charles Wright is currently Professor of English at the University of Virginia in Charlottesville, where he lives with his wife and son. He has also taught at Iowa, Princeton, Columbia, and the University of California at Irvine.

The following conversation took place on 3 April 1986. Interviewers were Stan Sanvel Rubin and William Heyen. Mr. Wright began the interview by reading two poems, "The New Poem" and "Ars Poetica."

The New Poem

It will not resemble the sea.
It will not have dirt on its thick hands.
It will not be part of the weather.

It will not reveal its name.

It will not have dreams you can count on.
It will not be photogenic.

It will not attend our sorrow.
It will not console our children.
It will not be able to help us.

Ars Poetica

I like it back here

Under the green swatch of the pepper tree and the aloe vera.
I like it because the wind strips down the leaves without a word.
I like it because the wind repeats itself,

and the leaves do.

I like it because I'm better here than I am there,

Surrounded by fetishes and figures of speech:
Dog's tooth and whale's tooth, my father's shoe, the dead weight
Of winter, the inarticulation of joy . . .

The spirits are everywhere.

And once I have them called down from the sky, and spinning around and
    dancing in the palm of my hand,
What will it satisfy?

I'll still have

The voices rising out of the ground,
The fallen star my blood feeds,

this business I waste my heart on.

And nothing stops that.

Rubin: You read two poems about poetics and poetry. I'd like to go back to the first of the two, "The New Poem," which says that it will not offer us consolation and it will not be able to help us. What can we expect from "The New Poem"?
Wright: That poem was written in the time of the Vietnam War, in the late sixties, when political poetry was, if not *de rigueur*, certainly all the vogue. There were read-ins against the War, as you remember, and political poetry was experiencing a kind of rebirth, as it were, in this country. My point in that poem is only about political poetry—not poetry itself—which is not going to help our children over there. It's not going to be any consolation. It won't do the job; something else has to stop the

War. As Auden said, "Poetry makes nothing happen." He meant it in that kind of political sense. That's what I mean in that poem; I don't mean it as encompassing all of poetry, because I think poetry can change your life; but it can't change a war, or it couldn't change that one.

Rubin: You won't even grant Shelley's "unacknowledged-legislators" claim that poetry is somehow changing the world?

Wright: Again, I have to tip my nonexistent hat to Wystan Auden and say that the "unacknowledged legislators of the world" are now the secret police and not the poets.

Heyen: The poem says, "It will not attend our sorrow." That line makes me sad. I want the poem to accompany my emotions through the world.

Wright: Certainly the political poem can't. Accompanying us through the world could be the poem's finest moment, and ours as well. But I don't think it'll help us on the battlefield. That really is beside the point, because what the read-ins were about was changing the government, and it wasn't the poetry that changed the government's mind, but *all* the people finally getting together. Maybe poetry had a little to do with it, but it was the inevitability of the asininity of the enterprise that finally changed things.

Heyen: When I first read that poem, I wasn't connecting it with you and Vietnam and the time you wrote it; I was reading it as a kind of prophetic statement—that's how readers will come to it.

Wright: I hope that if they will not read just that poem but something else I've written they will see that "The New Poem" is not a total "Ars Poetica," or poetic statement on my part.

Rubin: Now the other one you just read is an "Ars Poetica." You say in that poem, "I like it because I'm better here than there."

Wright: "Here," because if I had been reading that poem before an audience live, instead of an audience out there behind the glass I would've said that *here* is where I write, my little room, and *there* is the rest of the house or the world. I am more myself when I'm writing than when I'm out doing daily things. Somehow my job is to bring what's *here*, *there*. My business is the metaphysics of the quotidian.

Rubin: Then the act or process of writing *does* offer you something of value.

Wright: Oh, it changed my life totally, when I started writing! I was just someone looking for something to do, and then I found it.

Rubin: The line, "This business I waste my heart on," implies a certain degree of irony or pain, or both.

Wright: It's a self-inflicted pain, of course. It's what we all do as writers. You waste your heart on it, because it's never quite right and it never quite is satisfying; but it's the closest thing to being satisfying that I've been able to come up with in my life.

Heyen: This is maybe a bad question because it has to do with "idea" and I think you'd agree that we find out what we know and feel by writing; but you did just now use the phrase "the metaphysics of the quotidian," and yet when I read your poems they're always edging toward something beyond that. You say, "The spirits are everywhere," for example; and you say that you want to get to that "still, small pinpoint of light at the center of the universe," where all things come together and intersect—this is a romantic view of the integrity and the harmony of the universe out there. So the focus is on the here and now, but there does seem to be something inside you of a greater connection or a greater feeling.

Wright: Certainly a greater aspiration; and one can only get there through the tangible, tactile things of the everyday, I think. There's a passage I came across in the letters of Paul Cézanne in which he says that colors were to him numinous essences beyond which he *knew* nothing—"the diamond zones of God remaining white." For me if you replace the word *colors* with *words* and *white* with *blank*, you would get how I try to find out what those "zones" are. I admit that I think they exist; I'm just not very sure of them.

Heyen: Roethke says, "The flesh can make the spirit visible." Richard Wilbur says that Poe's aesthetic, for example, is insane. He uses the word *insane*; that is, Poe tries to knock people out into some aesthetic realm out there, forsaking the earth.

Wright: I think that's very foolish. I won't try to top Mr. Wilbur's word, but it seems fairly accurate from my point of view because I don't think it works that way. If Lowell was right that "I myself am hell," then you can fill in the blank in "I myself am ———."

Heyen: There is so much "thingness" in your poetry—the heavy, drenched thingness of the world. That's one of the most beautiful things about your poems, I think.

Wright: You only get to the invisible through the visible—an old idea, but it seems workable to me. As Frost said, "What worked for them might work for you." That's why I say that almost all of my poems seem to be part of this ongoing argument I have with myself over my rather foolish enterprise of . . . what? Perhaps the possibility of salvation—again I go back to what Cézanne was saying because that's as close as I can get to it in any rational way.

Rubin: Has that always been your motivating impulse? Is that what got you started writing in the first place?

Wright: It's been my motivating impulse ever since I realized what I thought I was about. What got me interested first in writing was the fact that my mother used to date William Faulkner's brother at the University of Mississippi and used to talk about it at the house and I thought writing would be a great thing to do. Like everyone else I tried to write stories in school, but I can't tell a story—I'm the only Southerner I know who cannot tell a story.

When I got to Italy in the Army, I went to a place called Sirmione, where the Latin poet Catullus supposedly had had a villa. Someone handed me *The Selected Poems of Ezra Pound* and said, "You should read 'Blandula, Tenulla, Vagula'; Pound wrote it right here in Sirmione." It was like a lightning bolt out of the sky. I read it, it was beautiful; it was a poem about a place I was sitting in, and it wasn't *narrative*. It wasn't Mr. Frost. Much as I love his poems, I can't write those long narratives. This was associational, imagistic, fabulous! It worked the way my mind worked, in jumps and starts, synaptically, and my life was changed. So I tried to rewrite the *Cantos*, a very foolish enterprise, which I gave up after a few years.

I showed up at the University of Iowa, thinking I wanted to go to graduate school; but I had neglected to get myself accepted into the program. It was so unstructured at that time that no one knew I hadn't been let in, so I just signed up for classes and started going. The very first class, I walked in and sat down—I think it was Mark Strand who was in my class that said, "I don't think the iambic pentameter line is working very well here in this poem." I'm dead, I thought. I was a history major in college and I didn't even know what an iambic pentameter line was! So I shut up for two years and listened very intently.

To answer your question, it was the desire to be a writer that made me get started and once I got started, somehow all my life's obsessions, my ten-year lover's quarrel with the Episcopal Church and all the accoutrements of growing up in East Tennessee with the country music and all of that life-and-death, lyric theme in country music started to well up in me and I knew what I was interested in—this constant struggle with, well, Will we be, or won't we be?

I'm one of those few people who think there is a difference between content, subject matter, and form. The content remains like a Greek chorus behind everything I write—the contemplation of the divine, if you will. The subject matter is how you tell the story to get to that content. The form is however you put it together.

Rubin: Pound was important to you, as you said, because of the movement of mind, I suppose.

Wright: The whole associational modernist way of putting together a poem was important to me. Pound was the first poet I ever read. I think anybody's first poet whom he really reads is very important. If you're lucky, you get a great poet; if not, you still like the one you started out with.

Rubin: Were there other poets who were important to you in a shaping way in terms of this content, the contemplation of the divine?

Wright: Wallace Stevens. He said that "the proper study of all poetry is the contemplation of the divine." There are obviously other things that are important in poetry: restitution of the past, rescue from oblivion—a lot of things are important as content. This happens to be the one that obsesses me, and if you don't go with your obsessions, then you're kind of faking it, you know. I intend to continue with my obsessions, although I hope the story lines and the examples change from time to time; but the main idea of what I am worming my way toward would be there.

Pound was important for me, as I said, because he was the first poet. He also allowed me to try things that you weren't supposed to try when I was learning to write poems, particularly at the Iowa Workshop, which was much more structured and formal. I was, to a certain extent just because I didn't know anything, a slightly odd thorn in that context. Iowa was very good for me, because I spent three or four years trying to learn forms. If you don't know them, then you can't do the other. You've got to know what you're *not* doing.

Heyen: You've said that in the beginning your music was the music of the stanza, and you worked awfully hard on stanzaic integrity and stanzaic balance. In general you've moved toward a more free-flowing or synaptic or associational poem. I guess this is a question of form, content, and subject matter all at once. How do you think you came to that other way of writing?

Wright: I'm a fairly—that's not true—I'm an *excessively* orderly person. Stanzas seemed to me the proper study of poetkind. Which is to say if the poem isn't in stanzas, it's all kind of unorganized. Wrenching order out of chaos is one of the things we know poetry does. During those three or four years I was trying to write formal verse, I fell into stanzas, because if you're trying to do sonnets or quatrains. . . .

I had a fortunate occurrence. I mentioned to you yesterday that I used to have a little shack at the back of my house in California. When my son was born, the first several years were very hectic and there wasn't a lot of free time to do things. I would start a poem and I'd get the idea, and maybe a stanza, and then I'd have to rush off to do something else. The next day I'd come back to it and write another stanza. After a period of time, I started to realize that the stanzas were all cohering to the title, but they weren't necessarily narratively following each other.

This was a great discovery for me, because it went back to my original idea of how things worked in my mind, which was synaptically, and I'd been trying to force myself into a logic of narrative, just because I thought I should learn how to do it. Unbeknownst to myself, I was breaking back out into where I should've been in the first place. *But* with the great exception that I had learned that the organization was very important as well, so I was leading from organization instead of leading from chaos. As the stanzas got larger and looser, there still remained the idea of a stanzaic or a patterned organization. And no matter how long the poems get—my last one is forty-two pages—they are still built up of stanzas, but you really wouldn't know it to look at them.

Heyen: I looked up that word *synapse* this morning, and it has to do with impulse from nerve to nerve. But it also has to do with the way that when a cell divides the chromosomes are realigned again somehow.

Wright: One of my pet little theories is that most art—and certainly poems—tends toward the condition of circularity: we try to make things complete. The artist's job, or at least my job when I'm writing a poem, is to try to keep it from meeting completely, because once it meets completely the energy stops. So what you should be doing is keeping it apart and working in that synapse—that's where the sparks are—in that synapse from nerve to nerve. Again, that goes back to the stanzaic pattern, but not a *complete* stanzaic patterning. That's one of the things I don't like about—even though I love many of them—accepted forms. The accepted, given, traditional form—if it's executed perfectly, it's a completion, a circle. Since I truly believe that considerations of form are at the heart of all poetry, all considerations of poetry are considerations of form—I don't mean forms, but *form*—then one should try as hard as possible to generate forms that are one's own, but out of the given, out of the tradition. I don't mean standing in a field and lighting your hair on fire and jumping up and down saying, "Look, I'm doing something new and different."

Form means everything to me. Larkin said, "Content means everything to me, form is nothing." Form means everything to me, content is nothing. I don't believe that, of course, but it's a provocative thing to say, because people say, "What do you mean?" My point is that once you know your content, the way Larkin knew his forms, then it's not something you have to think about any more.

Heyen: The older I get, the more I understand what Williams meant when he said, "The only way to stay alive is through technique." He uses the word *technique*, but he means the exploration of the form.

Wright: And he talks about the "measure"—that's the word nowadays. It's not the metrics; it's the measure. I have to admit I'm dedicated to free verse the way Frank Stella says he's dedicated to abstract art. You know, he knows a lot, if not everything, about the history and traditions of art. That is where he's staked his territory; this is where I stake mine.

When I talk about formal organization, I'm always talking about working in free verse. It's the one meter where the rock hits the water as far as I'm concerned.

Rubin: I suppose once you found prosody at Iowa, it never let you go.

Wright: It's true. I love formal poems, and I teach a course in prosody. It's endlessly fascinating to me—the variations in iambic pentameter and tetrameter, and syllabics, accentuals, and all of this; but at this point I'm not particularly interested in working in those meters. I'm interested in what those meters can give to the free verse I try to work in, which is not really all that "free." It's quite ordered and structured, and its idea of line comes from having studied the formal line.

The trouble now with most of the kids is that they don't know what the formal meters were so they don't know that lineation really exists as lineation. They're thinking in sentences and ideas, so they write them down and sort of just chop the line wherever it looks good. Lineation in free verse originally came from traditional meters. All of the great modern masters of free verse—including Whitman—always wrote in accepted, traditional meters before they broke away. They had a sense of the line; they knew what a line was, or had been. If you don't know what a line has been, how the hell can you make it different?

Rubin: I'd like to push this a little further into how you actually work. How conscious, for example, are you of syllabics and stress while you're writing?

Wright: Totally. I count the syllables of every line I write, and I tend to work in lines from, say, three to nineteen syllables. Mostly they're an odd number for some reason.

Heyen: You count them consciously? That's very surprising to me, because I sensed a more intuitive engagement with your music as you wrote—which I guess is a good effect when I read your poems.

Wright: I love you for saying that, because that's what, of course, I would like it to be. I'm conscious of stress only to try not to make it regular. If you're working with a thirteen-syllable line, you're going to have somewhere between four and seven stresses. Stresses, in a way, tend to be like little staples for me to keep the line down, as the line gets longer and longer. I'm listening to syllables; I'm listening to the sound and to what used to be known as quantitative meters, which we cannot write in, because the English language will not accept them; *but* the idea of them—the weight, the duration, the length, the syllable, is very important in my line. That's what Pound was talking about in the "sequence of the musical phrase": he was trying to get the idea of quantitative meters into English and not to work with the metronome or syllable stress.

So, yes, I count them all. I find that after ten or fifteen years of doing this I hear what they are before I've counted them and I know basically where I want a long one or a short one. Music—to use the word you brought up—is extremely important to me. Sound is extremely important to me in my poems, I hope not to the detriment of what I'm trying to say, because as we all know there is the "how" and the "what." Someone said, "Great poets write the 'what,' minor poets write the 'how.'" But you can't get to the "what" except through the "how." You can't just start with the "what," as many examples of beginning poets will show. They have something they want to tell you, but they don't know how to say it. To make "how" you say it an end in itself seems foolish because then you end up with this gorgeous structure out here in the middle of the desert.

It's not very fashionable, but I'm extremely interested in style as well. Style is a dirty word in poetry now, because it seems to imply surface, and surface only. I don't think it has to. Painters know that style is important. You can get fifteen painters to go out and paint the exact same motif, and the great painter will make a great painting out of it and the others will just make a painting out of it. Ultimately I would like to be able—if you put ten poems on the wall as they do paintings in a muscum—you'd be able to say, "Oh, that's the one by Charles Wright."

Heyen: The trouble with words like *style* and *content* and *subject matter* is that you can only talk about one of them at a time. This is something that is very much on my mind right now. Robert Penn Warren once said that he went through a school as an English major and didn't realize until he was done that he'd never really had a course in literature. All the courses were courses in history, philosophy, biography—whatever. Everything except poetry. What is the "poetry" of poetry? What is the essential experience of poetry, beyond the other talk we find ourselves doing?

Wright: All I know is that essence is not ironic. Emily Dickinson says, "When the hair stands up on my head, I know it's true poetry."

Heyen: I think it has something to do with not being able to separate the "dancer" from the "dance," when you're in the *presence* of the poem at least.

Wright: You read my mind! I was going to say that I wrote down in this little journal or commonplace notebook I keep, "If you can tell the dancer from the dance, one of you is not doing his job." There is no division between form, subject matter, and content.

It seems to me there are three stages you go through. When you're a young writer, it's the singer, not the song—you're learning how to do it. When you hit your prime, it's the song, not the singer. Then, in old age, you go back to "It's the singer, not the song." Of course, the great poet knows it's always both at the same time. *The Divine Comedy* is the singer and the *song*.

Rubin: Does the concept of voice, which is such a catchword in workshops, mean anything to you?

Wright: I never really—I know sort of what I think of as voice, and someone has his own voice and so forth—no, it doesn't mean a lot to me. So many people mean different things by it: the authority of the way the poem is presented, the style, the manner that is being brought to it, either from tradition or some newfangled way. I never know quite what voice is.

Tenor and voice—tenor and vehicle—voice and subject matter. I have no answer for that.

Rubin: The persona poem, the poem as if spoken by someone else?

Wright: That's an obvious voice; but it's a different kind of "voice" from what a lot of people mean.

Rubin: That seems really beside the point for you. It's a kind of poetry that people write in abundance these days. It would seem almost an evasion of the real work as you are describing it.

Wright: I've written one book that I think is in a persona, and all the rest of the I's are thinly disguised me.

Rubin: Are you thinking of *China Trace*?

Wright: That's the only real persona poem. It's interesting that, when you think about Keats and the "negative capability" of submerging your own personality or voice for the voice of the character, he says that there's only one person who can't do this and that's Wordsworth because of the "egotistical sublime." When he walks through a field of daffodils, he can pull it off; everyone else had better work with "negative capability." Surely there's been some fusion now after almost two hundred years of the Romantic movement. Maybe it's an egotistical necessity or a negative sublime—maybe I write out of a negative sublime. I don't know.

Rubin: Does all this attention to form that you've been describing and all this care for the "music" imply a lot of hard work and revision in your writing process?

Wright: Yes, it does. I've been sitting here talking a lot of theoretics, but when it gets down to the work you have to just write, and in my case erase. Most writers don't erase; they just cross out, because they want to save earlier versions for posterity. I revise constantly. I used to revise whole poems; now I revise as I go along, from line to line. Sometimes I erase so much I tear a hole in the paper.

I don't believe in "first-thought, best-thought." I know that when Allen Ginsberg talks bout that, it's a Zen concept; but you can't get into that until you've put yourself into a Zen condition where you're completely empty and ready to receive. *Then* first thought may be best thought, but don't tell that to young poets unless they're practicing Zen Buddhists. First thought is usually worst thought—you have to work at it!

Heyen: *He* has reworked every one of his poems, including "Wales Visitation."

Wright: I think that was "first-thought, best-thought" with "Wales Visitation," which used to be called "Wales Visitation Sutra." It's one of my favorite poems of his. The way he uses the line is so strong and so hooked together—the way he says he's learned from Cézanne about one word hooking into another. I thought that was a fabulous poem. I wish he hadn't even changed the title.

Heyen: Charles, we need to hear you read one of your poems.
Wright: All right, I'll read "Dog Creek Mainline." It's about a little town in Western North Carolina I lived in at the age of six. It's a poem about memory and how we change memory, how memory changes and memory becomes imagination. And imagination becomes language. Last night when we were talking about this, Bill added a coda: language goes back into memory again. I liked that so much I thought I'd repeat it here.

There are some place names here I should explain. Ducktown and Copper Hill are two little towns in East Tennessee.

The poem ends up commenting on itself, on the process of memory and how it becomes imagination—how it becomes true in its untruth.

Dog Creek Mainline

Dog Creek: cat track and bird splay,
Spindrift and windfall; woodrot;
Odor of muscadine, the blue creep
Of kingsnake and copperhead;
Nightweed; frog spit and floating heart,
Backwash and snag pool: Dog Creek.

Starts in the leaf reach and shoal run of the blood;
Starts in the falling light just back
Of the fingertips; starts
Forever in the black throat
You ask redemption of, in wants
You waken to, the odd door:

Its sky, old empty valise,
Stands open, departure in mind; its three streets,
Y-shaped and brown,
Go up the hills like a fever;
Its houses link and deploy
—This ointment, false flesh in another color.

                        *

Five cutouts, five silhouettes
Against the American twilight; the year
Is 1941; remembered names
—Rosendale, Perry and Smith—
Rise like dust in the deaf air;
The tops spin, the poison swells in the arm:

The trees in their jade death-suits,
The birds with their opal feet,
Shimmer and weave on the shoreline;

The moths, like forget-me-nots, blow
Up from the earth, their wet teeth
Breaking the dark, the raw grain;

The lake in its cradle hums
The old songs: out of its ooze, their heads
Like tomahawks, the turtles ascend
And settle back, leaving their chill breath
In blisters along the bank;
Locked in their wide drawer, the pike lie still as knives.

*

Hard freight. It's hard freight
From Ducktown to Copper Hill, from Six
To Piled High: Dog Creek is on this line,
Indigent spur; cross-tie by cross-tie it takes
You back, the red wind
Caught at your neck like a prize:

(The heart is a hieroglyph;
The fingers, like praying mantises, poise
Over what they have once loved;
The ear, cold cave, is an absence,
Tapping its own thin wires;
The eye turns in on itself.

The tongue is a white water.
In its slick ceremonies the light
Gathers, and is refracted, and moves
Outward, over the lips,
Over the dry skin of the world.
The tongue is a white water.)

Rubin: Earlier you mentioned the poem "Dog Creek Mainline" as the first poem you wrote that was *yours*. What did you mean by that? What makes it "yours"?

Wright: Well, it's about my own life. I spent ten years learning to write, and I'm still learning; but those ten years were extremely important to me, because as I've been saying I was learning more traditional forms and learning what might work and what might not. As I look back at them, there's not a bad poem in the bunch that I saved; there's not a good one either. They're just all O.K. Anybody could've written them. There they are—well put together, nice little Lego assemblages.

Then I discovered that I had a childhood, a past, something I wanted to say; and that's the start of finding my own burden and my own job of work, as they say down in East Tennessee, and my own language, since I had chosen writing as my job. This is the first poem that came out of my own life directly, the first poem that nobody else could've written, because no one else had been there and had had the same experiences.

Rubin: I wonder if you could say something about what you're trying for now in your work.

Wright: What I'm working on now is something I call "verse journals." They are quotidian situations I write about in a journalistic fashion, but in verse. It started out as an exercise in lengthening the line and how far up against prose it can go before it stops being a poetic line. This seems to be the right kind of format, since journals are supposed to be prose, so let's see what one can do with them.

What I'm after is what I've always been after—to make the "diamond zones" unblank. I just say to myself, "Good luck," because I need it! I don't know that I can be any more expansive in form after this; I may try to go back and write short poems. But the intent will still be the same—to punch a hole through the invisible.

Rubin: Hearing you read aloud is for me, and I think for others, a revelation in telling us how to read you. Do you speak your lines aloud in the privacy of writing?

Wright: No, I write for the inner ear; but I'm very conscious of my inner ear. I say them over and over to myself, but not out loud. But they *are* oral; they are *all* oral.

"Affectionate Arguments"
A CONVERSATION WITH WILLIAM MATTHEWS

William Matthews

William Matthews was born in 1942 in Cincinnati, Ohio. He was educated at Yale University and the University of North Carolina at Chapel Hill. His seven books include *Ruining the New Road* (Random House, 1970), *Rising and Falling* (Atlantic-Little, Brown, 1979), *A Happy Childhood* (Atlantic-Little, Brown, 1984) and *Foreseeable Futures* (Houghton Mifflin, 1987). In addition to poetry, Mr. Matthews has written many reviews and articles and is co-translator, with Mary Feeney, of the prose poems of Jean Follain.

William Matthews has been the recipient of several awards, among them fellowships from the National Endowment for the Arts, the Guggenheim Foundation, and the Ingram Merrill Foundation. He has recently served as President of the Poetry Society of America where, under his guidance, the membership has been greatly expanded. His work has received critical attention from such writers as John Hollander, Michael Benedikt, Peter Stitt, David Kalstone, and Bonnie Costello. His work is characterized by humor and irony and this was noted by D. A. Barton in *Choice*, saying, "Matthews has emerged as an interesting and serious poet who uses wit to reveal what is so often hidden."

Mr. Matthews has taught at numerous colleges and universities. He is presently Professor of English at City College of New York and claims that he may not move again.

The following conversation took place on 16 July 1987. Interviewers were Stan Sanvel Rubin and Judith Kitchen. Mr. Matthews began the interview by reading his poem "Whiplash."

Whiplash

That month he was broke,

so when the brakes to his car
went sloshy, he let them go.
Next month his mother came
to visit, and out they went
to gawk, to shop, to have something
to do while they talked besides
sitting down like a seminar
to talk. One day soon he'd fix
the brakes, or—as he joked
after nearly bashing a cab
and skidding widdershins
through the intersection
of Viewcrest and Edgecliff—
they'd fix him, one of these
oncoming days. We like
to explain our lives to ourselves,
so many of our fictions
are about causality—chess
problems (where ?! after
White's 16th move marks
the beginning of disaster),
insurance policies, box scores,
psychotherapy ("Were your
needs being met in this
relationship?"), readers' guides
to pity and terror—, and about
the possibility that because
aging is relentless, logic too
runs straight and one way only.

By this hope to know how
our disasters almost shatter us,
it would make sense to say
the accident he drove into
the day after his mother left
began the month he was broke.
Though why was he broke?
Because of decisions he'd made
the month before to balance
decisions the month before that,
and so on all the way back
to birth and beyond, for his
mother and father brought
to his life the luck of theirs.

And so when his car one slick day
oversped its dwindling ability

to stop itself and smacked two
parked cars and lightly kissed
another, like a satisfying
billiards shot, and all this action
(so slow in compression and
preparation) exploded so quickly,
it seemed not that his whole life
swam or skidded before him,
but that his whole life was behind
him, like a physical force,
the way a dinosaur's body
was behind its brain and the news
surged up and down its vast
and clumsy spine like an early
version of the blues; indeed,
indeed, what might he do
but sing, as if to remind himself
by the power of anthem that the body's
disparate and selfish provinces
are connected. And that's how
the police found him, full-throated,
dried blood on his white suit
as if he'd been caught in a rust-
storm, song running back and forth
along his hurt body like the action
of a wave, which is not water,
strictly speaking, but a force
that water welcomes and displays.

Rubin: I'd like to begin the discussion by going to the poem you read, "Whiplash," which is from A *Happy Childhood.* It involves so many concerns that run through your poems that one could really start any-where, but there is a view of life there and it balances causality against what you might call free will. I wonder if we could just ask you, does the poem relate to any particular accident, any source in reality, or does it come out of those kind of thematic issues?

Matthews: Well, some of both. It doesn't relate to a particular automobile accident. I'm fascinated by automobile accidents. I've written four poems, of which I liked two well enough to publish them. I also have a plane-crash poem. I love disasters apparently, and I think what I like about them is that they create swiftly and melodramatically, because poems are so small, a need for the righting mechanism—a need to rediscover not just a lost but a shattered and violently rearranged poise.

This poem is about any number of enormous emotional shocks or disruptions, or about simply any one of a long series of discoveries that the very things that have saved us and propelled us can seem both wisdoms and an almost shameful form of self-deception.

Rubin: You invented the notion of the accident?

Matthews: The accident itself was invented to be the embodiment of the kinds of violations of balance and restorations of balance by which I imagine all of us living.

Rubin: And the poem runs through a whole series of these whiplash shocks that culminate, I think not uncharacteristically, in music, in song.

Matthews: Yes, without me ever having particularly planned it consciously. I return to music again and again; it seems fair to say that in lots of my poems the presence of music is the point at which a sort of outcry begins to become an emotion, "carved in time," as Pound says—not just an expression of pain or an involuntary utterance, but the beginning of shaping the kind of utterance that will be restoration and song. The presence of song is already the presence of healing in most of my poems, I realize.

Rubin: I began by asking the kind of literal question, because this character in the poem, this poor guy, is so locked into causality, into the material circumstances, into the psychological decisions he's made, into everything that precedes his conscious choice and will that if you didn't allow him to decide at the end it'd be an awfully grim poem. There's a real balance between the fatalistic and the self-expressive. I wonder if you would say if this relates to your sense of what poetry is about for you.

Matthews: Certainly there is some serious element of whistling on the way past the graveyard in most poetry, and, God knows, in mine. You said that very nicely: the guy in the poem is desperate for an explanation of what is after all on some level only an extraordinary version of the ordinary hurts of being human; he would like to have a theory of hurt and he would be more than willing to add to the weight of the stuff already in the pan all of World War II and major plagues. He would give anything for an adequate explanation. But somebody for whom a romantic relationship has ended asks, "Why did he leave me?" and the answer is, "Because your eyes are blue." There is no answer, there is no adequate explanation. I feel slightly more willing than the character in the poem to say that these things happen to us because our eyes are brown or blue. He's more desperate than I am because he wants to have everything explainable. I certainly share with him the urge to have explanations, but I'm growing sceptical that they're going to arrive.

Kitchen: The accumulated weight of all his explanations seems to culminate first in a sort of humor, because at some point none of us can buy all of these explanations, and then in a moment where the poem itself has whiplash, so that you come to *form*, in some sense, and from that moment on we, as the readers, seem to travel back up the spine of the poem to see what form has done for this poem. So there's a shaping principle in this poem; it seems to teeter.

Matthews: I like the notion of the force running down the poem and bouncing back up. I wanted the formal energy of the poem to seem apparently very informal, chatty, and almost casual at the beginning, but for the form to come out of the poem from the inside out, the way the water gets shaped from inside by that physical pattern of force that can be called a "wave," which isn't water and therefore you can't see it—you know it's there by the way it causes other things to act. That was what I had in mind for the formal behavior of the poem.

Rubin: So we're saying that you don't need a theory if you have a poem.

Matthews: Yes. And if I had to pick one or the other, it would always be the poem.

Rubin: We're going to stick to this poem, I guess, another minute. Another thing about it that suggests your work generally is that, in a sense, it appears to be kind of a discursive mini-essay on a topic, on a thought, as you say. This is material that you've been making your own for some time, material that involves the meaning of human behavior, the ways we try to explain things to ourselves. I wonder if you'd say something about your own feeling for this. Am I on target in saying this? And can you describe how it's come to be?

Matthews: I think the impulse is double-edged, and I'm going to refer quickly to a moment that happened this morning in the class that Judith and I are co-teaching. It's been fun, because when you're co-teaching you divide the roles. Somebody had written a particularly beautiful and rather heart-breaking poem, and Judith was able to say, That poem is really about the things in life that make us want to read poems. It's about what it feels like to be alive; it's about mortality; it's a serious poem. I love it that you wrote a poem this serious. I was then able to make a joke, which indicates both my agreement with Judith and my sense that every time we start to get serious we're faintly ridiculous. I'm absolutely interested in all those questions if I can express both of those points of view simultaneously. I'm absorbed by the possibility that life has meaning, and I'm absorbed by the possibility that the search for meaning is implicitly silly and ridiculous. My interest in that material is that I can continue to come at it with that strange combination of belief and doubt.

Kitchen: Let's talk about the book itself then, because it does seem to me—I've been reading Bill Matthews for a few years and when A *Happy Childhood* came out, there was a difference. It felt like a new Bill Matthews, maybe he was recognizable but there was something new in it, and some of it I think you just touched on. You allowed yourself to play even more with these philosophical questions, less personal, and you have several poems with opposite titles—"Good" and "Bad," "Right" and "Wrong,"—and you're playing a philosophical game with wit and verve, with a love of language, and I'd like you to talk about getting yourself from "there" to "here" into this book.

Matthews: Part of the impulse for the book came from the preceding book, called *Flood*, a collection of poems in three parts, the middle of which is another series of disaster poems called "Flood." By writing a series of poems that kept working in an obsessed way around recurring fascinations, I discovered that there is something very powerful and liberating for me in not having to get it right in a single poem, in being able to look at something similar in the next poem and the next poem. I thought, The next book I write is going to be a whole book that works like that. So I set out to write a book, rather than a collection, when I wrote *A Happy Childhood*. The book that I set out to write evolved so much that the distance traveled from the first idea to the last is enormous. I blundered into a notion that the whole book was going to be about the need for us to have stories and the need to distrust deeply the possession our stories take of us and to meditate upon that through a series of things, from childhood with good and bad, right and wrong, to Freud—there are several poems that are really affectionate arguments with Freud, one of which describes psychoanalysis as the study of survival and self-deception. There are poems like "Whiplash" which don't work out of the polarities but try to include them, and poems like "Manic" and "Depressive" which deliberately play off polarities. I think of the book as a long poem, disguised as a collection.

Rubin: Let's talk a little more about the book as a whole, how you worked at it when you were doing these series of poems. Are they in fact published in sequence? I'm speaking of an individual poem, like "Flood" in the other book, or like "Wrong" and "Right." Are they published as they were written? Do you do them over time? This sort of thing.

Matthews: I sometimes work on them simultaneously, because if I've got eight in a sequence something I do in number seven will make me go back and change something in number three, so they're all part of each other. While I need to put them in an order and I pick the one I think is best, the one they appear in for the book, I may publish them in magazines in a completely different order as if they were individual poems or as if they could be read in another sequence. I do think it's possible in those sequences that, if you turned the handle and they all shifted a few positions, like facets in a kaleidoscope, they would read almost as interestingly in the next arbitrarily discovered sequence as in the one I finally decided for them.

Rubin: This answers my next question, which was going to be, Do you

have a sense of a dialectic going through one of these serial poems, that the thought is getting somewhere or getting nowhere, or just proceeding? And I guess you were saying you don't; it's more an aesthetic kind of play.
Matthews: Well, I do feel that some of them come toward a conclusion—the last of the sequences in the book certainly comes to a conclusion and there is an assertion toward the end of that poem. It's a poem about people who like discovering errors and like being able to say what's wrong—maybe the commonest form of mental illness is ethical superiority—and the poem just started out as thinking about what it means to love to find out wrong, that there was something a little terrifying about the discrimination-making personality. Then at the end I wind up saying that the only error was to be alone, a line that I had no idea I was going to write. That's a line which certainly sounds as though it has some of the elements of a conclusion; on the other hand, I do want to reserve the right to make fun of the idea tomorrow. So I would like the idea that the dialectic could continue past the eighth poem: that I could say something ringing and I could get up the next morning and think, Did I say that?
Kitchen: I don't think there's a problem because the poems, rather than following a line, circle back on themselves and on each other. And I noticed that even more in the next book; that's why I began to feel that, although it was a new Bill Matthews, it was in transition toward *Foreseeable Futures*. I'd like to move into . . .
Rubin: I have one more question about the structure of the book—"Manic" and "Depressive" are quite logically on facing pages, but "Right" and "Wrong" and "Good" and "Bad" have been carefully separated from each other. I wonder if you would say something about the arrangement of the book.
Matthews: Those four were distributed throughout the book. It begins with one of them and ends with one, and dividing the book into approximately equal thirds are the remaining two. What I really had in mind was that, underneath the very adult fascination with definition and the hope that we can say certain things that are useful to us and the very adult suspicion that that very activity traps us and makes us less flexible and responsive to ourselves and to others, is the world of the child. I had in mind that good and bad, right and wrong, would be the four compass directions of the child's world. The book in that sense would be circular and like a globe.
Kitchen: There's one poem in the next book that, as I was reading it, felt like the one that "got away" or that came later, after *A Happy Childhood*. That was "Lucky and Unlucky," and, of course, even just its title sort of lit up in neon. It belonged with those polarities, and yet it does something different. I wonder if we could read that one, partly because the other

poems are very long. This one is shorter, and it would move us into the
very newest material.
Matthews: This is a poem in which the title continues grammatically into
the first line of the poem—I think the only time I've ever done this.

Lucky and Unlucky

mean the same thing, like *flammable* and *inflammable*.
Four crows bicker on the peak of my roof, then three
rumple upward like charred paper lifting from a fire

with the malarial torpor of the poorest tropics.
But it's Seattle in February, and alder smoke
uncoils from the chimneys; it's Saturday:

errands and children, errands and loneliness.
Is the future the history of memory or forgetting?
The cleaners, the drugstore, the lumber yard . . .

At home the crow just sits there, the color of blue-
black ink still drying, each of its eyes as big
as a hummingbird. Whatever those yolk-yellow

eyes can see through the sifted rain, the pear-
shaped crow just sits there. Through streets
slickened by mist I drive home to that crow.

Kitchen: I have one more question that I think comes logically out of
looking at that poem on the page as opposed to hearing it read aloud.
Almost every poem in this book is a poem written in three-line stanzas as
though in some sense you were finding a form that, by being so strict,
would liberate you to play some of the other linguistic games and
philosophical games. I wonder if you could talk a little bit about form and
structure and whatever else comes to mind.
Matthews: I had never done that before—taken a form and asked of
myself that I would write a large number of poems that would be "in the
same form." I'm thinking here of the private game of form as opposed to
the public aspect of form that the reader gets. The private game of form is
that part of form which helps the poet write the poem; then there is the
public aspect which may make the poem more or less accessible to the
reader, but that comes after. The private matter of honor was that each of
those poems would occupy that apparently same form in a quite different
manner, so that no poem would feel formally as if it had learned how to

feel from any of the other poems. I partly wanted to see if I could do that. I probably wrote about fifty poems in that form before I found the thirty-five that I put into the book. There may be a reader who disagrees, but I came to feel that I had in fact done just that—solved each poem's formal problems differently. It's partly the usual perversity and cussedness of the writer: I wanted to try it because I had never done it before. With hindsight I come to see other things that are interesting about it. The book is called *Foreseeable Futures* and is seriously occupied with the questions, How do we think about the future? Why do we find it so difficult? Can we think about the future without the shadow of death over it every time we look at it? One of the things I discovered and one of the reasons the title became plural is that it occurred to me that we don't think of *the* but of simultaneous futures—if A, then B; if X happens, then I would probably respond by doing this. One surveys the future the way a skillful chess-player might survey the chessboard. It's full of ramifications and paths, and there's some way you see them all simultaneously, and they're all comments and parodies on each other. I thought I wanted fairly short poems, but I also wanted a long line, to really let the sentence unravel. So I wound up with a form that had a rather long line, but I also wanted that sense that certain forms like the sonnet have of beginning to impose, as you grow nearer to it, the need for an ending. However, I didn't want a poem that behaved, as the sonnet can, like a closure machine. I like the baggy brevity of it, and I like the fact that it didn't at any point divide into thirds. The sonnet seemed to me to divide into thesis and antithesis and synthesis all too easily. I didn't think I was going to get anything that had the surety of a syllogism, and if I did I should watch it. So what I wandered into without doing any of this thinking consciously was finding a form that frustrated the kinds of certainty and aphorism that the sonnet approaches while rewarding some of the same kind of compression and that by this kind of opposing relationship reminded one of the sonnet's history of argument, because lots of these poems are arguments: if this is true, then that is true. And, of course, the arguments all tend to fall apart in a clatter toward the end of the poems, because the poems are about things that we can't know as well as what we can, but sometimes they come to conclusions too.

Rubin: Why does this kind of poem argument, internal argument really, self-reflexive argument, why does this attract you? Why do you find yourself working in it, do you think?

Matthews: The simplest answer would be that I prefer the way of pro-ceeding which allows into poems the largest amount of emotional activity like that I really carry around inside me on a given day. I feel less and less of the real emotional and psychic and intellectual activity that is the inside of a person during a given twenty-four hours is left out as I push toward this form. More of what we sometimes call "inner life" can get out and be expressed and made words, made something outside myself, as if to say, Is this what it feels like for us to be human? Do we walk around like this? I don't know. I hope so. That's another question. I feel that this procedure has allowed me to be more inclusive, to get more stuff in, even if some of the stuff is static and waste paper and so on. In fact, I slightly like getting shabby stuff in there, because I think that other kind of poem that I'm trying not to write is a poem that works by being beautiful and by being tasteful and leaving out everything that conflicts with that. I really want a little garbage and a dead cat in the poems, as well as the things that are aesthetic and polished and beautiful.

Rubin: This clearly describes a kind of difficult method of getting to truth. The poems don't, for example, attempt to make immediate emotional claims and identify truth with emotion *per se*.

Matthews: No. Surely the truth of one's emotional life is a major ingredient in whatever we wind up feeling is the truth about our lives. But one who has been habitually—I think in some ways it would be fair to say since the very first book—as interested in self-deception as a subject as I am is somebody who has an embattled and loving but slightly adversary relationship with emotional life, which is, I feel, very hard to talk about. What the hell is an emotion, and how is it we sometimes don't recognize one until it bites us on the nose? And yet everybody knows intuitively what emotional life means, though talk about it that goes much farther than that becomes wildly abstruse. It seems to be easier to embody emotions than to describe them. That may be one of the things poetry and music do uniquely well. But emotions are not all the truth of our experience, and I love them and I hate them.

Kitchen: The poems do seem to reflect the life of the mind. When you say you ask if this is what it's like to be human, my first reaction on reading the book was, so this is what it's like to be Bill Matthews. But to move inside the moving brain is, it seems to me, what this book has allowed us to do. It hasn't allowed us into someone else's heart in quite the same way as it's allowed us into someone else's thought process, and it's almost insidious how easily we slip into your way of thinking. I love that effect, but I always wanted to come out and somehow think that way myself, and of course it wasn't possible. I guess I'm making a statement about the book, that it shows us both how like other people we can be and how unlike, as we step back outside the poems. That's not a question; that's a statement.

Matthews: I think that's certainly true. As you said that, it suddenly occurred to me that sometimes you look at the progress of your work and look at early poems, and you think, I wonder what fairly close but slightly demented relative of mine wrote those poems? And you realize that it's you that wrote them, but an earlier you. There's something about the way you phrased that—that you realize both how like other people and unlike other people you are—I mean, as you described your relationship to the books in that way and I looked at the actual books, seventeen years of compressed history in Stan's hands, I myself felt that way. I think of that combination of kinship and strangeness—I wouldn't call it anything like what philosophers call The-One-and-the Many problem (which I think of as being a chicken-and-egg problem, which can only really be solved by refusing to accept their terms) but whatever the real emotional equivalent of that is, that sense of how you could be so isolate and strange and belong so deeply to a culture and a language and a kinship system and all those things, that if one could get both of those things going simultaneously, if it's true that my book does anything remotely approaching that, I'd be very pleased indeed.

Rubin: It seems that, thinking about the seventeen years, there is clearly less use of the "I" in the more recent books; these poems are all distanced in a sense, or displaced: there are characters, or semi- or incomplete narratives, as in "Whiplash" that you read at the beginning here. Were you conscious of this? What does this mean in terms of your sense of the use of personal material?

Matthews: I feel in one way as I said earlier that it has more stuff in it: I'm able to include more of what it really feels like to go through a day; in that sense it feels to me more personal than anything I've ever written. On the other hand, I think whatever claims the poems make on the attention of the reader are not made on the basis of "I-am-the-man-I-suffered-I-was-there." There's some—I don't know how to paraphrase whatever claims they are making, and I don't know how effective those claims are, because I can't read my poems as if I hadn't written them. I would like it if they said, Why don't you come in and look at this; it's kind of weird, but you might be able to figure out a way that it's part of your life. The other way of thinking about that is to remember that you are in some way all the characters in your dreams—a staple of how you talk to clients about dream interpretation in certain schools of psychoanalytic practice. It's always attracted me that there's a possibility that it's also true of all characters in poems. If that's the case, then you can take a guy like that slightly panicked rationalist in "Whiplash," who is in some ways very different from me but whom I must contain: if I don't contain him, I can't quite write about him. In some way he represents part of me, but I don't very often offer anything like an autobiographical "I" any more, because one thing I've found is that that guy got in the way of all these other characters coming and talking, and I'd rather have more voices.

Rubin: Psychoanalysis is an interesting kind of referent for this, because, as you've noted, you have so many poems around that theme, around that subject matter that interests you, and obviously it's a dialogue of self and other, or, in some more contemporary formulations, a dialogue of self and other—which is the analyst—*and* Other, or the subconscious. The reason this interests me is not for obsessive scholarly reasons you're referring to, but the poems as you describe them, and I think as I read them, seem to be making interesting truth claims. You know, poetry notoriously has no ability to make a claim on truth, except for some of us who wish to believe it does. You seem to go more than half way toward wanting it to have a claim on the truth, the truth of human nature, the truth of the split you're embodying in the form.

Matthews: I'm willing to rush toward truth as far as the word *accuracy* today, and to say that I do think poetry can embody a kind of accuracy of registration about what it feels like to be alive. I make such claims not especially for my own poems but for the very best poems written in any particular era. It seems to me that we may get the fullest account of what it felt like to be human in that particular era in a poem. A poem can contain many contradictory things; a poem is not required to make arguments that are internally consistent the way certain other kinds of discourse that want to make truth claims have to do. Poems are not required to go back and solve the same exhausted dualisms by which Western thought falls in a cluttered heap. You don't have to have to solve all those problems in the first chapter of every book if you're a poet; if you're Elizabeth Bishop, you can give a particular sense of what it was like to be alive in a particular era, which is irreplaceable, and which seems to me the fullest account. I feel that experience is being lost far less fast when I read Elizabeth Bishop than when I read any other kind of thing. I don't know if that's a truth claim, but it's a claim for not being trapped in the self and not being trapped in the present. The advantage of poetry over other forms of discourse is that it can be incomplete, even surrealistic. You don't have to obey argument's rules, and poetry's rule is a kind of accuracy and a willingness not to take yourself too seriously, but to take yourself absolutely seriously indeed.

Rubin: Do you have a sense of what, if anything, you'd like these poems to do to an audience? Do you have a sense of an audience? You've done seven books of poetry; does that enter into your writing at all?

Matthews: I think I have a stronger sense of audience from the last two books than I'd ever had before. For whatever it means, those books have made people come forward in conversation and try to describe what the encounter with the book felt like to them. Before that, people would say, "Hey, I liked your last book," and there were welcome pleasantries from fellow poets; but something about the earlier books made readers less inclined to describe what their experience of any book was like. Not that there is an audience I would write *for*, but that if I indulge myself in writing these poems they will find people who will be interested by them and who will want to make something of them, and even in some cases will want to bring a report of that activity to me. I quite love that, but the way I got that audience was by ignoring it. So that's how I'm going to continue.

Rubin: We are at the end, unfortunately, of a discussion which seems to have focused rather unremittingly on the theme of self-knowledge, and I think it's apropos to your most recent books that we should end with the reading of the poem from *Foreseeable Futures* of that title.

Matthews: This poem is called "Self-Knowledge."

Self-Knowledge

High above the slant snow and sludged traffic,
smug as Horace on the Sabine farm and twice
as indolent, I read Horace until the gray is wholly

drained from the afternoon. The docile sheep,
the fire fed by a servant, those jars of Falernian,
for which the occasion is pleasure itself,

maturing in the cellar like negotiable bonds . . .
I could send out for Chinese food. I could
pop a Bud Powell tape into the box. I could

wrap myself in wrath and my oldest coat
and scowl through the slickening streets, looking
for someone to haunt, and who would it be?

I'd know his limp anywhere, his stoic jokes,
that battered coat. The poor, pained, brave
son of a bitch, I'd know him anywhere.

"The Making of the Music"
A CONVERSATION WITH MICHAEL S. HARPER

Michael S. Harper

Michael S. Harper was born in Brooklyn, New York, in 1938 and attended high school and college in Los Angeles, and graduate school at the University of Iowa Writers Workshop. Since 1970 he has published nine books of poetry, including *Dear John, Dear Coltrane* (University of Pittsburgh Press), *Nightmare Begins Responsibility*, and *Images of Kin*, which won the Melville-Cane Award from the Poetry Society of America. His most recent collection is *Healing Song for the Inner Ear* (University of Illinois Press, 1985).

Mr. Harper has won awards given by the National Institute of Arts and Letters and the Black Academy of Arts and Letters, as well as fellowships from the Guggenheim Foundation and the National Endowment for the Arts. He draws upon the traditions of jazz, improvising on the art and life of such artists as John Coltrane, Miles Davis, Charlie Parker, and Billie Holiday. His work has been described, by critic Paul Breslin, as "attempting . . . to use the whole range of his intellect, emotions, and experience, rather than clinging to some narrow domain of the 'poetic.'"

Mr. Harper is Israel J. Kapstein Professor of English at Brown University; he has taught at Brown since 1970. He lives with his wife and three children in Taunton, Massachusetts.

The following conversation took place on 20 February 1985. Interviewers were Stan Sanvel Rubin and A. Poulin, Jr. Mr. Harper began by reading his poem "*It Takes a Helleva Nerve to Sell Water.*"

"It Takes a Helleva Nerve to Sell Water"

> Frederick Douglass never moved
> to Washington in this address;
> his statue is in Rochester,
> in a city park,

a windbreak, my canopy.

In the 60s at LAX
he runs for office;
my brother's dark hand
stretches out in greeting—
no student of the Revolution,
he's selling water to the quake
victims in Santa Monica:
he's in his white uniform,
but nobody's buying
Arrowhead Spring Water!

He takes his hand
surrounded by security;
the eyes of the governor,
still as a pockmark
at Playa del Rey,
becomes the country's monogram,
markings of the movies,
a concertina of light.

I tell him how in 1934
they closed the WPA theater
midtown, Orson fell down
the trapdoor before *Citizen
Kane*, before black *Macbeth* uptown:
the black choral section stood
in a one-night stand,
sang spirituals below the poverty
line, below the stage threshold:
these blacks were thespians too,
Roosevelt loved the stage,
the New York Yankees came to power
in spring training; one night at the *Savoy*
Chick Webb battled Count to a standstill
on radio.

For the cameras my brother asks the governor
in his white uniform—will you govern for all
the people? He had given away his water
while others sold theirs, that he was a scout,
that the Lake is no stranger to him,
bowie knots and trails familiar to his tent.
We were tokens then, in shallow water,
integrating the camp swimming pool,
now embarrassed as headmasters on patrol.
There were redwoods; you could find snakes;

among the spruce and sycamores
the sansei boys were quick to break camp
selling all the water they could find
in the flooded pastures of their homeland
where we lived. Those who want crops
without digging in the ground
won't see the harvest in the movies.

Rubin: I would like to begin by asking you to explain the history which is at the center of the poem you just read.

Harper: First of all, the poem begins with a reference to Frederick Douglass and ends with the improvisation of a cautionary note that Douglass left to his brethren, the citizens of the United States, particularly Black Americans. Douglass spent some time trying to educate his populace; he was a great rhetorician and statesman. He said, of the "crops" to be expected in this land, that agitation would be part of whatever the "fruit" would be. There is a literal reference to one of the cardinal principles of his talks, improvised at the end of the poem. You don't have to know that, but the poem is very rhetorical.

The thing that sets the poem off is the question of the speaker, because the title is a quote. I first published this poem under the title, "Inauguration Blues," and the present title, *"It Takes a Helleva Nerve to Sell Water,"* was its epigraph. I decided that "Inauguration Blues" was a little self-indulgent, so I changed it.

The poem is really about something that happened to my brother, not me. He was the figure who sold Arrowhead Spring Water and gave it away during the Santa Monica quake. He was the one who confronted the then-Governor, now President of the United States, at a press conference. My brother was not a politically engaged person; he had married young and was trying to raise his young children. He had tremendous ambitions, but they ran along entrepreneurial lines.

It is also about our experience as young kids growing up in Los Angeles at a time when we were consciously beginning to expand our historical understanding of where we had lived and why the land that we occupied had belonged to the Japanese-Americans who had been relocated in these centers. One of the most moving things that happened to me in high school was when I saw pictures of these Japanese-Americans, mostly young kids, lined up at Santa Anita race track, waiting to be carted off to the centers. These young people were my classmates in school, and they were terribly ashamed to even talk about what had happened to them during World War II. This was during the early fifties.

So it's a memory poem, and Douglass is mentioned because during

Reagan's inauguration he made this citation about the great Founding Fathers—Washington and Jefferson—and he's looking out over the monuments. The poem's first lines are my usurpation of his utterance to add another hero that would never come to Reagan's mind because Douglass is simply not part of his pantheon, as he is, of course, a part of mine.

Another element that is not in the poem, because I thought it would be too much to put it in, is what W. E. B. Du Bois said of Frederick Douglass—that he was the greatest man of the nineteenth century. Of course, Du Bois knew about Abraham Lincoln and others. The scale for evaluating someone as resourceful as Douglass is still not fully seen, I think. So much of his life was dictated by events that were not in his control, and he had to make some very difficult decisions. In his three autobiographies, there is a good deal of detail about the processes of his thinking, and you see there the process of a man working out of the ethos of his country. It gives you some respect for what polity means.

I haven't made any systematic study of Frederick Douglass, but I can't come to this area of New York State and not think about him. There is that wonderful statue of him in downtown Rochester. I carry in my briefcase a picture of him as a young man. You know, the pictures of Douglass that most people see have that fiery expression on his face, often in an agitated pose, haranguing his constituents, and he has this white mane of hair and beard. Douglass was a formidable figure throughout his life. To think that as a young man in 1845 he wrote the autobiography that he did is extraordinary. It's an American document—right up there with the best autobiographies ever written.

Poulin: I have some questions about the titles of your books that strike me as being genuine flags to your central subject matter and themes. Let's begin with *Images of Kin*.

Harper: Kinship is more than family. Ralph Ellison makes this marvelous distinction between ancestors and relatives: you can't choose your relatives, but you can choose your ancestors. He's talking about literary creation, about the application of voice and the framing of certain formalistic principles that go into novel-writing, in his particular case. When I say *kin*, I'm talking about those particular epiphanies—often configured around personalities but sometimes events—that make up a pantheon of nourishment that I get, not only as a human being but as a writer. My kinship, then, is in part the family lines, the "blood lines," not only related to my kinfolk but also appropriations of others. The two great poets of kinship for me are Robert Lowell and Robert Hayden. They're very different in the ways they solve poetic problems such as voice and themes. But they are extremely instructive poets, people that you can improvise against.

I also mean by kinship "portraiture," which is again a way of framing an image. The technique of recession and highlighting is usually talked about in relation to painting and photography, but there are verbal equivalents. I have spent some time trying to do my own kind of portrait-framing and creating my own galleries.

Rubin: You use history as a framing device.

Harper: Yes. I think it was Williams who said, in his book *In the American Grain*, "History for us begins with murder and enslavement, not with discovery." We as Americans have this terrific problem with amnesia—we can't remember things very long. I think it has to do with the way the country was formulated. When you write down on a piece of paper all the values you're supposedly trying to live up to, it takes a while to improvise your way through that landscape, which is very treacherous and full of contradictions. You don't have a uniform, homogeneous populace—the forces that go into nation-building are extremely complex.

Poulin: That introduces us to *Nightmare Begins Responsibility*, doesn't it?

Harper: Very much so. You know, I get teased about that a bit, because I was aware of Yeats's "In dreams begin responsibilities," and, of course, I know about Delmore Schwartz's story with that title. I knew what the title was going to be before I wrote the poem. It doesn't happen that way often, but it was one of those occasions on which I was carrying the poem around in my head, and I had to create the occasion whereby I could sit down and write the poem. Talking about responsibility, I said in another context, "The responsibility to nightmare is to wake up." We as a people have horrific things to deal with in our past. I've tried, as best I could, to deal with my own personal nightmares, but my conception is expansive, even when I'm being self-indulgent. And I think all poets are being self-indulgent when they write too much about their own lives, and they don't develop the smokescreens to diminish or to put into perspective their own personal insights, griefs, losses, gains. When I say "self-indulgence," I mean it as a warning: to be careful of making too much of what we think to be our own importance. This is an *American* phenomenon, by the way, and it goes along with the innocence that we as a people have. We're terrifically innocent people, which is one of the reasons why we're surprised all the time.

Poulin: Your mentioning "perspective" reminds me of your statement in a recent essay about Coltrane: you spoke of his problem with a reed that made it very painful to play, but there was no way to get around it. You end with the statement: "There was no easy way to get that sound. Play through the pain to a love supreme."

Harper: I remember that very well. Coltrane was a great tenor saxophonist in the tradition of Coleman Hawkins, Lester Young, and Charlie Parker. He was losing his teeth—because of self-indulgence—

and he was trying to find a craftsman who could make a reed which would allow him to maintain a level of intensity—a purity of tone—and at the same time would alleviate the pain he got in his jaw and his teeth. He spent a lot of time trying to find somebody to duplicate the sound that he was afraid of losing; at the same time he knew that he was losing his teeth so that he would not be able to play the same. After a long and arduous attempt to find somebody to make that mouthpiece, he gave up; he realized that he couldn't find anything that would ease the cost of playing.

There's an important thing to be said here. Each musician, particularly the player of a wind instrument, has a "signature," the way in which the mouth is made—the way in which the lips and teeth come together as a principle of organization and arrangement. Those tonal qualities are individual; no single person can duplicate perfectly the way in which another individual plays through a reed into an instrument. Coltrane had to understand that at the very personal level. His reasons for doing what he was doing were musical or technical but also personal. I didn't go into all the details when I made the comment, but I had that imagery in mind: certain things that have to do with individual style or the way in which you approach your life *cost* something. The way in which we understand the cost in general terms is the amount of pain it costs, because that gets your attention. Pain always gets your attention in a way that pleasure does not. One remembers intense moments of pain in ways one cannot easily forget. I use this as a general approach to my own struggles—artistic or personal. I guess that's what I meant by self-indulgence. We have a tendency to get too involved in our own personal struggles, not understanding that somebody else has always had it tougher.

Rubin: Would you say a few things about the creation of the poem, "Nightmare Begins Responsibility"?

Harper: First of all, the poem was written in answer to a terrible problem I had with whether enough had been done by the medical people in saving two children that I lost, that were born prematurely. As a father, and as a person who is very suspicious of technology, I had all kinds of problems coming to terms with these deaths, and the poem was my way of dealing with it. The poem is meant to be read very quickly. I'm trying to duplicate the process of birth in it.

Poulin: Are you interested in musicians because as artists they become an instrument of the art and we know nothing about *them*? In other words, if you play the piano, you can pour your whole experience into your playing and your audience will never know what it is.

Harper: There is a certain equivalency to my identification with musicians. I have always admired the way in which a musician could, night after night, make the commitment to play as deeply as he or she could, despite how he or she felt, and that the process of playing was a kind of expiation, a freeing from whatever the personal difficulties were in living. And we all have our difficulties. The *process* of making the music was liberating in such a way as to create a conduit, a spiritual flow, which for that particular moment, was transformational. That whole concept has been deeply ingrained in me, since I was young. The maker of the music and the music itself are two aspects of a relationship which I think are just extraordinary. Since American music is primarily improvisatory, jazz music in particular, there's a kind of cultural statement to it. It speaks again to the placement of the individual in society.

I have an image in my head that I can never forget—Earl "Fatha" Hines playing the piano in Chicago in a nightclub owned by Al Capone, and what it must have been like for him to go to work every night, knowing full well that anything could happen. That kind of "grace under pressure" is extraordinary to me! That's the social background, but in Earl "Fatha" Hines's head was the desire to make the best music he could make. If you want the social commentary, you go to listen to what he's witnessed. What you pointed out is something deeply ingrained in me and implicit in much of my writing, even though I don't always make a point of it. It's a guideline; it's something that's standing there as a kind of sentry.

Poulin: I want to ask a question, out of genuine ignorance. Various critics have written about the influence of jazz on your work. I've done it, too; now I must confess that I don't understand that! How *does* jazz influence your work? [*Laughter*]

Harper: Let's take a particular poem that I wrote. Maybe that's the best way to look at it. My first book was called *Dear John, Dear Coltrane*. I was accused by many Black Americans of writing a book that was kind of "in-house"; in other words, "Why are you writing about something that is sacred to us?" The white media thought the title was sentimental, because it sounded like a " 'Dear John' letter." So there is this terrific gap between the denotation and the connotation of real meaning of a title. Most of the people who were being critical were not poetry lovers. They were going to buy the book to display on their shelves, but they were not going to take the time to read it, and they were not going to ask me any penetrating questions about why I wrote as I did. We have this technical gap between practitioners of the trade—people who try to write—and those people who are commentators, in a peripheral fashion. I think what people probably mean is that I make a lot of references in subject matter to musicians.

Last night I read a poem called "Strong Man," which has a contrapuntal give-and-take, "I"-and-"we," call-and-response pattern. The poem "Dear John, Dear Coltrane" had that same pattern, which is reminiscent of the Black church, or any ritualistic setting where there is dialogue. That organizing principle is both a cultural phenomenon and a poetic one, because there are lots of precedents for it, if you look for them. But most people were not familiar enough with the traditions out of which I was working even to comment. I don't think too many people—maybe you, because you're a good anthologist and you read widely—would know who Sterling Brown was. I spent literally years telling people that a man named Robert Hayden knew a great deal about technical things like pattern, when I was teaching my students how to write sonnets and villanelles and all the rest of that sort of thing. My own approach is somewhat different: I like improvising, and although I might have a pattern or an idea, it does not come across directly. I've written a few poems in rhyme and meter, which have a kind of framing technique, that we might call tightly prosodic, but I don't usually work that way.

There is a problem with vocabulary in trying to make equations between the requirements of writing a poem and the requirements of being a musician. We would have the same problem talking about the requirements of painting and poetry. What we have is a confusion here between subject matter and technique: I make a lot of references to jazz musicians, but the references don't necessarily have very much to do with my own technical interests in writing the poem. I think it was Frost who said that writing free verse was like playing tennis without a net. Now that's good as a kind of metaphor for what I'm trying to talk about.

I get a great nourishment from musicians because of what they can do technically, but the making of the music is what's important. The technique is there, because they can't move you without the technique, but most musicians don't spend a whole lot of time talking about scales. They talk about tunes, and maybe they talk "in-house" about changes, but they don't talk about technique. And I find that poets generally—except in workshop situations—don't either. Hayden, who was a great technician, spent very little time talking about technique. If you asked him a specific question, he could give a reference, which was technical.

So we have a cultural problem here, and we also have the problem of segregation. There is a lot of segregation in American letters; we might as well be clear on this. One of the reasons I talk about Frederick Douglass is that I think he would be good for any course in autobiography. I don't care who's teaching it; I don't care what other autobiographies are being studied. At the level of language and form, there is a great deal to be learned by reading Douglass's autobiographies.

Regardless of what my subjects are, I either write good poems or I don't, and people can either respond to them or they can't. The fact that I drag in Coltrane or anybody else is really immaterial. Finally, for my purposes, I'm trying to write as good a poem as I can.

I can understand the difficulties, though, because I have done concerts with musicians, and sometimes they work and sometimes they don't. It really has something to do with the quality of the people that you're playing with. It doesn't have anything to do with technique, it doesn't have anything to do with format, it doesn't have anything to do with discussing anything and saying, "Now we're going to do this and that and the other." It has to do with the quality of the people you're improvising with: if they're good musicians and they're sympathetic, then it works out. But we never confuse the two. Which is to say, a poet doesn't assume that he is playing a saxophone, and the saxophonist doesn't think that he's writing a poem. The two are not translatable; they're different media. Sometimes they go together, but what brings them together is the human voice. When we say, sometimes in idle and whimsical fashion, the "voice of the poem," we are in fact talking about a very profound and very cultured article. We could take pages defining what we mean by "voice."

Let's take Rilke as an example. In Rilke's great sonnets, there is a particular voice which a translator has to capture and I don't think that's a problem that can be solved by going to technical things. One has to go to more intuitive things.

The tenor saxophonist most closely approximates the human voice. That's one of the reasons it moves us so deeply. It's not magic. That's one of the reasons Coltrane is so important to me.

Rubin: One other thing music and poetry have in common is transformation—the voice transforms one kind of energy into another. Would you speak about transformation?

Harper: My primary reason for writing is to activate. I'm trying to *make* something that hasn't been made. What is often the activating principle is presentation. That's what separates something which is authentic from something which isn't—that activating principle. The Greeks defined the word *poet* as "maker," and I think that's good enough; I don't think that we've improved on it.

Rubin: Can a poet transform history?

Harper: If he's a good poet. He'd better be a great poet; he'd better be Dante or Shakespeare. There's a great word that Hayden uses—*timeless*. He's talking about more than quantity; he's talking about quality. How *does* one make something that lasts? One makes *well*.

Rubin: That leads us to your latest book, *Healing Song for the Inner Ear*, whose first section is concerned with Hayden.

Harper: It's really dedicated to him. The first part of the book is called "Re Persons I Knew," and there are three poems for Hayden.

The book itself has given me a good deal of trouble. I hadn't published a book in about seven years, and the organizing of this book was extremely difficult for me. I had too much material, and I wanted to make a statement which was organic, so I had to wait. When I'm in a situation where I can't make a decision, oftentimes it's not that I haven't tried as hard as I can to make one, but it just won't come. So I waited.

The sections are "Re Persons I Knew," "Ends of Autobiography," "Goin' to the Territory," "My Book on Trane," and "Peace on Earth." I begin with Hayden, because Hayden was as close to being a poetic mentor as anybody; if I had met him earlier in my life, he could have saved me a lot of time. He's a tremendous poet, and this poem called "Memorial Meetings" opens the book. It comes out of a time when he and I read together at Yale.

Poulin: You speak of "healing songs." Doesn't this get us back to the question, "Does poetry make anything happen?"

Harper: Of course. You know, I'm on both sides of the fence—I'm schizophrenic—on that one. I agree that "poetry makes nothing happen," but I don't think that the resonances that poetry offers to people can be evaluated or judged in the same way that one can look at and evaluate events.

Poetry is a qualitative thing: what it does for your spirit, what it does for your sinews, is not anything that can be measured. How can anyone say what the value is of something which is finely made? Let's just say it's a piece of pottery or an African sculpture. It has a certain function or use; but it also has a certain abstract quality: the composition of the object, apart from its function, has a value. Maybe that value can't be quantified, and maybe you can't sell it, but it gives you some image of human aspiration, and it gives you some connections.

Hayden was a quite developed spiritual man, so much that he could talk at multilevels; and his simplicity, his directness, his empathy was a decoy, because Hayden was an extremely complicated, philosophic, intellectual man who masqueraded as though, because he was born in the Detroit ghetto, he was not the most disciplined and articulate and literate man. Now here's a contradiction.

The question is, where did it come from? It didn't come from studying with W. H. Auden, although I'm sure that helped him. It came from some mysterious place which has to do with those distinctions which make individuals what they are. I think that we spend too much time on technique; we have to have it, but the making is a process which is magic. It really is magic, and it doesn't always turn out easily. The effort is the important thing. Jean Toomer, the man who wrote *Cane*, said that years and years ago: "The importance of effort is to make it."

"The Steady Interior Hum"
A CONVERSATION WITH LISEL MUELLER

Lisel Mueller

Born in Hamburg, Germany, Lisel Mueller came to this country in 1939 and has lived near Chicago for many years. She is the author of four collections of poetry, including *The Private Life*, winner of the 1976 Lamont Poetry Prize, *The Need to Hold Still*, winner of the 1981 National Book Award for poetry, and *Second Language* (1986), all from Louisiana State University Press. She is the translator of *Selected Later Poems of Marie Luise Kaschnitz*, *Whether or Not* (short prose by Marie Luise Kaschnitz), and *Three Daughters*, a novel by Anna Mitgutsch.

Ms. Mueller says of her work, "I'm often asked if I consider myself a Midwestern poet, and my answer is yes and no. I dislike categorization of this kind, and I trust my poetry has scope and meaning beyond such restrictive boundaries. Still, there is the fact that when landscape appears in my poems it is a Midwestern landscape; I have lived almost continuously in the Midwest since my arrival, and my children were born and raised here. Let me say what countless other displaced persons must have said: I am more at home here than anywhere. At the same time I am not a native; I see the culture and myself in it, through a scrim, with European eyes, and my poetry accommodates a bias toward historical determinism, no doubt the burdensome heritage of a twentieth-century native German."

Ms. Mueller has served as a member of the faculty on the Warren Wilson M.F.A. Program for Writers and has supported the efforts of many younger writers. She lives with her husband about 35 miles northwest of Chicago.

The following conversation took place on 1 December 1981. Interviewers were Stan Sanvel Rubin and William Heyen. Ms. Mueller began by reading her poem "After Whistler."

After Whistler

There are girls that should have been swans.

At birth their feathers are burned;
their human skins never fit.
When the other children
line up on the side of the sun,
they choose the moon,
that precious aberration.
They are the daughters mothers
worry about. All summer,
dressed in gauze, they flicker
inside the shaded house,
drawn to the mirror, where their eyes,
two languid moths, hang dreaming.
It's winter they wait for, the first snowfall
with the steady interior hum,
only they can hear;
they stretch their arms, as if they were wounded,
toward the bandages of snow.
Briefly, the world is theirs,
in its perfect frailty.

Rubin: I'd like to ask you about the poem you just read, "After Whistler." You've said it took twenty drafts. Does it normally take that kind of effort to complete a poem, and if not, what was it about this one that made it more difficult?

Mueller: This was an extreme case. I don't usually go that long without giving up; I was being stubborn. It took me so long because it was a poem written with nothing to start on. I usually don't force myself to write poems but wait until I get some kind of language fragment going through my mind that will start the poem and generate more language. In this case, I didn't have anything, but since I hadn't written a poem for a long time, I decided I simply had to write something. I let my mind go blank and used the first image that came. That's very unusual for me.

Rubin: Could I ask how you chose the title?

Mueller: Originally it had nothing to do with Whistler. It was a poem about white mist, because the first image that came when I decided to let my mind go blank was one of whiteness, probably since I was sitting outside and it was a very bright day. About halfway through the process of writing, the poem wasn't getting anywhere very fast and I decided I had to hang it on some sort of frame. I thought of James McNeill Whistler's famous painting *The Little White Girl*, the one in which a girl who is dressed all in white is standing in front of a mirror; she is holding a Japanese fan, and there are flowers next to her on the floor. She's a very fragile-looking creature. I felt that in order to make a poem about whiteness stick I had to give it that title and connect it to even a small extent with that Whistler painting.

Heyen: I like the poem very much, right from its beginning, "There are girls who should have been swans." I'm reminded of a William Stafford poem that begins, "My father owned a star." It's a beautiful beginning.

Did you say that you thought, in general, that poems that came more easily were your best ones? Why do you think that's true?

Mueller: I don't know. It probably has to do with spontaneously generated language being less labored, and the connections are more easily made.

Heyen: And maybe your subconscious works on what will be the poem for a long time.

Mueller: I don't know. There are certain times when I seem to be open to the possibility of seeing in a new way. I can walk along for weeks and look at all kinds of interesting objects that suggest nothing to me, and there are other times when all of a sudden I make some kind of connection. I see something or hear about something, and it connects with something else in my mind; therefore, it becomes metaphor, or at least contains the possibility of metaphor. And I don't know why that only happens at certain times and not at others.

Rubin: When you're in such a state, do you feel a desperate need to do something about it, or do you wait until something comes?

Mueller: I've learned to be pretty patient most of the time. At first I used to be frightened—you've heard it a million times and maybe you've even heard yourself say, "I'll never be able to write another poem; I've dried up"—but it's happened so many times that by now I'm pretty confident that the juices will start flowing again.

Heyen: And maybe now that you have three good-sized collections behind you, you can relax about that kind of thing. Could you tell us how you started writing poetry?

Mueller: I didn't think about becoming a writer for a long time. I did write some poems while I was in college—some very bad poems. They were overly romantic, very flowery. But it was a natural way for me at the time to release tension or express emotion. A lot of people who never become writers do that when they're adolescents. After I left college, I really didn't think about writing very much; I just assumed that it was the kind of thing one does when one is young. I was twenty-nine when my mother died. I felt a great need to express my grief in a poem; it seemed the only way to get some relief. It was at that moment that I really wanted to be a poet.

Rubin: In the poem, "After Whistler," you have the phrase "steady interior hum." That's the kind of thing I imagine a writer always to have going. You must have heard that "hum" before you took poetry seriously.

Mueller: It must be true that I did have that steady interior hum and that need to use a rhythmic language which is very important to me. My poetry is very rhythmic, and it's probably a rhythmic drive that really gets me going. It must have been there all along, but I didn't know it. I did read quite a bit of poetry during those intervening years, and that perhaps allowed me to use language in a way that became publishable.

Rubin: You were in a bilingual environment, weren't you?

Mueller: Not really. When I came over here, I was fifteen, and, of course, I lived with my mother, father, and sister; so as long as I lived at home I was in a bilingual environment. I graduated from college very young, at twenty, and I was already married at that time to the man who is still my husband. He is a native American, so I spoke very little German after that.

Rubin: But you're still fluent in German.

Mueller: Translating from German into English or reading German is no problem for me at all. But the kind of fluency in speaking that you have to have in conversational German or in writing letters really dried up for me, and translating helped to bring it back. Strangely enough, I found when I became deeply involved in German again—and in English too, since you go very deeply into both languages in translating—that I had not forgotten German to the extent that I thought I had. Perhaps it's like swimming or riding a bicycle—if you once learn it, it's always there.

Heyen: Probably about ten or fifteen years of poems went into *Dependencies*, I assume. I see that your title is from Wallace Stevens's "Sunday Morning." I noticed other echoes of Stevens. Was he the most important poet for you of that generation? I hate to ask these questions about influences, because I know they're tough to answer.

Mueller: I don't think I write at all like Stevens. I can't recognize any influence of him in my work, but I would love to write like him. He's my favorite poet of that generation.

Heyen: When you look back on your own first book now—it goes back to 1965—how do you like it? What do you think of your first poems?

Mueller: A lot of it I don't like anymore. Many of the poems seem overly decorated, too metaphorical. Some are sentimental. I've come to write barer poems. But I'm still fond of a few poems in *Dependencies*. Maybe about ten poems in that collection I'm happy to have written.

Heyen: I care for many of them. Somehow, though, it's a more "literary" book than your others: more poems are based on other writers, and on paintings or music.

Mueller: That's true.

Heyen: What change did you sense in yourself, then, toward the next book eleven years later? Was there some other emotional complex that went into *The Private Life*?

Mueller: *The Private Life* has two main springs. One was domestic, the experience of family: my husband, my two daughters as they were growing up. There's a lot of material in the book that has to do with recognizing human growth through the examples of my children and the relationship between parents and children. The other was the Vietnam War, which affected me deeply. It made me think about the interdependency, certainly in our age, of the private and the public life. There's no way anymore for the individual to escape from History, the public life we all share. Being European-born, I felt this very strongly. That is the story of my parents, who were born shortly before World War I, and their whole life was determined by History. Everything was imposed on them from the outside, because the twentieth century in Germany was catastrophic. We came over here as a result of the Nazis in Germany, since my father was political. It's reinforced in my next book, *The Need to Hold Still*—that sense that came to me as a result of the war in Vietnam.

Heyen: There's a beautiful poem in *The Private Life* called "My Grandmother's Gold Pin," which ties many of these things together. Would you read it?

Mueller: This pin was sent to me after my grandmother had died. It was the only piece of hers I had because all her other things were lost during the war. I'm talking in the poem about all the objects that I remember my grandparents having when I was a child. They lived in the same city, and I was with them a lot and fingered these objects from the Edwardian period. In fact, they were very poor when I was a child, but they had at one time been better-off. So the objects are really metaphors for an historical period that is gone.

My Grandmother's Gold Pin

The first fleur-de-lis is for green-stemmed glasses with swirls
which were called Romans / for the cow with the brown fleece,
which said moo when we bent its neck / for the elegant braids
on my grandfather's shabby jacket; my grandfather, who was
poor and proud and loving:

The second is for the upright on which my aunt played Schubert
Impromptus (though we shivered with joy at "Rustles of Spring") /
for the cactus which bumped the ceiling / for the silk and
ebony fans that clicked into bloom in my grandmother's cold
bedroom / for the same dark dress she wore every day, making
her bosom cozy under her round smile / for snowdrops with
modestly lowered heads, which we bought at the corner for
every one of her birthdays, rushing spring by two days:

The third is for cherry soup, beer soup and chocolate soup,
served in thin china bowls with gold edges / for grandfather's
walking stick with its silver head swinging, when we walked
past red rhododendrons and ponds full of hand-fed swans / for
the hours of pachisi / for the card tricks up my grandfather's
sleeve; merry secrets of one who was totally deaf, who was
gentle and gay and a child among chldren:

The fourth is for a white china hen with fresh eggs in her
belly / for darning days, when my grandmother traded us
mended socks for crisp brown flounder / for my grandfather's
treasure of butterflies / for Roman candles, his credible
galaxies / for the red leather albums of postage stamps, precious
untouchables which went, one by one, for the roof over their
heads:

The pearl in the center is for remembrance / for never
forgetting the war, flight, madness and hunger which killed
them / for never forgiving that death in an animal shed /
for the flowers I'd bring, if I could, to the grave on the
other side of a Wall which should be a metaphor or a bad dream /
and for the passion of sorrow, senseless and pure, which is
all I can give in return to them, who were truly good:

And that, my daughter, is why I wear it / and because it is
all I have left of an age when people believed the heart was
an organ of goodness, and light stronger than darkness,
that death came to you in your proper time:

An age when the dream of Man nearly came true.

Rubin: It does catch up all the things you were speaking of.
Mueller: One of my daughters asked me why I wore the pin so much
when she was small. The poem is my answer to her.
Heyen: In another poem, you say, "I know enough to refuse to say that
life is good, but I act as though it were." I sense in poem after poem the
same struggle to believe in something, but with the knowledge of a
terrible history behind you. Even in that poem, when you speak of their
"death in an animal shed," you want to say what you don't want to say.
That holding back leaves a lot to our imagination. It's a very personal
poem, but at the same time it's a poem within its own language.
Mueller: Simone de Beauvoir said, "In language I transcend my particular case."
Rubin: Your mentioning Beauvoir reminds me that there are poems in
the book that deal with being a woman and a poet in America. Would
you say something about that in your work?

Mueller: It's not something that I'm ever conscious of when I write poems. I naturally write in a feminine voice, and the experience I know best has to do with being a woman. When I write a dramatic monologue, which I do frequently, I assume the voice of a woman more often than that of a man. Other than that, I'm not really conscious of being a "woman poet" as opposed to being a poet who happens to be a woman.

Rubin: Do you speak your poems aloud while composing? Do you feel that energizes your sense of language or interest in drama?

Mueller: I like to assume someone else's voice. When I was young, I would have loved to be an actress. Maybe it stems from that, that possibility of being in someone else's shoes and imagining how the person feels. I find it boring to be constantly writing about myself. There are so many other more interesting people in the world, or have been. At the same time, I have the satisfaction of taking the liberty of trying to be that other person and imagining how I would feel had I been that person. So there is a double satisfaction in being someone else and still being myself.

Rubin: There was a ten-year gap between your first book, *Dependencies*, and your second, *The Private Life*. How did you come to *The Need to Hold Still*? What sources does that collection draw upon?

Mueller: I don't really know, except that the book contains several long sequences. That, I suppose, was a change for me. Another change was trying to explore my subject by writing a set of variations or a seminar-rative poem. That was reinforced by coming back to fairy tales or folk tales, from which I really started.

As I told you, I began writing in earnest when I was twenty-nine, after I had been a student in the graduate program in folklore at Indiana, where I studied myth and fairy tales. Of course, as a German child, I was brought up on the Brothers Grimm; but I reread and studied them at Indiana. It seemed as though I had found some kind of metaphoric world that I could draw on for the imagery in my poetry. I think I came back to that more strongly in *The Need to Hold Still* because there is that whole sequence that stems from folk tales.

Rubin: I'd like to ask you to read "The Story" from that collection, because it pulls together what you've said about coming back to stories and about your relationship with your children.

Mueller: This was written almost in one draft. It came out of the title which I'm quoting here. It was such an intriguing title to me that it immediately suggested something else.

The Story

You are telling a story:

How Fire Took Water to Wife

It's always like this, you say,
opposites attract

They want to enter each other,
be one,
so he burns her as hard as he can
and she tries to drown him

It's called love at first
and doesn't hurt

but after a while she weeps
and says he is killing her,
he shouts that he cannot breathe
underwater—

Make up your own
ending, you say to the children,
and they will, they will

"The Why of the World"
A CONVERSATION WITH STANLEY PLUMLY

Stanley Plumly

Stanley Plumly was born in Barnesville, Ohio, in 1939 and grew up in the lumber and farming regions of Virginia and Ohio. He was educated at Wilmington College and Ohio University. His books of poetry include *In The Outer Dark*, which won the Delmore Schwartz Memorial Award, *Out-of-the-Body Travel* (Ecco, 1977) and *Summer Celestial* (Ecco, 1983). In addition, he has written numerous articles, which are being collected in a book of critical prose.

Mr. Plumly has held a Guggenheim Fellowship and a fellowship from the National Endowment for the Arts and served as the poetry editor of *The Ohio Review*. His work has been cited by such critics as Peter Stitt, William Meredith, and Robert Penn Warren, who said, "Plumly has established a new sort of ratio between the poet and his subject—or even his poem. It's a new turn of language, in haunting, visionary pieces."

Stanley Plumly has taught at several colleges and universities, including the University of Iowa, the University of Houston, and Columbia. He is presently at the University of Maryland and lives in Washington, D.C.

The following conversation took place on 30 June 1982. Interviewers were Stan Sanvel Rubin and Judith Kitchen. Mr. Plumly began the interview by reading his poem, "Valentine."

Valentine

In summer they bunched like fruit, green
over green, lemon and lime,
darker on the sun side. Picked,
they looked like paper hearts—
pinned on paper, the way
we hung them up to dry at school.
They'd dry the color of the season.

This season I'm remembering climbing
onto the muscular branch of that
linden just to breathe, those nights
the second-story heat was bad enough
you had to sit it out. Moonlight
was cool coming down through the leaves—
it smelled of the earth dug at the root.

I let it cover me. I let it gather
on the ground into shadow
and small places, like water.
I'm remembering how clear things were
three or four in the morning twenty
feet above the day—I'm remembering
how I knew I had a soul because

it felt so good breathing this good air.
Luck is a tree branching to the roof
outside your window. I sat there, half asleep,
pulling off leaves, watching them disappear,
By dawn they were everywhere under me, gold,
silver, green, each the size of the hand
we lay on the sleep of children.

Rubin: The poem, "Valentine," which you just read, has a theme that has been identified with you—memory. Does every poem for you have to contain a memory?

Plumly: Well, the muse of poetry is the daughter of memory. It's either "recollected in tranquillity" (or anxiety), or pulled out of a long past, more or less involuntarily. The latter is the memory I deal with, the involuntary, Proustian kind—omniscient, omnipresent. In a way it's not even memory, in the sense that it's always *there*, as though I'm always nine years old, or six, or twelve, as well as the forty-three which I am now. I don't see a clear demarcation. What I try to plug into is that pipeline to the past and to read my emotional life as an adult through the past. To use the past that way is simply a way of framing the event for me.

Kitchen: I've always been interested, as you are, in approaching memory in the present tense. So many people use the past tense for their memory poems. Could you talk about time and the way it functions in your poems?

Plumly: As I said, it's all a continuum, contiguous and coherent. Once I get a book of criticism done that I have planned, I would like to go on to a book of prose and revisit much of the material in the poems to fill in the spaces that the poems naturally and inevitably provide with further connections to different events in the past. It is my sense of time that it has a "plot," and it's not simply sequential; I certainly don't believe it's a series of non sequiturs, but there is a pattern, a cause-and-effect relationship between events. That's the basis for even my metaphorical thinking, the way I make a metaphor or simile. The "why" of the world permeates the nature of my poems, I think.

Rubin: Maybe I could make a distinction between a poem as a memory brought to life and recreated, and a poem as an act of trying to remember. Your poems seem to contain both. In "Valentine" you say: "I'm remembering how I knew I had a soul."

Plumly: It's a way of identifying sources or saying to the reader—and to myself, I suspect—that these sources are still very much alive. In a way the poet is the medium between the expression or the poem itself and the source. That's why I would like to think that my poems are preoccupied with the self and the I, and yet are not egocentric. I place myself at the center, but I also see myself as a kind of invisible presence in the poem. I'm not really in the way of the material. Remembering is that present, progressive way of saying the past is coming through me. In this case the focus is on that linden tree and the air around that tree, the ambiance of that tree, and what that outward life, that object life, suggests about where I come from, what I care about, what's valuable to me.

Rubin: It crystalizes around that one image, that one moment.

Plumly: It is a focusing apparatus.

Rubin: You said "Proustian" at the beginning. These poems are so personal, so felt. How do you come to one of these?

Plumly: These poems tend to be like windows in a long hallway—different windows, different sizes, different-colored glass, but it's the same hallway. Similar sources that make a poem possible for a poet are there consistently. There's a tremendous carryover of energy. One poem satisfies the arrangement of the objects and the single event, but that's not all there is to it, and I have to go back again.

Kitchen: It seems to me that the book, especially *Out-of-the-Body Travel*, was a larger poem, clearly and carefully ordered to create that sense of an organic whole.

Plumly: I think of *Out-of-the-Body Travel* as a novella. It has a narrative, horizontal volition, or movement, and the poems are those vertical rhythms that interrupt or arrest that continual drive into the future that we call time, coming from the past. At some point in the career of the book, I realized that there was a presiding metaphor of travel, the sense of mind that telepathists call out-of-the-body travel; for me it's a metaphor that describes coming out of my mother's body, and yet being inevitably attached to it forevermore.

The book which followed it, *Celestial Summer,* is very much about losing that attachment, for she's at one end of the scale and I'm at the middle of it, so to speak. When she dies, what happens to the connection? Does the connection change, and does that pull me in her direction? Not back to the womb, but into the grave.

But there's also the metaphor of moving out of the body into the inanimate world, the spiritual world, the world of inference. And then there's also the literal travel by train. That's different from flying, or even going in a car, because a train is unique in the sense that you have your own body on your hands. You're moving close to the ground, a realistic speed, at the speed of an animal, say, a horse.

Rubin: What period of time is represented in the poems of *Out-of-the-Body Travel?*

Plumly: You mean, how many years did it take me to write them? Three years, or three and a half. Some of it was done in a cluster, and some of the other poems came much later. I submitted one manuscript a year before the final manuscript. It had a long section of prose in the center, and my editor wisely said, "I like the prose, but it's not appropriate for this book." Even though we had a date set for the publication of the book, I agreed that something needed to be done. Most of the poems in the center section of the book come out of that prose. In a way this other book of prose I'd like to do, this autobiographical book, is a reversal of that process.

Rubin: How secure were you in the ordering of these poems?

Plumly: There comes a point where you have to say, "That's it! It's no longer mine; it belongs to itself, and other hands have to come to it." Those new poems would be in the center; that's where they logically belonged, and so it all fell into place. Once you have a few poems in place, the rest fall in between.

Kitchen: In the new manuscript, are you finding that by having some kind of concept of the overall collection you are filling in gaps continuously? Do you ever write an extraneous poem, one that won't be included in the book?

Plumly: Yeah, I have a couple of extraneous poems that I didn't think were good enough and I didn't like the material. In fact, I stole a line or two from them for other poems.

I don't have the energy to write the way some people write. I have to focus on a poem at a time, and it has to be the best poem that I can make out of the material.

Kitchen: Do you ever write a "best poem" that doesn't fit a particular collection?

Plumly: No, that's not possible.

Rubin: Let's follow through on your working methods on a more fundamental level. Do you keep notebooks? Has a poem like "Valentine" gone through a lot of drafts?

Plumly: I go through a lot of drafts, but I don't keep notebooks. I'm a firm believer in not doing journals and in not keeping notebooks. I don't need that information. It would depress me, scare me. I wouldn't want that information, because that's *my* information. I want the poem to have its own secret life, its secret ambiance. I keep the drafts of poems simply because a library wants me to keep them and might find them interesting. Otherwise, I wouldn't want them.

Rubin: That fits the dreamlike or reverie quality of these poems, as if they had been received whole. One wonders what's behind that.

Plumly: Those tricks are mine.

Kitchen: You sound as if you wouldn't have been Sylvia Plath with those coming out one after another.

Plumly: Absolutely not! That's not knowledge to be shared.

Rubin: Would you talk about music and language? You've written very interestingly about the directions American poetry has taken in the last several years and about its sources in the nineteenth century. Has your feeling for the music of poetry changed, say, as a marking point, since *In the Outer Dark* in 1976?

Plumly: I write a longer, more flexible line. My lines are longer because there's more information in them. But I'm also better able to pace them.

What I've been trying to say in much of my criticism is that American poetry is essentially a free-verse experience and that the formalizations of free verse have to be described. It's difficult because we all have our own ways of doing it. There are some generalizations that can be made, but you have to examine a poet's work to talk intelligently about free verse. That's true also of so-called "formal verse," but we just haven't done much of it. I don't think that there are enough poets talking about poetry. Writing criticism is hard work. I hate it, but at the same time I have a lot of opinions and, I would like to think, some insight. So criticism is the only place to go. You can't really do that in your poetry; some poets have tried—Emerson and A. R. Ammons come to mind, but I don't find that work as interesting or as supportive as real poetry.

Kitchen: Would "This Poem" come close to what you have in mind? Could you read the poem for us?

Plumly: Yes, it comes as close as any poem I've written. It's the last poem in *Out-of-the-Body Travel*, and I saw it as a kind of underlining—not underpinning—of the concerns and sources of the book. When we talk about sources and putting a book together, I see myself on the landscape or in a room, and it's a certain time of the day; I see myself in a dramatic circumstance. That's not so much where the poems come from as it is where the poems as a group order themselves. "This Poem" is a poem that looked back at all of that and said, "This is a gesture of explanation." Images and voices are not very distinguishable in my synaesthetic mind. I hear what I see, I see what I hear. It's a Roethke perception.

This Poem

It is familiar language, like the lifetime leitmotif
of a vowel, the one pure sound you will ever make,

what you say to yourself in the little litany
of breathing.

                   But nothing like *the bicycle lay out*
all night on the lawn. The first voice I ever heard
I still hear, like the small talk in a daydream.

Przewalski's horse on the wall at Lascaux is language,
as in a child's drawing the voiceprint is simply visual,
what the eye overheard. Every voice we imagine will

eventually take form, as those we remember are
         written down.

Here and here and here.

Rubin: Part of what you've said about prosody is that you've seen a turn from the line to the sentence. You identify that with a kind of narrative thrust.
Plumly: Absolutely! The English sentence is a narrative instrument. There is simply no way around that. If you examine the work of "deep imagists," or the work of surrealists, you'll notice that one of their needs is to purify the image by divesting themselves of those syntactical relations. I'm not saying that's not legitimate; I'm just describing what is, in fact, the case. The thrust of the sentence is narrative, and that's the secret of what we understand as free verse.
Rubin: How significant is the individual word to you?
Plumly: It's absolute—that's how significant! But it's not just the single word I concentrate on. It goes then to the logic of the phrase, the clause, the simple sentence, the compound sentence, the compound-complex, and so on. As I've said in some of my prose writing, on hearing a free-verse poem, it's unlikely that you can tell line breaks, without the text in front of you. But you can tell sentences, and you can interpret rhythms in those sentences. Good writing will always break at the right places. It will have a sense of its own.

Kitchen: Then, when you think of line breaks, you're thinking of the poem as it looks on the page?

Plumly: We make a mistake in talking about line breaks. That's not the issue. The issue is what can the line sustain; what can it hold. It will break itself.

I teach a lot of poetry writing, and I find that the students get hung up on line breaks, without really understanding or even paying attention to what the value of the line itself is. They are more interested in terminating, when the issue is *sustaining*. I'm concerned with writing whole lines, full lines, and hopefully rich lines that have a certain texture or sense of their own.

Kitchen: Please talk about language—*sound*—how that adds to the larger picture, not just thematic concerns.

Plumly: Language, sound, and music in poetry. I wonder. It's all rhythm, inside and between the words and among the words. Rhythm is what passes through and over the words as they move within the length of their expectation. Frost's blank verse can never be mistaken for Stevens's blank verse. It's in the voiceprint, it's in their feet. Who's the best dancer—Yeats, Eliot, Pound, Stevens, Frost, or Williams? Dickinson, I'll bet.

Rubin: How is your sense of all this related to the reading that you do? You're a widely respected reader; what does it do to your own inner music?

Plumly: There is no better way of hearing a poem than to read it before an audience. You just have a third ear that you don't have in the privacy of your study. Until you "go public," you don't have the extra tension, that extra pull on your interest, that forces you to hear and to see what you probably wouldn't otherwise. In fact, the reading may even reinforce what you liked in the poem but didn't understand.

Kitchen: What about your reading in private of other people's work?

Plumly: It gets more and more difficult for me to read new work. I think I'm not unusual in that regard. The older I get, the less new poetry I read. I read literary magazines, but I don't find the work very interesting. Occasionally you'll discover some wonderful stuff, but I read people I've read before, whose work I admire. I read some of my contemporaries, and I go back to certain poems by Yeats or Keats. Those are the standbys. And I think it's a function of age more than anything else. Maybe it's also because I teach so much and I'm forced to read so many student poems that the magazines seem . . .

Kitchen: . . . one long student poem?

Plumly: . . . one more step in that direction.

Kitchen: What *is* the function of the literary magazine? You've edited one, and you publish in them.

Plumly: There is a handful of really good magazines that I do read. You find some terrific work there. That's one function of the magazine—first exposure. And I suppose for some people it's an act of self-editing, a way of saying, "Do I really want this poem in the book?" It's a kind of testing process. I've done a lot of editing myself, and it's terrible, difficult, painful work editing a magazine. Those who do it well deserve all the credit they can get, because when it's done well, it's incredible.

Rubin: Did you have one particular reader or editor who made a lot of difference to you early on?

Plumly: Daniel Halpern had a great deal to do with the success of this book, because he's the one who said the prose had to go. Before that, absolutely not. I wish I'd had someone, because I wasted a lot of time. Most of my time was spent alone. I had no poetry workshops. I was in graduate school with Bill Heyen, and we mostly spent time fending off the fiction writers. Our instructors were not the best people to help poets, to be honest about it; but maybe that was for the best.

Rubin: So many of your poems have to do not only with memory but memory of your mother or father.

Plumly: Yes, as totemic figures.

Kitchen: Your mother and father are as much absent from the poems as they are present.

Plumly: Absolutely! Frankly, that's one of the smartest things anyone's ever said about my work. I get so tired of people saying to me, "You write mother poems or father poems." They're not mother poems or father poems. They are as absent as they are present.

Kitchen: You really mean that they are "totemic figures."

Plumly: They *are*. They really serve a symbolic function. They are antagonists or sources of a gravitational pull. They take me out of myself, into the world.

Kitchen: Into a sort of history?

Plumly: It's history only because they are part of history.

Kitchen: I'd like you to read "Say Summer/For My Mother," because it illustrates what you've have talking about.

Plumly: It's the only poem, or maybe one of two, that came in a single sitting. I sat down and wrote it out the way it is. It is, in effect, a single sentence. There are a couple of periods, but it has one motion. It comes out of a simple incident that in itself couldn't be the poem, but around which the light made its way.

Say Summer/For My Mother

I could give it back to you, perhaps in a season,
say summer. I could give a leaf back, green

grass, sky full of rain, root
that won't dig deeper, the names called out
just before sundown: *Linda back, Susy back,
Carolyn*. I could give you back a supper
on the porch or the room without a breath
of fresh air, back the little tears in the heat,
the hot sleep on the kitchen floor,
back the talk in the great dark,
the voices low on the lawn
so the children can't hear,
say summer, say father, say mother:
Ruth and *Mary* and *Esther*, names in a book,
names I remember—I could give you back this name,
and back the breath to say it with—
we all know we'll die of our children—
back the tree bent over the water,
back the sun burning down,
back the witness back each morning.

Rubin: If *Out-of-the-Body Travel* is concerned with time, *Summer Celestial* seems to be predominantly concerned with place, or space (as the title would suggest). But each of these concerns is only a means to a larger end—memory, how the mind in the present carries its past. Could you talk a bit about that?

Plumly: Time and space and memory are abstractions, except as manifest. Their particular emphasis in my work has finally to do with other, emotional causes. Time is emotion—its spatial relations have to do with the simultaneity of context: the blackbird in time is moving, actually and emotionally. The information clustering around an event, a moment, an experience will rather quickly have to act or be acted upon: then you have motion, emotion, mortality. Space is emptiness to be filled or divested. Memory is temporal, of course, by definition—that's how it gets made, through time. Yet memory remembered, memorized is a spatial order, a cluster, intensifying, energizing, manipulating the moment. Memory is the mortality of the moment. *Summer Celestial* is obsessed with this.

Kitchen: There is a curious concern with *naming* in *Summer Celestial*. Or lack of name, the elemental existence of the object without a particular name. Is that a worry for you? Something you are exploring yourself? You end *Out-of-the-Body Travel* with the concept of an anonymous father, and then seem to pick up that thread, and extend it in the next book.

Plumly: The object named into the world becomes an almost infinite palimpsest—fingerprinted, voiced-over, trans-touched *ad infinitum*.

Once named it never dies—only changes. Anonymity is the suggestion that you could ever get back to the utter silence of the original object. Even the skull, we've found, is reconstructible back into its face. The clues are everywhere—in the ground, in the stones, into the dust in the sunlight, in the immortality of water. Anonymity is the recommendation of first causes, first things, the source.

Rubin: How does *Summer Celestial* extend your work? What themes do you see emerging again, or working through to some conclusions?

Plumly: It is bigger, richer, more filled. It has more mind than the last book, but not any less heart. The themes are likely the same, but their dimensions have changed. Form has a way of growing with the spirit, with experience, with the pressure of ultimate concerns and deadlines.

Kitchen: It has been noted that one of your major concerns is memory, not *what* you remember, but how, and why. *Summer Celestial* seems to be concerned with the process of memory—what will trigger a particular memory, how they will "stack up" like light. They become part of the present. Could you talk a little about that? About your own process and how it begins to show you the meaning of a given memory?

Plumly: Memory is not a continuity—it is a series of accidents, a "mess of shadows," ruins and fragments, pieces and piecemeal, habits and severed connections that somehow won't break. It comes in panels, like the rain, and looks a lot like smoke and pollen-drift. With patience it resembles the sequence of colors in leaves. In congregates, like light. The same memory cannot be held the same more than once. Say it twice and you'll have two memories.

Kitchen: The layering effect of your memories gives the reader a way to experience the present. To see with your added vision of the past. Where do you go next? Will you simply mine the depths some more, or are you finding that the new work is heading in new directions?

Plumly: The new book of poems, *A Doctrine of Signatures*, is the most symbolist work I've done yet. The poems are longer, wider, thicker, denser, jumpier. They push and pull. They run no straight lines. The older I get, the more digressive I become. After forty, ideas have to pay their own way.

"The Oracle in the World of Experience"
A CONVERSATION WITH CARL DENNIS

Carl Dennis

Carl Dennis was born in St. Louis in 1939 and educated at the University of Minnesota and the University of California at Berkeley, where he received his Ph.D. in 1966. He is the author of five volumes of poetry: *A House of My Own* (Braziller), *Climbing Down* (Braziller), *Signs and Wonders* (Princeton), *The Near World* (Morrow), and most recently *The Outskirts of Troy* (Morrow, 1988).

Of his poetry, the late Richard Hugo wrote, "These poems are so true and telling they seem to fly into our lives like bright birds of surprise." His work has appeared in such magazines as *The New Yorker*, *The Georgia Review*, and *Salmagundi*. In 1984, Mr. Dennis received a Guggenheim Fellowship in poetry.

Mr. Dennis now lives in Buffalo, New York, where he teaches in the English Department of SUNY Buffalo. In 1987, he joined the staff of the M.F.A. Program for writers at Warren Wilson College.

The following conversation took place on 11 November 1986. Interviewers were Stan Sanvel Rubin and Judith Kitchen. Mr. Dennis began by reading his poem "More Music."

More Music

This one thinks he's lucky when his car
Flips over in the gully and he climbs out
With no bones broken, dusts himself off,
And walks away, eager to forget the episode.

And this one when her fever breaks
And she opens her eyes to breeze-blown,
Sky-blue curtains in a sunlit house

With much of her life still before her
And nothing she's done too far behind her
To be called back, or remedied, or atoned.

Now she'll be glad to offer her favorite evening hours
To Uncle Victor and listen as he tells again
How the road washed out in the rain
And he never made it to Green Haven in time
To hear the Silver Stars and the Five Aces.
And she'll be glad to agree that the good bands
Lift the tunes he likes best above them to another life.
And agree it isn't practice alone
That makes them sound that way
But luck, or something better yet.

And if Victor thinks he's a lucky man for the talk
And for his room in his nephew's house
Up beneath the rafters, and the sweet sound of the rain
Tapping on the tar paper or ringing in the coffee can,
Should we try to deny it? Should we make a list
Of all we think he's deserved and missed
As if we knew someone to present it to
Or what to say when told we're dreaming
Of an end unpromised and impossible,
Unmindful of the middle, where we all live now?

Rubin: That's a strong and very interesting poem. In many ways it's emblematic of the style and concerns of the book as a whole.
Dennis: Some of the concerns of the book are there, certainly. The fact that the people the writer talks about in the poem are trying very hard to accept their lives and accommodate themselves to their lives, even to find luck or good fortune in lives that are in some sense impoverished, touches on one of the themes I'm interested in exploring. At the same time, the speaker works against that concern, because he finds it strange or even troublesome that these people are trying so hard to accommodate themselves. That tension between the desire to accept and to make do, on the one hand, and the desire to resist the actual world, which doesn't fulfill our hopes, and to demand something more, is an important tension in the book.
Rubin: There is a real narrative underlying this and a real sense of character—the girl and Uncle Victor sound like people you know, in the same way a short story writer seems to know his characters. Are they, in fact, people you know?
Dennis: No, I made them up. This is the kind of theme that for me works

best when I can think of a dramatic situation outside myself, because it's hard to avoid a certain kind of self-advertising if you treat yourself with too much sympathy, too much understanding, too much veneration. To make sure that the tone that I want here, the slight outrage in the speaker's voice, is credible to the reader, I have to turn toward others.

Rubin: You say "the slight outrage." It's very muted, if "outrage" is the word. I suppose it has something to do with the tone of the last lines: "If Victor thinks he's a lucky man / . . . should we try to deny it? / Should we make a list / of all the things we think he's deserved and missed?" But isn't he, in fact, a lucky man?

Dennis: He thinks he's a lucky man, and in some ways thinking you're lucky makes you lucky. Your attitude toward your own life is one of the crucial elements in whether or not it's a successful life.

Kitchen: But the premise of the poem is that we realize our luck only after the fact, or when it's been threatened.

Dennis: That's a part of these characters' notion of themselves—they're lucky to be alive. But the narrator has more ambitious hopes for human nature: he feels that these characters are leading more narrow and impoverished lives than they should have to lead, that they deserve more, and that, therefore, he would like to appeal to some cosmic force for a little more justice for these people. But he realizes that there is no one to whom he can make this appeal. And he's disgruntled because these people themselves don't ask for more.

Rubin: In the middle of the poem, the speaker talks about how the girl agrees with Uncle Victor that these bands actually do something beyond the ordinary; there's a kind of transcendence now that Victor and the girl can believe in, talking about the band he didn't get to see. This seems characteristic for you—whatever transcendence we can believe in has to do with something that doesn't exist.

Dennis: It's true, though that doesn't mean one simply should accommodate oneself to the ordinary. I try to get in these poems a dialogue between the ideal and the real. It relates to the double function poetry performs: on the one hand, to hold out an ideal standard of behavior the world has forgotten or betrayed, and, on the other hand, to accept, bless, celebrate what is. Both elements are important in poetry. If it expresses only an unembodied ideal, it's cut off from the ordinary world; if it defines its role as mere accommodation, it loses its power to criticize and inspire change.

Kitchen: I'm glad you mentioned criticism, because you would like us to recognize the limitations of this world before we begin to accept and celebrate.

Dennis: Yes. Honesty about limits has to precede meaningful accommodation. In times like our own, when poets have serious doubts about their authority, it's tempting to write only about the need to face limits and live with failure. It's much harder to write poems offering models that challenge our ordinary behavior.

Rubin: You seem to have perfected, here and in your earlier work, a kind of flat or transparent style that doesn't want to call attention to itself as performance, but rather wants to focus on the story it's telling or the characters it's describing.

Dennis: I would certainly prefer the adjective "transparent" to "flat." Of course transparency is an ideal that remains out of reach, and a poem today has to show an awareness of the limitations of its own point of view, the difficulty of escaping a purely subjective stance. Surely it shouldn't make extravagant claims for the purity and the power of its language. But to stop with this kind of self-reflexive criticism means, to me, to abandon the social function of the imagination. After all, it's the imagination that tells us what we most want to know about others, that allows us to intuit inner states of mind from external evidence.

It's partly for this reason that I like to write poems about other people, though another reason is simply that I can imagine lives that are more interesting than my own. I don't dislike autobiographical poetry, but I think you have to be blessed with a life that's particularly representative for autobiographical poetry to work well. Because of his ancestors and his New England roots, Lowell seems to me the poet for whom there is a certain kind of American history embedded in his own personal life that makes his "autobiography" symptomatic of the culture.

Kitchen: You don't think that could be true for any poet?

Dennis: In a way. That's the other point to make: it's true for any of us who are willing to reconstruct our lives according to certain demands of the imagination. The danger of autobiography is assuming that without effort your life is going to be poetically interesting, and ignoring the need to transform the facts.

Rubin: What would you say have been the major influences on your own poetry?

Dennis: The most important influence was Yeats. The book that I was writing in my twenties but never published was full of Yeatsian imitations. I guess what I learned from him was what a poem is and does and how the practice of poetry might be a noble calling. And I was impressed by the way he was able to transform autobiography into something larger. Later, reading his doctrine of the mask, I came to realize how theatrically he conceived of the self in his poems. I'm impressed by his distinction between the ordinary, everyday self that shaves and eats breakfast and the voice that he cultivates in the poems. The voice I want in my own poems is always in part a construction, though if it's successful it will seem natural. Of course there's no point in constructing a voice that doesn't feel congenial, that doesn't allow you to explore fully all your concerns.

Rubin: Your lines are very tight, very controlled, but the poems do seem to move toward an oral state that would be at least superficially conversational, very easy to hear. You work in a period, your syntax is extremely normal, and the poems unfold in large, almost paragraph units. Would you talk about this particular style?

Dennis: It has to do with a desire to give the sense of someone speaking in the poems—how we talk aloud to ourselves or to a single listener. Feeling that someone could actually say the poems prevents me from writing solipsistic poetry. And imagining the listener as single prevents me from making the utterance too oratorical or public. As for the rhythms, I try to make them carry the emotion of the speaker. I want to avoid the opposed vices of prosiness and predictability, prosiness that is emotionally bland and metrical regularity that is unnatural.

Rubin: Have you been interested, perhaps earlier in your career, in more traditional form?

Dennis: I have. In fact, that book I threw away when I was about thirty was by and large rhymed poetry. I used refrains and imitated Yeats's Crazy Jane poems. Most of it was formal, in the way Yeats is formal. I had real trouble working away from metrical pattern, too, and what bothers me now about my first two books is mainly the rhythm. They seem too metrical, too formal, a little stilted. Writers today often begin with prosiness and work toward a more formal control. I had to work the other way.

Rubin: Along the way, was there another poet who became more important to you than Yeats?

Dennis: No one all that important. All the other influences were smaller ones—Frost, Eliot, and later on William Carlos Williams.

Rubin: You just spoke of your first two books. How did you know you were ready to put together a collection?

Dennis: I thought I was ready before I really was. It's nothing more mysterious than finally getting a group of poems that you are satisfied with, and continue to be satisfied with for a year or two. I wonder sometimes how many of those poems I'd keep now; I think I'd have to go back and revise most of them.

Kitchen: Like W. B. Yeats?

Dennis: Yes, I was thinking about Yeats, who went back and rewrote his earlier books.

The other thing that bothered me about my earlier poems was that the self seemed too modest. Along with the formality in those poems is a certain self-belittling quality in the voice. The speaker is too meek, too willing to treat himself as an object of easy dismissal. I would like now to speak as authoritatively as I can, without sounding dishonest or self-important. That doesn't mean that I can't try for a variety of tones; but I want to get a richness in the poem less by playing with voice and more by exploring the subject matter of the poem as deeply as I can.

Rubin: Could we shift ground slightly and talk about your working methods? Do you keep a journal?

Dennis: Now and then I write things down; but actually it's not a daily habit for me.

Rubin: How do poems grow for you?

Dennis: In a variety of ways. Totally accidentally I might hear something on the news, a story from Nicaragua, say, which makes me so angry that I sit down and try to write something.

Kitchen: But this anger seems relatively new. Could you talk about your stepping into the political arena?

Dennis: It has less to do with feeling more political than I used to and more to do with feeling that I can now accommodate in my poetry materials that I used to have difficulty accommodating.

Kitchen: What made them troublesome before?

Dennis: That self-belittling voice I just mentioned. To write political poetry you have to claim for yourself a certain kind of political insight and moral indignation that I was reluctant to claim or unable to dramatize.

Rubin: Do you revise much?

Dennis: All the time. I write by sketching in and then redoing the whole poem, rather than working line by line, so that gradually the contours of the poem take shape. I try to keep a poem around for several months, showing it to close friends, before I'm ready to send it out. Almost every poem that appears in a magazine will be altered before it appears in books. In fact, I have to be careful about that, because I alienate editors when I come back with desperate appeals for change. Usually, though, when a poem comes out in a book, it's stopped moving around.

Rubin: *The Near World* has four parts. Do you pay a lot of attention to the ordering of poems in your collections?

Dennis: I am excruciatingly concerned with the ordering of poems. If you read the book in sequence, you gain things that you don't if you read hit and miss. I am very concerned with the way the poems work with each other, enter into dialogue with each other.

Kitchen: I hear a voice in *The Near World* that is confident enough to find fault with some of the external situations in which people seem to find themselves.

Dennis: I would hope that's true. Getting authority means in part confronting things in the world as well as in yourself that trouble you. That's one of the reasons I've turned now to writing some political poetry. I'd like to feel increasingly responsible for confronting the mess of the world. This means, at times, feeling responsible for the mess itself.

Rubin: This might be a good time to ask you about the long poem you

wrote in the persona of an inmate at Attica Prison. Would you talk about
the origin of that sequence and perhaps read from it?

Dennis: It comes out of my correspondence with a man in prison. I met
him about seven or eight years ago at Attica when I was helping a friend
give a workshop there. He was trying very hard to write well and his
seriousness impressed me. We've been corresponding regularly ever
since. He was born, like me, in 1939, and it's hard for me not to see him
as someone I might have been had I been given a less lucky life. He
makes me think about the inequality of life, the lack of fairness at the
heart of things, which is always in danger of becoming a dead truth,
obvious to the head but not to the heart. I'm trying in a poem like this to
do justice to someone whom life has not done much justice.

This is not an uncommon motive for writing, though perhaps more
obvious in novelists. Melville is a good example. He was impelled to
write in part because he needed to tell the stories of people who were not
accommodated by their society, who were too heroically wild or com-
bative like Ahab, too good like Pierre, too innocent like Billy Budd, but
who represented certain important values, which, though doomed, deserved to be commemorated.

I used dramatic monologue here because when I tried to write about
him with the poet as the speaker, the poem seemed too much about the
poet's reactions, not about the man himself. I wanted to give him the
opportunity to conduct his own defense. Also, the poem is true in its
letter form to the way his thoughts most often actually get to me.

Letter from John

"We don't want troublemakers at Attica,"
The man said, so last month they moved me here
After seven years, north to Dannemora.
Otherwise I'd have written sooner.
I'm glad you liked my poem.
Your comments were helpful.
The stanza on death I can see now
Is overdone, said better earlier
In the figure of the flooded quarry.
I meant the woman in rags you ask about
As the moon, cloud-streaked that evening.
But the gray dust you take as metaphor
Is real. Dust from the concrete floor
Floats in the air all over Dannemora.
In the morning you see it clearest.
"Mottled green" is the color of the chipped paint

On the cell walls, which I contrast to the dark green
Of the one hill outside the window.

Hard to put into words what you feel
When the steel door slams behind you.
They drove me here through open country.
Huge skies stretched down to hills.
I saw the Hudson from the Newburgh bridge,
Clean and shimmering.

Handcuffs and leg-irons for two days,
Stripped and searched each night and morning.
They hate it if your back is straight.

The reference to the ocean near Montauk,
Though it seems to you dragged in from nowhere,
Suggests what the gray, forty-foot wall
Reminds me of. Not a perfect likeness, I admit,
A way not to bring the wall close but to push it back
For a spell of privacy, a little breathing room.

The poet here has misinterpreted the prisoner's poem—he has confused the metaphorical and the real—because his world is so different from the prisoner's. The prisoner is trying to straighten the poet out.

Kitchen: And in doing that you are making the reader more aware of what the *real* world is.

Rubin: There are a number of things going on in this beautifully textured poem. One is this thing about metaphor—that the dust is not metaphor but real. This sense that metaphor is a kind of illusion that can mislead us runs throughout the book. In "Beauty Exposed," you have a line "the spectral world of metaphor," in which certain things can seem true that in fact are not.

Dennis: It's part of the voice that wants to be absolutely honest about the limitations and, therefore, sees metaphor, at times at least, as a way of evading what is actually there. On the other hand, the other voice, the lyrical and assertive one, would like to be able to use metaphor to unify things that are apparently discrete or to make assertions about value in a world that apparently is resistant to value. Though you can take one particular poem and find one particular voice in it, I try to get a tension between them.

Rubin: You get another kind of tension in the reader ultimately questioning his or her own processes of dealing with life. In the poem, "Letter from John," John certainly has achieved in his poem—which we never see—a transformation of the really mean conditions of his own life.

Dennis: His poetry is an act of resistance to the world he's given: it allows him to see it in larger terms and to oppose to his restricted world some other world that he knows he would rather be in. That goes back to that tension we were talking about earlier—that desire to hold up a model which is unembodied in the world as well as the desire not to lose contact with the world.

Pound is talking about the transcendental model for poetry in "Hugh Selwyn Mauberley" when he describes his efforts at translation as attempts to bring an "Attic grace" to the modern reader. He opposes this effort to the undemanding art that "the age demands," an art that flatters rather than inspires, that gives us an image of our "accelerated grimace." I think he's right that too much art tries to give us the pleasure of easy recognition. Maybe one of the appeals of the movies is that the camera can turn surfaces into art merely by shifting them to the screen, without probing them deeply. We seldom expect movies to challenge our assumptions.

Rubin: Always tugging behind the scenes, there is the sense of a possible moment at which we could break through into some new kind of honesty that would transform everything. This is what we were talking about earlier as outrage or resistance.

Dennis: Yes. There's always the hope that honesty can lead to a moment of clarity where we see what we should really be doing, a vision that is obviously going to be partly informed by past notions of alternatives.

Kitchen: In many ways these poems construct alternatives to what we think of as *poetry*. They seem to resist some of the idealized versions of our lives or of the world that we're handed in poetry. For instance, in "Charity," you don't let the blind girl find any more fragrance in the flower than anyone else would with an equally adept nose.

Dennis: There's an ideal side of that poem, too, but you're right that it tries to be absolutely honest about the way in which we confront the unfortunate, and honest about the ways in which we try to avoid confrontation by pretending, say, that there are compensations for certain kinds of suffering, when we know that there aren't. Obviously if we think there are, we don't have to be compassionate, we don't have to feel the brunt of what we're seeing. So I agree that the poem is trying to be honest, but it's also trying to redefine sympathy in a way that challenges and demands more than . . .

Kitchen: . . . the easy answer. You seem to be saying that we as poets have allowed ourselves the luxury of not being quite so honest.

Dennis: I must say that I was thinking more in terms of the way in ordinary life we handle suffering around us, rather than feeling that fellow poets have not engaged the issue directly.

Charity

Time to believe that the thin disguise
On the face of the blessing in disguise
Will never be pulled off,

That the truth that's still in hiding
Will stay there, far in the dark.
All that can be revealed is revealed.

All that can be learned from the burning house
Was learned the first time, when the smoke
Blackened the walls in every room.

So much for more experience. What can grow
Has grown; what's small now stays small.
No portion waits for those who deserve more.

The flowers in the yard of the blind and deaf girl
Will never smell any sweeter to her
Than they smell now to any of her visitors.

The music she imagines will never compare to ours.
Her best day will brighten with no joy
That hasn't brightened our day more.

Time to admit that her steady cheer
Is the burden she assumes to keep us here
Touching her fingers for a while.

I wanted to give her a kind of heroism at the end—the dignity of knowing how fragile the sympathy offered her really is. Her cheerfulness is not a sign that she's found some compensation but only her strategy to hang on to human contact as long as she can, knowing that if she were sullen she would drive away what little society she has. I was trying to give her the dignity that comes with knowing absolutely the conditions that she's faced with.

Rubin: This poetry seems very concerned with revising not just the way in which we think about our individual lives but the way in which we treat one another. Your reference to Melville suggests that you think you're in the American vein in terms of the tension between the ideal and the real; but I wonder what you think of the relative success of American poetry in doing this business of getting us to treat one another better.

Dennis: Any good poem can help widen our sympathies merely by introducing us to a perspective on the world different from our own. Some poets I admire also make a particular effort to understand people who are very different in temperament, values, and experience. Lowell is a good example. Take his poem "To Alfred Corning Clark," an elegy for someone with whom the poet has very little in common, a high-society failure whose string of marriages are the major item in his obituary. What you see in that poem is Lowell's struggling to find something to praise in that old schoolmate with whom he has shared little and to whom he feels in many ways opposed. By the end of the poem, in a series of almost casual gestures, he's moved from a state of ironic distance to real intimacy. I'm impressed by that kind of progression, by a poet's taking on the challenge of feeling empathy for someone difficult to like. The differences and difficulties can't be fudged. Nothing is less useful than a statement of unearned sympathy. For a poem to work, it has to overcome resistance.

Rubin: How would you feel, then, about the poets who came to be known as the "confessional poets" and that impulse with which Lowell in particular became associated?

Dennis: You have to see them engaged in a necessary rebellion against certain rigidities in the poetry of the forties and fifties. That poetry tended to be formally conservative, ironic in tone, emotionally dry, and, for all its linguistic density, cut off from the actual world. Many of the "Confessionals" began their careers writing poetry like this and then felt the need to open their work to the flow of ordinary experience. For all of them the change proved a big step forward.

Of course the confessional mode brings with it certain liabilities. One is the danger of assuming that anything that happens to you, just because it happens to you, is worthy of notice. Another is the tendency to see the poet as the object of historical forces, as the passive recorder of experience, rather than as an active participant. I think Lowell and Wright, among others, are pulled in this direction, towards an elegiac passivity, though they manage to resist the pull in their best work. Take a poem like "For the Union Dead." It begins with the solitary poet musing among the broken images from his Boston childhood and ends with bardic rage at the moral failures of America.

Rubin: This "bardic rage" is obviously something that appeals to you.

Dennis: Actually, the notion of the poet as bard is an important concept in American literature. It begins with Emerson, who reacts against the innocuous, coffee-table poetry of his time by insisting on poetry that judges society rather than serves it. He uses his own reading of Anglo-Saxon poetry and his radical view of poetic inspiration to support a lofty conception of the poet as a prophetic visionary who castigates his contemporaries for betraying the heroic possibilities of human nature.

Of course, he had only limited success in putting his theory into practice. His poems work best when he gives up on his theory and writes in chastened blank verse as in "Days" and "Hamatreya." When he wants bardic sublimity and excess, he has to construct mythical voices to speak for him, figures like Merlin and Bacchus, who step in to make the grand demands that he can't make directly.

Whitman manages to give Emerson's inspired poet a distinct personality, to be both bard and a son of Manhattan. His catalogues express both scrupulous observation and bardic excess, the creative redundancy of nature itself. And even Emily Dickinson, though Whitman's antinomy in many ways, is influenced by Emerson's grand view of the poet's function. Like Whitman, she manages to make her voice personal and impersonal at the same time. She is both a woman and a sybil, a constrained sufferer and a riddling, all-knowing oracle. As a result, her voice has a peculiar authority.

Rubin: This strain you're speaking of could be accused in another light of giving support to the kinds of idealizations that your own poetry resists—this notion that you must have something ultimate and oracular to pronounce, or you won't have significance in your poetry.

Dennis: The oracle has to live in the world of experience. But without the ambition, which only certain kinds of idealism can produce, you can't have tragedy, can't experience the kind of failure that produces insight. You have to fall from a height to know loss. You can't fall if you've never climbed.

"Longing for the Unconditional"
A CONVERSATION WITH GREGORY ORR

Gregory Orr

Gregory Orr was born in Albany, New York, in 1947 and educated at Antioch College. He received an M.F.A. from Columbia University where he won an Academy of American Poets prize. He is the author of five volumes of poetry: *Burning the Empty Nests* (1973), *Gathering the Bones Together* (1975), *The Red House* (1980), *We Must Make a Kingdom of It* (Wesleyan, 1986), which won the 1984 Virginia Prize for Poetry, and *New and Selected Poems* (Wesleyan, 1987). He is also author of a critical study, *Stanley Kunitz: An Introduction to the Poetry* (Columbia University Press, 1985).

Critical articles on his work include "Transparency and Prophecy" by Greg Kohl in *American Poetry Review* and "Falling and Returning: The Poetry of Gregory Orr" by David Wyatt in *Pequod*. Critic Bill Christophersen wrote, "The heart of Orr's poetry, now as ever, is the enigmatic image that is his signature . . . [its] most arresting feature is its juxtaposition of death and desire."

Mr. Orr is Associate Professor of English at the University of Virginia and poetry consultant to the *Virginia Quarterly Review*. He lives with his wife Trisha, a painter, and his two daughters in Charlottesville. He also serves on the faculty of the Warren Wilson M.F.A. Program for Writers.

The following conversation took place on 25 October 1984. Interviewers were Stan Sanvel Rubin and William Heyen. Mr. Orr began the interview by reading his poem "The Lost Children."

The Lost Children

For Mark Strand

Years ago, as dusk seeped from the blue
spruce in the yard, they ran to hide.

97

It was easy to find those who crouched
in the shadow of the chicken coop
or stood still among motionless
horses by the water trough.
But I never found the willful
ones who crossed the fence and lay
down in the high grass to stare up
at the pattern of stars
and meandering summer firefly sparks.

Now I stand again by the fence
and pluck one rusted strand of wire,
harp of lost worlds. At the sound
the children rise from hiding
and move toward me:
eidolons, adrift on the night air.

Rubin: The poem you just read, "The Lost Children," has a terrific sense of loss in it. Would you say something about that?

Orr: A great deal of my poetry is based on memory and childhood, and a sense of both loss and the possibility of recovery through the poem. Saying that, I suspect that I'm describing the lyric temperament. It seems to me that lyric poetry tends to locate itself in the intensity of a given moment. Often lyric poets begin writing with an impulse—or maybe it's a continuing impulse throughout their lives—to seek the origins of the self in past moments, and, of course, that would be in childhood, that place where the self is born, where the most significant and therefore the most intense moments have occurred. That has to do with the lyric or, let's say, the *dramatic* lyric, the lyric where the self is locus and focus of an event.

Heyen: You speak of "strand of wire, / harp of lost worlds." That theme of the lost children, of now wanting to draw the past together, reminds me of a lot of your earlier work. In fact, I heard just now the word *crouched* which also shows up in *Gathering the Bones Together.*

Orr: There are recurring words for me. I've worked on the poetry of Stanley Kunitz, and he talks about key images as recurring throughout the poet's lifetime. I have discovered key words which recur again and again in my work—*crouched*, for example, or *muck*, which is a rich word that I love to use. *Kneel* is another.

Heyen: This is a personal question, and if you want to, you can just tell me to shut up. But, some people say that one becomes a lyric poet because of a deep and long-lasting hurt, some sort of trauma. When this terrible thing did happen to you, when you were a young man and in an accident killed your brother—do you think you'd be here in this person, as a poet now, if that had not happened?

Orr: I'm afraid to say that I actually do believe the deep hurt theory. I have a continuing argument about that with dear friends whom I respect a great deal; that is, whether poetry comes out of hurt or out of health and exuberance. The more I deal with it, the more I come back to the feeling that lyric poetry, at least, has a source in hurt, in the wound. What draws us to poetry is that—not the expression of the wound, but a sense ultimately that the wound can be transformed, that poetry is a healing process. That does not mean poetry is therapy. That does not mean that the poet must necessarily be a confessional poet. But the history of personal lyric poetry (starting with Sappho) is the history of obsession, and obsession begins in hurt.

Of course, terrible hurt or terrible events in one's life are not unique to poets. Everyone suffers some hurt or loss, but frequently we look at poets and say that the early deaths of a father or a mother were formative events. On the other hand, certainly not everybody who loses a parent early becomes a poet. But I think there is a connection, and I don't think it's a connection that one has to be ashamed of; nor do I think it's one that makes a poet live a fated life of being forever haunted. For example, I don't experience the intensity of being haunted by the events that I once did, and yet I don't feel that this threatens my existence as a poet.

Rubin: When did you begin as a poet? What was your earliest consciousness of these matters that you're discussing?

Orr: It would be hard for me to relate the earliest work, let's say the first book, to these particular biographical events. In a sense, they're at the source of the work, but they weren't present in the first book in any overt way.

The first book is a typical lyric poet's first book, melancholic and intense. I did not have the skills of language at that time nor the psychological skills to approach my own life. The first book of poems used as its model what I would call the lucid dream, a dream that is sharply focused and precise but still mysterious. It's certainly not discursive, it's presentational: event follows event, and metamorphosis takes place. Those are the structural elements of that first book.

But, part of that world of dream was an evasion of my own personal history and biography; it was a psychological evasion but also an evasion in terms of needing to develop the skill to give form to that experience, to shape it. A poem that has no absolute structure, no sense of wholeness, is a failure.

I knew from the very beginning of writing that I would need to write about my brother's death and my mother's death. Their deaths haunted me, and I hoped poetry might release me. I was haunted by personal guilt and also a sense of the suddenness of loss, a sense that people existed and were then obliterated, overnight—both my brother and my mother died very suddenly. That people could simply cease to exist seemed an unbearable horror that defeated all meaning.

Therefore, you write poems because they assert meaning. They create meanings, or they discover them. I'm a very pessimistic person—I believe poems *create*, not discover, meaning for the most part. That's an important distinction, but it's not one that I like to dwell on. I'd like to think they discover meanings that are already there in the world, but I fear that the poet's imagination out of its own need creates meaning. Finally I felt the need to come closer to that personal experience and to try to discover if there was any meaning in it or to create some meaning in it, some meaning that sustains life, which seems to me the purpose of poetry. The forces that work in the poet's consciousness are the mythic forces of Eros and Thanatos, love and death. Even in its encounter with death, the poem has got to discover some meaning, some life force, something to celebrate.

Rubin: By the time of *The Red House*, was there a conscious coming together of these concerns?

Orr: Some of my intentions, in retrospect, were misguided. There's much more of a narrative at work in *The Red House* poems. I have come to the conclusion I'm not a narrative poet. Lyric poets are always haunted by the sense that they can't extend their poems to take in the world—or at least I was.

I wanted also to do justice to a certain historical world that I knew. The "red house" of the title is where I lived with my family in the country from the time I was six to eleven years old. That was a time that I regard as almost idyllic. I was very happy and there were a lot of interesting things there that I wanted to celebrate.

The Red House itself is a sequence of about thirteen poems that begins early on and tries to move up through adolescence, through brief narrative lyric poems following this boy figure. But at a certain point it became biographical: the brother's death enters and then the mother's not long after. I was trying to go back to that point where I could find the basis for celebration.

One thing I tried to do in *The Red House* and some of the earlier poems in that sequence was to present the ordinary life of an adolescent boy growing up in this rural environment, in such a way that what is ordinary is elevated either by the music itself, by language, or by imagination, by discovery of something being more than it is. I was interested in the way light falls through a barn and the vertical slats of a barn, as if the light was like sword blades piercing a magician's box, that transformational imagination or something like that perhaps, but still to stay in the waking ordinary world, very much opposed to the dream world that my early work first came from. What I learned from that descriptive enterprise is what I could do and what I couldn't do. I find that what I lost was what I value most—intensity. That's a lyric value. That's brought me back away from narrative, from an attempt to be descriptively adequate to the world's variety. I can admire it in others, but that's not my gift.

Rubin: Surely there's lyric intensity in *The Red House*.

Orr: I hope so. If for some reason I was placed against a wall and asked, "What is it in one word that you value most in poetry?" I would say, "Intensity."

Heyen: You know, when Stan and I hear you talk—and you're extremely articulate about these things—we really hear a "mind in the act of finding," as Stevens says. In your essay on Robert Bly, you say, "What the art and act of poetics demand is a form of intense, naive enthusiasm. By naive, I simply mean that a poetics must be an unexamined intellectual and emotional energy flowing outward; as such, it is opposed to logical analysis and critical thinking: it cannot be balanced. It's a crystallization in essay form of heart truths." I'm thinking about this in terms of your book on Kunitz, too. How much as a poet do you want to be in control of what it is that you're doing? How much do you want to know about what you're doing? And, how much of this kind of thinking is concurrent with the act of the poem itself, or is this an afterview of your books when you're done with them? What about your sense of poetics as you were writing the book on Kunitz?

Orr: It's difficult to say. The constant struggle is to believe that you can become more and more conscious and aware of the processes of your own mind and your own imagination, and yet at the same time when it comes time to write the poem all prayers go toward a total silence of your mind and a reception in which you hope you hear a voice inside you saying anything, saying some word whose meaning you don't know, that will begin to form a poem.

In one of the recent poems I read last night, I said, "I hear a blessed humming in my head and I'm its glad amanuensis." That's an accurate description of a certain historical time when I was simply hearing voices a lot and simply listening and writing down, beginning a poem there. I contrast that with the time when I worked on the critical book that was a general introduction to the work of Stanley Kunitz.

Kunitz was my teacher; he's still my teacher and friend, I hope. I learned a great deal from the long three and a half years of studying his work, trying to articulate what is going on in his poems, what they mean and how they work. My original plan was that I could occupy the critical part of my mind with that and continue writing with the other, so that the right hand wouldn't know what the left hand was doing. But it didn't work.

I learned a great deal. It forced me to slow down in my own writing. I learned a great deal about how his poems work and how poems work. As anyone would by writing about another poet, I learned what I believed about poetry. It's inevitable that you project yourself and your own values and perceptions into someone else's work. What you hope is that it's an accurate projection, that it also discovers something authentically there. When the book appears, you can decide whether I'm talking about Kunitz or Orr. I had certain opportunities to see things in his work because of similarities in attitude and experience.

In my own writing while I was working on the Kunitz book, I went even further toward a literary poem with a density of meaning and allusion, which is characteristic of a phase of Stanley Kunitz's work. His work has gone through a lot of changes. But he's certainly one of the most intelligent people I've ever encountered—I mean intuitively intelligent, an associative intelligence. His close friend was Roethke, and they have a similar intelligence, although for Kunitz I think it was the associational intelligence and for Roethke an emotional, gut-level intelligence.

Kunitz's minor at Harvard was philosophy, and that's not ever to be forgotten. His emotional intensity was transferred up into the intellectual and the literary. I think that affected my work as I wrote the critical book; it became more dense, and I began in the middle of the Kunitz book to reconcile myself to the idea that I would write five poems a year. But those five poems would be so compacted and dense with meaning and history and music, as to reconcile me to the loss of the pleasure of writing poems. I like to write. It's fun to sit there every morning and write a new poem or work on old ones. The idea of five poems a year struck me as very sad.

When I finished the Kunitz book, it was as though I'd closed a door to a part of my life. Suddenly I began writing poems that were utterly different, much less literary, almost as a kind of reaction against what I see as both a nobility and a dangerous grandiosity inherent in the Romantic tradition.

Rubin: In that vein would you talk about one of your new poems, "After Botticelli's 'Birth of Venus'"?

Orr: One wants all the resonance of history and culture, yet not to be trapped in it. Someone once described a free-verse poem as a poem in which over the poet's one shoulder Literature was looking down at the page and over the other shoulder, Speech. These two forces are impinging on that page and the language on it. In the earlier work, while I was working on the Kunitz book, I was paying more and more attention to the advice I was getting over the shoulder from Literature. The poems got so dense and so compacted that my voice literally couldn't lift them up off the page; I couldn't speak them in a voice that approximated anything but somebody reading aloud a poem, and that seemed terribly frightening to me and solemn and dense in a sad way. A lyric poet finally believes in the incantatory magic of language. Also I wanted to get some of the variety of tone that you get from speech. I wanted things I'd never had in serious poetry: humor, nastiness, vulgarity—all those things that are important human traits.

"After Botticelli's 'Birth of Venus'" is based on the fifteenth-century painting, which probably everyone has seen reproductions of on postcards or in perfume ads. She's the goddess who's born of the ocean, and blown on a shell toward shore, where she's being greeted. The tone is flippant, and yet I hope that beautiful and magical painting shines up through the poem, since Venus or Aphrodite, the goddess of love, seems very worthy of being worshipped.

After Botticelli's "Birth of Venus"

Aphrodite, foam-born, blown
shoreward on her wise shell
with the breeze tickling her bottom
and a large crown gathered
on the beach to greet and gawk.
The authorities there, too—
men with large batons, trained
in mob control.

                Someone
selling hot dogs and souvenir
brochures of the obvious.
Meanwhile the goddess herself
has that blissed-out, postcoital
expression that indicates
she's not all there—were she a boxer
with a decent manager he'd recognize
that look; right now he'd be
tossing in the towel, reaching
for a bright silk robe to wrap his pal.

Rubin: There's a very interesting blend of colloquial idiom with mythic reference in the poem.

Orr: I was interested also in the boxing images. There's the manager's signal—you throw in the towel to stop the match. The mythic is that sacred history that lyric poets believe in as opposed to the linear history, the history of time which we hate. Time is death.

Rubin: Time *is* the opponent for the lyric poet, but he's not against ideas, is he?

Orr: I hope not. The lyric poet expresses the very human longing for the unconditional, for the eternal moment outside of time. In its intensity and its anguish, that longing could seem at odds with culture and intelligence, but I don't think it is. I think it's a form of human consciousness.

Heyen: I sure do like Venus's "blissed-out, postcoital expression."

Orr: A standard theory is that Botticelli was doing these paintings for the Florentine Platonists. Within this intellectual movement, sponsored by the Medicis, they were translating all of the works of Plato, Aristotle, and also all these strange, mystical texts of Hermes Trismegistus. All this was happening in Florence in this space of about thirty or forty years, and it was an attempt to reconcile pagan mysticism and Christianity in Plato. Which is, of course, absurd. But it was a wonderful, imaginative task. They suspect Botticelli was commissioned to do paintings to express that impulse toward reconciliation. Aphrodite is a pagan goddess, and what you should be painting is the Madonna and Child, if you're a reasonable person at that time; but they convinced themselves that Aphrodite was a part of the search for the Good. She was this earthly beauty who was unearthly and would lead us higher toward an ideal beauty. But, of course, she's also a very sexy lady, and in the Botticelli painting you get this odd combination of earthly, fleshly beauty and unearthly beauty— what they call temporal beatitude. That seems to me what all lyric poems want—temporal beatitude.

Rubin: Your poetry has numerous references to art, to literature, to ideas. Yet there's also this concern with the most minute, transient kind of natural life. For you, the two—nature and culture—don't seem to pull apart as sources.

Orr: It seems to me that the struggle in growing is to bring together those different things.

Rubin: Does that have something to do with how you write? Are you in a frame of mind where you'll be very attentive to passing natural life and you'll be thinking about Botticelli or some key work?

Orr: That's an interesting question because it's very much *not* that way, very much *not* an awareness of the world in any way such as that, where I see something and write about it. It's never happened that way.

There is a block of time from about eight to noon during which I have written for about fifteen years now as a daily habit. Any other time of the day I do not give a single thought to writing poems or to what I'm working on at all. I don't think about the poems. I don't look for a poem. I don't consider myself a poet. It simply doesn't happen that way.

I have two theories about my composing. One has to do with dreams, as models for how disparate things come together and become part of the same story. In dreams things from greatly different times and cultures, along with different people and elements you're not even aware of, suddenly come together in a strange, little visual story that you're taking part in. I experience the world, as many people do, as extremely fragmented and fragmenting. In the morning, I'm fresh from dreams, a state of consciousness where things have been made into wholes. Maybe it's not a whole that we understand, but it does form a beginning, a middle, and an end, which seems to me what story is as opposed to narrative—a sense of a beginning, middle, and end, all of which are in some kind of meaningful proportion to each other.

The other theory is that all sorts of sensations and phenomena are entering our consciousness in all different ways through all the different senses all day, but as in that old movie about the cosmic rays just passing right through the body, only a few actually hit that strange identifiable shape inside you we call the self and bounce back out. What I use in my poems are not historical or literary references that I've encountered in books but that little word or image that went inside me and came back out again. I'm getting it on the way back out when it's somehow bounced off some part of this thing called the self. Out of the thousands of facts and phenomena a day, most have no real significance to the self, and therefore our connection to them is not the stuff of poetry. But with those few that hit something inside, you try to listen with your ear pointed inward, trying to hear them on the way out again. I have to either see some image or hear some language to start a poem. I've never *chosen* a subject. Or, when I have, it's been extraordinarily ill-advised.

Rubin: Do you revise much?

Orr: Constantly. Until I went to graduate school, I couldn't revise at all. I'd never been in a workshop, so nobody had really told me what poetry was, but I was writing a lot of what I hoped were poems. In retrospect, they were just struggling to be poems. If something failed or somebody said the poem was no good, I'd write another one. I never felt that I could alter it. It wasn't ego, just ignorance. Revision is extraordinarily profound and painfully difficult for a young poet to learn. At least it was for me. If one of our secret desires is to be loved as we are, then a corollary secret desire is that the poem be perfect as it first appears.

Heyen: I don't know if you'll agree, but I think revision should be no more conscious or rational and no less intuitive than the first writing itself. I like to keep myself in the mind that brought the first flow through, if I can.

Orr: Yes, I think that's true. I now love to revise. I do it constantly, and it seems to me that's where poems happen. If I have twelve poems that I'm working on, the initial products of twelve different days, let's say, then I have an emotional spectrum: this poem began in happiness, this poem began in a melancholy mood, and so on. In the morning I leaf through them and try to work on the one that most corresponds to my mood or my sense of the world that day. The idea that one can wake up happy and work successfully on a morbid poem is absurd. You're not in sympathy with it. For a lyric poet, the need to be in sympathy with a work is the access to the intuitive.

Rubin: Do you have a feeling or conception of audience at this point? Or, does that not matter to you in the process of writing?

Orr: It certainly does matter to me, in the process of writing. The narrative in *The Red House* was pushing in a direction that I hadn't sufficient gifts to make interesting or worthwhile to people. The reason for some of the literary density was probably also that secretly and unconsciously I had an audience in mind that saw the lyric poet as semibarbaric. I was trying to prove to someone that culture had not been lost on me. I think a lyric poet fears being accused of being a barbarian or a naive primitivist. I resent that, personally. I don't think that a formalist poet is necessarily more intelligent or cultured than a lyric barbarian like myself. I was trying to prove myself to an audience that wasn't appropriate, and I'd gotten too far from myself. I would much rather be intense and risk alienating people. I'm sure that my new work will offend, but that's a good test of art. If it doesn't offend somebody, there's really something wrong.

"From an Odd Corner of the Imagination"

A CONVERSATION WITH NANCY WILLARD

Nancy Willard

Nancy Willard was born and raised in Ann Arbor, Michigan, and educated at the University of Michigan and at Stanford University. She is the author of five collections of poetry: *Skin of Grace*, which won the Devins Memorial Award in 1967, *Nineteen Masks for Naked Poet*, *New Herbal*, *Carpenter of the Sun*, and, most recently, *Household Tales for Moon and Water*. In addition to the poetry, she has published a novel, *Things Invisible to See*, and a collection of essays and stories, *Angel in the Parlor*. Ms. Willard has also written over ten books for children. *A Visit to William Blake's Inn* was awarded the prestigious Newbery Medal in 1982.

The late Robert Hayden said of Nancy Willard, "She also achieves dramatic tauntness in poems wrested from pain and anxiety. She has a feeling for the grotesque and earthy, for the fanciful and surreal . . . her vision, irradiated by a sense of humor, affirms both life and the art of poetry." This is echoed by Robert Pack, who says, "In Willard's hands, the real and the imagined are joined and enhance one another."

Nancy Willard teaches at Vassar College in Poughkeepsie, New York, where she lives with her husband and son.

The following conversation took place on 3 December 1986. Interviewer was Stan Sanvel Rubin. Ms. Willard began the interview by reading her poem "Questions My Son Asked Me, Answers I Never Gave Him."

Questions My Son Asked Me, Answers I Never Gave Him

1. *Do gorillas have birthdays?*
Yes, like the rainbow they happen,
like the air they are not observed.

109

2. *Do butterflies make a noise?*
The wire in the butterfly's tongue
hums gold.
Some men hear butterflies
even in winter.

3. *Are they part of our family?*
They forgot us, who forgot how to fly.

4. *Who tied my navel? Did God tie it?*
God made the thread: O man, live forever.
God made the knot: enough is enough.

5. *If I drop my tooth in the telephone*
will it go through the wires and bite someone's ear?
I have seen earlobes pierced by a tooth of steel.
It loves what lasts.
It does not love flesh.
It leaves a ring of gold in the wound.

6. *If I stand on my head*
will the sleep in my eye roll up into my head?
Does the dream know its own father?
Can bread go back to the field of its birth?

7. *Can I eat a star?*
Yes, with the mouth of time
that enjoys everything.

8. *Could we Xerox the moon?*
This is the first commandment:
I am the moon, thy moon.
Thou shalt have no other moons before thee.

9. *Who invented water?*
The hands of the air, that wanted to wash each other.

10. *What happens at the end of numbers?*
I see three men running toward a field.
At the edge of the tall grass, they turn into light.

11. *Do the years ever run out?*
God said, I will break time's heart.
It lay flat as a carpet.
At least on its threads I am learning to fly.

Rubin: The poem that you just read, "Questions My Son Asked Me, Answers I Never Gave Him," is fairly well known, because it's such an effective poem to use with young people in programs like Writing in the Schools. Would you say something about how you came to write it and about the question-and-answer form?

Willard: There are two sources for the poem. The first is, of course, my son, who did ask those questions when he was four, five, six years old. I used to keep a notebook in the kitchen, where all the great events in our house seem to take place, and I would write down his questions, because I found them much more interesting than any answers I might have given him. By the time I put the questions into a poem, I had begun to think of the questions as riddles, like the Zen Koan, and I tried to get the quality of his questions into my answers.

The second source was my own teaching, from which a lot of my poems come. I do all my own assignments in the poetry writing course that I teach at Vassar. One assignment is to write a poem that consists primarily of questions. We look at the oldest question-poem—the last chapters of the Book of Job, where God asks Job, "Where were you when I laid the foundations of the earth?" We look at Blake's "Tyger," every sentence of which is a question, as if the tiger eluded an answer, keeping itself a mystery.

Rubin: Have you used that poem in working with younger students?

Willard: No, but I know that other teachers have. I just got a whole lot of letters from a class in Cleveland, and the teacher included the questions that her students had made up, and the answers. Both the questions and the answers had a kind of riddle quality.

Rubin: Your first book of poetry was published in 1967. Did that book represent many years' work? When did you first come to poetry?

Willard: I started writing as a child. I wrote poems and drew pictures; and I've never really stopped. That's one of the reasons I like to do books for children—I can illustrate and have a text too. That's also why I like Blake.

The first poem I had published appeared in a children's magazine. An aunt of mine submitted the poem without telling me. I was seven. I remember being very excited, because I had to sign a letter saying that it was my own work.

Rubin: What were your main concerns at the time of that first volume? What made those poems come together and cohere?

Willard: The poems in *Skin of Grace* were written within a fairly short period of time, and I think that makes them cohere—who you are at a particular time, the things you're thinking about, and the things you're doing.

Rubin: When did you start writing fiction?

Willard: I started writing fiction at the same time I started writing poetry. I go from one to the other. For me it's helpful to work in more than one form. Sometimes you have to ask yourself which form a subject or experience belongs in; but the longer I work, the more the form seems to choose itself.

Sometimes people ask me how I can find time to write both poetry and fiction, and I recall the answer William Carlos Williams gave when he was asked how he could find time to be both a doctor and a poet. He said that when a patient came to him, he lost himself in that patient, and returned to his writing refreshed. I think for anyone working in more than one medium the change also energizes.

Rubin: In *Angel in the Parlor* you have an essay called "Becoming a Writer," which is autobiographical and full of advice too. There you quote Williams too, about having his typewriter in his office and always finding time to write, around his patients. What is your working method? Are you constantly writing? You are so prolific.

Willard: The interesting thing I've found is that the less time you have the more careful you are in the use of it. Since I teach and have a family, I've learned to do a lot of writing in my head, so that when I sit down to write, I'm really ready to go. Something that has also helped me, especially with fiction and the children's books, is that I love to draw and to make things with my hands. Often the things I make—soft sculpture and toys—find their way into these books.

Behind A *Visit to William Blake's Inn*, there is a real inn; I know, because I made it. It's six feet tall and stands in our dining room. Sometimes people ask, "How long did it take you to make that?" and I always say, "I don't know," because I just sort of made it in my spare time. While I was making the inn, with all these characters in it, I was listening to a recording of someone reading Blake's poetry, so the listening and the making came together. Out of this came the writing.

For me, listening to poetry and reading it out loud are important. I grew up hearing literature, not just reading it on the page. The way people speak, or read aloud, or sing—all those things that enter the ear before they enter the eye are important.

Rubin: Your poems are very musical. In A *Visit to William Blake's Inn* you seem to want to enchant the ear of the young child reading that collection. Did you have any intention in directing the young reader to Blake?

Willard: No, I didn't. An editor at Harcourt Brace Jovanovich asked me if I'd be interested in doing a collection of poems for children. I had never thought of doing one, and it turned out to be not at all what she had expected.

I hope people do read poetry aloud to children. I think the reason Mother Goose has lasted so long is that she sounds great. Her poems were passed down by word of mouth long before anybody wrote them down. That is how I hope people will come to the poems in *William Blake's Inn* first—by hearing them. I should say that the audience for the book includes adults as well as children. My youngest *listener* is two years old; my oldest reader is ninety-three.

Rubin: I notice that you're clearly using Blake's four-stress ballad form.

Willard: That's one of the things I sometimes ask students to do: write a poem which responds to a poet in his or her own form. I think a student can learn as much about a poet by using that poet's forms as by writing a critical paper. In a way, that's what I tried to do with Blake.

Rubin: Would you read one?

Willard: All right. But first I should say that the book is about a child taking a vacation at this fantastic inn. And the real inn is filled with mirrors, suns, moons, stars, angels.

When We Come Home, Blake Calls for Fire

Fire, you handsome creature, shine.
Let the hearth where I confine
your hissing tongues that rise and fall
be the home that warms us all.

When the wind assaults my doors
every corner's cold but yours.
When the snow puts earth to sleep
let your bright behavior keep

all these little pilgrims warm.
They who never did you harm
raise their paws a little higher
and toast their toes, in praise of fire.

Rubin: Narrative seems very important to you—obviously, since you're a fiction-writer as well. You're praised as a lyric poet, for the kind of emotion and beauty in your work; but there's a strong narrative sense too.

Willard: Last semester I asked my students to name a narrative poem. There was complete silence, until finally somebody said, *"Paradise Lost."* I said, "A lot of contemporary poems are narrative. A narrative poem doesn't have to be an epic. You can be standing in one place, and a whole story can happen to you." So in that sense many of my poems are narrative.

Rubin: But you don't generally write long poems in the traditional narrative form.

Willard: No, I've never done that kind of narrative.

Rubin: Your feeling for language is the precise word and the shorter moment.

Willard: I read a lot of fairy tales and folk tales, and how can you tell a story more succinctly than some of those old storytellers did?

Rubin: When you began writing, was there someone you were consciously imitating?

Willard: That's an interesting question. I'm really not sure. I read a whole lot of different things when I was growing up—probably as much nonfiction as fiction. Natural science I continue to read. My father was a chemist. Folklore and fairy tales I've always read. I still read children's books, and I also read adult fiction. So it would be very hard for me to tell what would have been an influence.

I wrote a critical book, which came out of my dissertation, on Rilke, Williams, Ponge, and Neruda—Neruda is someone whose work I really love, because of the way he praises the things of this world that are there to be celebrated.

Rubin: That's something your poetry does, and beyond just praise, to find the magic in the everyday.

Willard: When you praise the everyday, you have to remind people what it is you're praising. For me, the way to do it is metaphor. An assignment I give my students is, take a common, ordinary thing like a green pepper or a potato and make me see it as new and marvelous. If I can find metaphors for the ordinary, I can begin to celebrate it and make it come alive for somebody else.

Riddles are nothing but metaphors. One of my favorites is an Anglo-Saxon riddle for icicles: "On the way a miracle: water become bone." So many of Emily Dickinson's poems without titles are really riddles; you have to guess that she's writing about a hummingbird or a cocoon. The riddle for me is a very sophisticated form.

Rubin: You write out of the everyday, and you find these metaphors to transform everyday objects and experiences. I want to ask you about your approach to personal material. You also write about your son or about being in your own kitchen. What kind of space do you feel you're working in when you deal with autobiography?

Willard: In many poems I'm telling a story, and the minute you begin to shape a story, you're making the personal into something impersonal. The poems in *Nineteen Masks* are all narratives, but in fact they are not as fantastic as they seem, because they are based upon the lives of two people—a poet and his wife, who was a sculptor at the time—we knew in New York City. For example, "The Poet Invites the Moon for Supper" is based on a supper we ate in their loft on Prince Street lit by moonlight. Many of the most fantastic-sounding poems have a realistic basis. They are the things anyone could see, but I chose to write about them in a somewhat peculiar way.

Rubin: Could you read that poem?

The Poet Invites the Moon for Supper

Tonight a stranger followed me home.
He wore an overcoat and feathers.
His head was as light as summer.
When I saw how much light he spilled
on the street, I knew he was rich.

He wanted to make me his heir.
I said, no thank you, I have a father.
He wanted to give the snow to wife.
I said, no thank you, I have a sweetheart.
He wanted to make me immortal.
And I said, no thank you, but when you see
somebody putting me into the mouth
of the earth, don't fret.
I am a song.
Someone is writing me down.
I am disappearing into the ear of a rose.

Rubin: Do you work differently on what you might call these "mask poems"?

Willard: Those were all written in about three weeks between semesters. I had been thinking about them for some time, and I just sat down and wrote like a madwoman during semester break.

Rubin: To go back to the essay in *Angel in the Parlor,* "Becoming a Writer," you say you did have a creative writing workshop, and what you really remembered from it were the people.

Willard: We never called it a "workshop." The same is true of the course I teach at Vassar: in the two-hour meeting, we spend the first half talking about literature and the other half critiquing the work of the students. The material being discussed is never exclusively student work.

Rubin: I'd like to ask you about another essay, "The One Who Goes Out at the Cry of Dawn," which formulates a little personal mythology of how writers are taken care of; there's the giver of dreams at night, the creative part of the psyche at work. How seriously do you take these personifications as the way you understand the writing process?

Willard: I think it's important to know how that process works, and I've heard other writers say the same thing. There is the critical part, which is very useful when you revise; then there is the primary source part, which is good for the first draft, and you have to keep the critical part at bay while you're doing that rough draft. In a rough draft, anything goes. When students tell me they have a block and can't write anything they like, I tell them to write something they don't like, just to get started. They can throw it out later. The fear of failure is that critical voice coming in too soon.

I sometimes ask my students, "What do you think your muse looks like?" That's one way of asking them to look at their own creative process, what works for them. When I asked myself the same question, I decided my muse is not a person at all: it's a train, because I do much of my writing on trains.

Rubin: In that same essay, you say that a writer can write too much as well as too little. If you keep notebooks, you may feel that everything in them has to be important. Do you keep a journal?

Willard: Yes, I keep a journal or rather a writer's notebook, since what interests me are not the things I do so much as what I see others do or what I hear them say. I find that writing them down keeps them in my head. Occasionally I've wanted to go back to a whole period of time, and I read over the notebook, but I don't use it as a resource, except in a very general way; for example, to get back to the feeling of someone I might have met.

The same is true when I'm doing research for a novel, such as *Things Invisible to See*, which is set during World War II. I wrote my story first, and then did my research, so I wouldn't be tempted to include everything I found. I try to keep the story in mind first of all, whether it's a poem or fiction.

Rubin: Do you do a lot of revising?

Willard: Some poems are gifts; but generally I do a lot of revising, especially in fiction. Characters in fiction are like people in a room that you keep coming back to, and as you get to know them better they tell you more about themselves. Revision is coming to see more of what's there.

Rubin: Have you ever carried a poem around for literally years and finally had it come right?

Willard: Sure. Which may mean you'll scrap the whole thing and keep one line. Sometimes you have to write it wrong to figure out what you really want to say.

Rubin: Does language feel the same to you whether you're using it in fiction or in poetry?

Willard: Not entirely. When I'm writing fiction, I'm thinking more of the way people speak, and when I'm writing poetry, I'm more aware of my own voice. A colloquial conversation might be wonderful to put in a story, but I'd probably have difficulty working it into a poem. The poems I like are formal, not the way we speak.

Rubin: Have you seen your own poetry changing?

Willard: I don't know. I see a continuity in subjects—family and a connection with the natural world. When I look back through these books, I sometimes wonder, Have I been gardening all these years? Have I pared that many vegetables?

I have no capacity for abstract thought. If I can see it and touch it, then I can relate to it. I was never any good in mathematics.

Rubin: How important is form to you?

Willard: It's important. Form is for me something I can hear. I was very lucky at Michigan to have a teacher who made us memorize poetry. This helped me to hear it.

I'm interested in the connection between poetry and music. Someone has set the poems in *William Blake's Inn* to music, and I was pleased to be told that he found it was easy to do because the poems sounded musical.

Rubin: What is the connection between poetry and music for you?

Willard: I used to sing in a church choir. And we sang a lot of poetry: traditional hymns, George Herbert's poems, psalms. You hear music and poetry together when you sing. For me, there's always been a connection between poetry and music.

In a book I've just finished for Random House, *The Ballad of Biddy Early*, I've gone to Irish barroom ballads and ancient Irish charms. The poems in this book are meant to be accessible the first time you hear them, like popular songs.

Rubin: Did you speak these poems aloud during the composing?

Willard: I tried them out loud. First of all, you hear it in your head and then you *say* it, to see if what comes out of your mouth is what you've heard in your head. I think it's very important to hear them.

Rubin: I think of metaphor as a visual form of transformation—one thing appears as another. Where do the metaphors come from? Are they a kind of gift?

Willard: They really are from an odd corner of the imagination. Sometimes I can think of the metaphors, but not the voice to hold the poem together.

A poem may be very ambiguous on first reading, but if it hangs together through the sound of it, the music, I know that I want to reread it because there's something there worth getting at.

Rubin: And you do write quite a bit about family, which you've indicated is one of your continuing themes. Have you worked on a poem that you have felt too personal to go on with, or do you transform it?

Willard: If it's personal, I'll probably transform it into a story or persona, because it's easier to get distance.

I read confessional poetry once in a while; I do like Sylvia Plath. But I guess what I've enjoyed is not her confessions but her brilliant metaphors.

Rubin: We seem to be in a period of clear reaction to that confessional impulse.

Willard: Yes, I think so. However, her poetry remains of interest because of these other qualities.

Rubin: You've written from an early age, and you've published in various genres. You must have diverse audiences—for your poetry and for your children's literature. Does it matter to you to have a sense of an audience when you're writing? How do you conceive of your audience?

Willard: I don't have a sense of an audience when I'm writing. Because I write in so many different genres, my audiencs are often very separate. I don't worry about audience, but I do enjoy talking with and reading to audiences.

Rubin: Is your work not particularly interested in history and politics? Is it ahistorical and apolitical because of your interest in folklore and archetypes?

Willard: I think it's political in the broad sense. I like the epigram that appeared in *Kayak*, "To the fish all lines are political." I can't really separate life and politics. Of course, we've been active in politics. During the Vietnam War, my husband ran as a peace candidate, long before Eugene McCarthy became one. I did write something about that, but it was nonfiction.

Some of the poems in *Carpenter of the Sun* are political—"The Graffiti Poet," for example, which I wrote to explore a voice, a personality—who is *the* graffiti poet? Who is this person, so lonely and anonymous, so outside the social structure that he has to write on the walls?

Rubin: Can poetry do anything for that person? Or, is that a romanticizing of him?

Willard: I think the lyrics of rock music have taken over many of the functions of poetry; in fact, that may have affected the audience for poetry.

Rubin: Poets as a whole seem quite chastened and guarded about what poetry can really do to transform communal reality.

Willard: I think it could do a lot. I was delighted when I heard of the movement to put poetry into the subways a couple of years ago. No one made a big thing about it; it was just there. If you wrote a poem for the subway, it had to fit into the space given to an advertisement. I love the notion of poems being out in everyday life, with no big fuss being made about them.

When my son was growing up, he was a very slow eater, and he would sit staring for hours at his broccoli, so I decided that he should have something better to look at. I took apart an old copy of *Songs of Innocence* and *Songs of Experience* and made the poems into placemats. Our whole conversation at dinner improved; our appetites did too. He sat reading Blake and enjoying the marvelously detailed pictures.

I tell teachers, "Make poetry a part of everyday life, not something rarefied, and your students will stop being afraid of it." Some people tell me they're afraid of poetry, because they're afraid they might not be able to understand it, or they'll fail at reading it.

Rubin: My earlier question about audience partly involved my sense that you do write autobiographically in essays and you do write about your sources and growing up and your opinions. And you do something else in your fiction. So maybe your poetry has its own particular place, its own particular need in a Jungian sense.

Willard: I've read a lot of Jung; I guess his work has influenced me.

Rubin: Could I ask you, before you leave, to read "The Graffiti Poet"? You seem to move toward a sense that the reader and writer identify and are one.

Willard: I think it comes from reading so much older literature—my interest in graduate school was medieval literature. I love being able to pick up a poem written seven hundred years ago and connect with it immediately.

William Carlos Williams writes of the "generosity" of art: "It closes up the ranks of understanding. It shows the world at one with itself." The sense of time *present*, that is all time.

The Graffiti Poet

Who are you?
I grew up in the schoolrooms of the Dakotas,
I sat by the wood stove and longed for spring.
My desk leaned like a clavichord, stripped of its hammers,
and on it I carved my name, forever and ever,
so the seed of that place should never forget me.
Outside, in their beehive tombs, I could hear
the dead spinning extravagant honey.
I remembered their names and wanted only
that the living remember mine.

I am the invisible student, dead end
of a crowded class. I write and nobody answers.
On the Brooklyn Bridge I wrote a poem:
the rain washed it away.

On the walls of the Pentagon I made
my sign: a workman blasted me off like dung.
From the halls of Newark to the shores
of Detroit, I engrave my presence with fire
so the lords of those places may never forget me.

Save me. I can hardly speak. So we pass,
not speaking. In bars where your dreams drink,
I scrawl your name, my name, in a heart
that the morning daily erases.
At Dachau, at Belsen, I blazoned my cell
with voices and saw my poem sucked
into a single cry:
throw me a fistful of stars.
I died writing, as the walls fell.

I am lonely. More than any monument,
I want you to see me writing: *I love
you* (or someone), *I live* (or you live).
Canny with rancor, with love, I teach you to spell
your name, which is always new,
and your epitaph, which is always changing.
Listen, and keep me alive, stranger:
                    I am you.

"Emotional Temperature"
A CONVERSATION WITH EDWARD HIRSCH

Edward Hirsch

Edward Hirsch was born in Chicago in 1950 and educated at Grinnell College and the University of Pennsylvania, where he received a Ph.D. His first book of poems, *For the Sleepwalkers* (1981), won the Delmore Schwartz Memorial Award from New York University and the Lavan Younger Poets Award from the Academy of American Poets. His second book, *Wild Gratitude*, was published in 1986 by Knopf, and received the National Book Critics Circle Award.

Mr. Hirsch has received an Amy Lowell Traveling Fellowship, an Ingram Merril Foundation Award, an NEA Creative Writing Fellowship, and a Guggenheim Fellowship for poetry. Such critics as William Meredith, Peter Stitt, and W. S. Merwin have praised his work.

At present, he is a member of the creative writing faculty at the University of Houston. He also serves on the faculty of the Warren Wilson Program for Writers and has written many articles and reviews for such places as *The New York Times Book Review.*

The following conversation took place on 8 October 1986. Interviewers were Stan Sanvel Rubin and Judith Kitchen. Mr. Hirsch began by reading his poem "Omen."

Omen

I lie down on my side in the moist grass
And drift into a fitful half-sleep, listening
To the hushed sound of wind in the trees.

The moon comes out to stare—glassy, one-eyed—
But then turns away from the ground, smudged.
It's October, and the nights are getting cold:

The sky is tinged with purple, speckled red.

121

The clouds gather like an omen above the house
And I can't stop thinking about my closest friend

Suffering from cancer in a small, airless ward
In a hospital downtown. At 37 he looks
Boyish and hunted, fingered by illness, scared.

When I was a boy the summer nights were immense—
Clear as a country lake, pure, bottomless.
The stars were like giant kites, casting loose. . . .

The fall nights were different—schoolbound, close—
With too many stormy clouds, too many rules.
The rain was a hammer banging against the house,

Beating against my head. Sometimes I'd wake up
In the middle of a cruel dream, coughing
And lost, unable to breathe in my sleep.

My friend says the pain is like a mule
Kicking him in the chest, again and again,
Until nothing else but the pain seems real.

Tonight the wind whispers a secret to the trees,
Something stark and unsettling, something terrible
Since the yard begins to tremble, shedding leaves.

I know that my closest friend is going to die
And I can feel the dark sky tilting on one wing,
Shuddering with rain, coming down around me.

Rubin: I understand that the poem "Omen" was drawn from a real experience, and at the center of the poem is a friend who was dying.
Hirsch: Unfortunately, it's true. When I was teaching at Wayne State University in Detroit, a very close friend, Dennis Turner, who was healthy and thirty-seven, had pains in his abdomen that wouldn't go away. He went into the emergency room of a hospital, where somebody he knew worked, and they kept him. After that, the news was relentless. He had liver cancer, it turned out, and he died three months later. I watched my dearest friend go from being healthy and very much alive to becoming an old man by the end of the summer. Mercifully, since the cancer was so brutal, he died in August.

I wrote the poem some time over the summer, when, as the news got more and more relentless, it became clear to me that it was going to happen.
Rubin: It's easy to understand that this kind of experience would move a

poet to poetry; but it's also a dangerous kind of material. How does one approach that material?

Hirsch: Whenever you're transforming an experience into language—I guess this is about as close a personal experience as I've had that I've written about in an immediate way—you try to hold your personal experience up at a certain distance. Part of that is the shaping and the making of the poem, transforming it from just your own feelings into something else. I realized, after I'd written it, that it wasn't a poem about my friend—which is the poem I wanted to write and still owed him and finally wrote later, "Fast Break." It was a poem about my own feeling of loss. The poem reads nature in a kind of Japanese way so that the landscape reflects what you're feeling and what you're trying not to feel. Rather than trying to have something that's already thought out in the poem, you come to it as you work through the poem. The writing of the poem is the process of understanding the experience.

Rubin: One of your real strengths for me is the way the poem moves relentlessly to that final stanza where you say, "I know that my closest friend is going to die"—just that inescapable factual knowledge that no poetry can avoid. That kind of moment recurs in a number of your poems.

Hirsch: That's the kind of relentlessness you're trying to hold off, but it keeps coming in on you. It's a poem that has a fairly high emotional temperature, and in that sense it takes some emotional risks; but I believe that's what poetry can and should do, so I'm willing to walk on that limb.

Rubin: It also has your typical pronoun "I" and the Other as central to the poem. Do you feel a necessity or impulse to have a poem derive not just from personal experience?

Hirsch: It depends on the particular poem. I feel perfectly comfortable writing about personal experience, but I've also written a lot of poems that aren't about personal experiences. When I started writing poetry, I didn't want to write personally at all, because I thought that there were too many excesses in confessional poetry. I wanted to write poetry more distanced from the self, where the self wasn't the only subject. I really don't think it is. What was initially a strategy to discover more things as a poet eventually became a straitjacket, and I started to write more personally.

Kitchen: You seem to make a real distinction between "personal" and "confessional."

Hirsch: I think of not so much the beginnings of confessional poetry but the ways in which it became misused. I began to get uncomfortable with the way poets were centering their own suffering as *the* primary subject of poetry, and by implication that they suffered more than other people. I love the breakthroughs of confessionalism, the emotional risks, the way poets like Lowell and Berryman and Plath began writing about their own experiences. I don't think we should underestimate the importance of that and I want to keep some of that risk and largeness and passion and the way they brought into poetry subjects that had been previously excluded. At the same time I became uncomfortable with the fact that there weren't enough other people in that poetry, and there were ways in which poets were prizing their own experience over other people's experience. I'm not trying to be moralistic about it; I just wanted to get other kinds of people and experience into my poetry. I wanted there to be a politics in my poetry as well.

Kitchen: Do you think the confessional poets gave enough permission to go in that direction so that now poets of our generation are trying to work through the confessional into something else? For example, the poem you just read, like many others in both of your collections, is quite formal in its stanzaic structure, as though you were looking for a distancing form for material you'd already been given permission to use.

Hirsch: It depends on the emotional temperature you feel comfortable with in a poem. I feel comfortable with a real hot one: I love passionate poetry. The poetry I love most is passionate, like the late "terrible sonnets" of Hopkins or those great Keats odes that are dark and highly personal. There is a difference between making a personal confession or writing a diary of your personal experience, on the one hand, and making a poem, on the other. For me the activity of finding the form in the poem, which is a way of finding what you want to say, is also a way of distancing your experience and turning it into something else. I believe firmly that a poem is a made object, and the making is an act of craftsmanship. The poem is not simply a lyric outcry. The poems I want to write have enough room to think about themselves a bit.

Rubin: What did you mean a moment ago when you said that you wanted your poetry to have room for "politics"?

Hirsch: One of the things that became clear to me when I began reading around in the history of poetry was that most of the people I had grown up with and the kind of experiences I had had growing up in Chicago weren't in poetry. It was nature poetry, Christian, rural, while my experience was ethnic and urban—the landscapes and people I knew in the city weren't there. One string in my bow was to write urban poetry. At the same time I was discovering with great enthusiasm what was for me a whole new world of painting and literature—the world of high culture that I didn't grow up with and knew nothing about—and I wanted to write about that too.

Rubin: So "politics" doesn't refer to any ideological or programmatic sort of thing.

Hirsch: No, it's not a didactic politics. There is a politics implicit in your subject matter, and if your subject matter is poor people or people who have been excluded from poetry or people who don't themselves have a voice, that implies politics to me. But it's not programmatic; it won't tell you who to vote for.

Rubin: When did you find poetry in yourself? Were there writers or others that mattered to you early on?

Hirsch: I began writing in a vacuum, out of a kind of emotional desperation. In high school most of my friends were jocks, and they certainly didn't know anything about poetry. I didn't either. I had to get rid of this load of adolescent turmoil and pain. Isn't that the way most of us begin to write?

It wasn't until I went to Grinnell College that I began to discover people who cared about poetry and ideas, and I began to read around in the history of poetry and decided, "This is terrific!" Then I started to think about what it would mean to "make" a poem, not just to spill my guts out. Some of my teachers were unquestionably important at that point. They'd say to me, "This is terrific, but I can't understand a word of it." So I began to think of making poetry that other people could read, and that's, of course, the transforming of personal experience into something else—something social and public.

Rubin: Was there anyone in particular?

Hirsch: At Grinnell there was a wonderful teacher, Carol Parson, who helped me to believe in myself as a poet and to believe that there was a place in poetry for what I was trying to do. At the same time, as she said later, she realized that I was all passion looking for intellect. She got me reading poetry—I hadn't read very much—and I think she was surprised how I took to it.

Suddenly I found myself immersed in poetry. Fairly early—perhaps my sophomore year of college—I decided I'd rather fail at poetry than succeed at other things. I don't know what a fate that would be! I didn't want to become a poet, because I didn't know any poets. I just needed to write poetry. And I found a way to live in the world. Wallace Stevens says, "The sound of the words can help us to live our lives." Poetry became a way to help me live my life, and to understand it. I set myself conscientiously to read as much poetry as I could.

Rubin: What contemporary poets mattered to you at that crucial point?

Hirsch: Initially I went on Yvor Winters's reading list, and I didn't read contemporary poetry, but the Metaphysicals. Secretly, on my own, I read Romantic poetry. At the time I didn't have a language for what the difference was. It was the end of New Criticism so the Metaphysicals were at the peak of the "stock exchange" of poetry. Later, I discovered poets who meant more to me and who helped me find a more characteristic voice.

I had to find models and learn how to write, then forget those models and break loose from what became a kind of straitjacket. I gravitated to poets of great emotional excess—Shelley, Hopkins, Williams—and what I had behind me was a sort of formal training and so I felt the tug of breaking loose from the classical restraints of poetry. I had learned the rules and then tried to shock myself by what I'd say to break them. If I went to Hopkins for feeling, I went to Stevens for imagination. Stevens was very liberating for me because of the way his poems move around and because the things in them are so extravagant imaginatively. Also he was important because of the way his poems think or meditate, especially "Esthetique du Mal" and "Notes toward a Supreme Fiction," because of what got included in them.

Rubin: Were you reading the "confessional poets"?

Hirsch: Yes, and I probably underestimate the ways that they were affecting me. I read all of Lowell and Berryman, in particular. I still fancy that late Berryman, those books that have taken such a beating in recent years—*Delusions, Love and Fame.* There's a lot wrong with them, but they're so extravagant and I like their large gestures. As you suggested before, I suppose those books helped give me permission to do what I wanted or needed to do.

Then I discovered contemporary poetry as well, and there's a whole generation of poets that were important to me; but I was a little older when I came to them. When I was in college, no one I knew really read contemporary poetry. There were no poets at Grinnell, and things kind of stopped with Eliot, Stevens, and Williams. A little later I discovered Berryman and Lowell, then finally the generation of Philip Levine and James Wright and W. S. Merwin and Anthony Hecht. At the same time I started reading translations of poets like Lorca and Vallejo.

Kitchen: Your latest title, *Wild Gratitude*, would suggest that you're still after some of that excess or wildness.

Hirsch: Well, you know, Ezra Pound says, "Only emotion endures." Isaiah Berlin, in *The Hedgehog and the Fox*, argues that Tolstoy is a "hedgehog," because he knows one big thing; Dostoievski is a "fox," because he knows lots of little things. I think of myself as a "fox with a "hedgehogian" belief in emotion. That's what I came to in poetry, that's why I started writing, and that's why I still write. That's why I'll always like a poet like the late Roethke. I love the expansive lyric and formal control in his work.

Rubin: Would you talk about *Wild Gratitude* as a collection? It begins with the personal, moves into history, and then returns to the personal. I'd like to hear how you shaped it as a whole.

Hirsch: I'm a lyric poet, and it's the writing of the individual lyric that matters first of all. For a long time I was just writing individual poems, but then midway, or three-quarters of the way through, I began to see a pattern and to think about the kinds of experiences I'd been writing about. I saw lots of connections, similar things that had moved me. At that point I began to write poems toward the book and to arrange the poems I already had.

I see the book in somewhat the way you do, but I see it more specifically as a descent into Hell—what St. John of the Cross calls the "dark night of the soul." That's both personal and historical. For me the culmination of that is the third section, which begins with a personal poem but then moves into poems about my grandparents, about some poets I deeply admire, and about events in middle Europe. That third section ends with a long poem about the siege of Leningrad, the nine hundred days in which the Nazis basically starved a city. The personal, for me, becomes part of the political and the historical so that you read your personal experience against the historical. At the same time the historical experience is related to personal and familial experience. Then we come out of that in the last section. The book is a kind of descent and rising. We live in what Elizabeth Bishop called the "worst century thus far," and it was some of those horrific experiences that I wanted to take on. Nonetheless I have a tremendous urge to celebrate in my work.

Kitchen: The final section begins with a poem called "Recovery."

Hirsch: Yes, that's a personal poem about someone who has been ill but gets well, the flipside of "Omen."

Rubin: And the last lines of the book are: "The simple astonishing news / That we are here / Yes, we are still here."

Hirsch: Yes, despite all, we survive, and even flourish. Theodore Roethke says: "In spite of all the muck and mire, the dark and dreck of these poems, I want to be one of the happy poets." For me that's the celebratory aspect of *Wild Gratitude*. The title's not ironic; I mean it as *wild* gratitude, the lucky feeling that we're still alive. Despite everything we've done to ourselves, we're still here.

Rubin: The book begins with a poem called "I Need Help." It's a very strong poem.

Hirsch: I wanted to begin with an ironic and plaintive plea. Sometimes when I read it, people feel sorry for me; but I think it's kind of funny. It's both ironic and desperate at the same time.

I Need Help

For all the insomniacs in the world
I want to build a new kind of machine
For flying out of the body at night.
This will win peace prizes, I know it,

But I can't do it myself; I'm exhausted,
I need help from the inventors.

I admit I'm desperate, I know
That the legs in my legs are trembling
And the skeleton wants out of my body
Because the night of the rock has fallen.
I want someone to lower a huge pulley
And hoist it back over the mountain

Because I can't do it alone. It is
So dark out here that I'm staggering
Down the street like a drunk or a cripple;
I'm almost a hunchback from trying to hold up
The sky by myself. The clouds are enormous
And I need strength from the weight lifters.

How many nights can I go on like this
Without a single light from the sky: no moon,
No stars, not even one dingy street lamp?
I want to hold a rummage sale for the clouds
And send up flashlights, matchbooks, kerosene,
And old lanterns. I need bright, fiery donations.

And how many nights can I go on walking
Through the garden like a ghost listening
To flowers gasping in the dirt—small mouths
Gulping for air like tiny black asthmatics
Fighting their bodies, eating the wind?
I need the green thumbs of a gardener.

And I need help from the judges. Tonight
I want to court-martial the dark faces
That flare up under the heavy grasses—
So many blank moons, so many dead mouths
Holding their breath in the shallow ground,
Almost breathing. I have no idea why

My own face is never among them, but
I want to stop blaming myself for this,
I want to hear the hard gavel in my chest
Pounding the verdict, "Not guilty as charged,"
But I can't do this alone, I need help
From the serious men in black robes.

And because I can't lift the enormous weight
Of this enormous night from my shoulders
I need help from the six pallbearers of sleep
Who rise out of the slow, vacant shadows
To hoist the body into an empty coffin.

I need their help to fly out of myself.

Rubin: Why do you call the poem "both ironic and desperate"?

Hirsch: It's a kind of litany of all the people I could imagine calling for help. There's a wry quality here; I'm calling on lots of people who I know can't help me: the inventors, the weight lifters. Also it's playful in its extravagance.

Rubin: I'm impressed by how different its tone is from the tone of your long poem, "Leningrad," about that enormous event which was a tragedy but ultimately a triumph, because somehow those people survived. Do you work differently on poems like these?

Hirsch: One is a personal plea for help, desperate yet comic, related to my own circumstance, whereas "Leningrad" is an historical experience to which I am trying to gain access. I ended up writing that poem from the point of view of someone inside the experience; I wanted to write it from the third-person, but it was just too distant. The experience was so relentless and nightmarish and in that way representative of the most awful historical experiences we'd suffered through in the twentieth century. It was also the details that I found so moving in reading about Leningrad—how people made bread and how the bodies began to pile up on sleds. I wanted to write a poem that would begin to capture that. It needed a certain length and a certain kind of historical litany; as I got deeper into the subject, the humor fell away.

Rubin: Did you do research on Leningrad while you were writing the poem?

Hirsch: I began with a long-standing interest in Leningrad and in Middle Europe, and I'd done a lot of reading. I had already written these personal poems when I began thinking about the kind of world my grandparents came from. Also in the long-standing fight between the politicians in Moscow and the intellectuals in Leningrad, I was sympathetic to the latter, since poets I cared about the most—Akhmatova and Mandelstam—came from Leningrad. Having read a lot of their work, I began thinking about what they had lived through—Mandelstam, through Stalinism; Akhmatova, through Stalinism and the siege of Leningrad. I had also read Harrison Salisbury's book on the siege; in it he describes how purely by accident the zoo had been bombed first, and for some reason that just got me going. I began this long poem—although I didn't know it was going to be a long one—with the surreal image of all these animals running wild through the city—which became an emblem of the anarchy that followed. So, I guess it was a combination of long-standing interest in the subject and personal concerns—the poem comes at the end of a whole section of poems set in Middle Europe and Russia. Then I started reading all the memoirs I could get my hands on for what Pound called "luminous details."

Rubin: How do you go about working at such an ambitiously long poem?

Hirsch: It's not just a long poem for poets who are used to doing long poems; but if you're a lyric poet, and you believe in keeping pressure on every line, as I do, a long poem is a kind of contradiction, as Poe said, because you're constantly condensing and trying to keep on the pressure as much as possible. At the same time you're expanding the poem and moving it outward.

I didn't set out to write a long poem but to write about the experience; that experience is so large that it demanded a certain kind of scope and relentlessness.

Rubin: How long did it take to complete the poem?

Hirsch: I spent one whole summer on it. Writing it was a little odd, because it's a winter poem.

Kitchen: I would like you to talk about "music." In both books you have a concern with music as well as the kind of "music" you can make yourself.

Hirsch: There's a jazz credo that "it don't mean a thing, if it ain't got that swing." There's a little bit of that for me in poetry: one of the ways I know it's poetry is that it's got rhythm. It's not pure music, but it is rhythmical speech, what Yeats calls "passionate syntax." And I do believe that the lower limits of poetry are speech and the upper limits are song. Most poems gravitate somewhere in between. "Song" tries to make that explicit.

Song

This is a song for the speechless,
the dumb, the mute and the motley,
the unmourned! This is a song for every
pig that was too thin to be slaughtered
last night, but was slaughtered
anyway, every worm that was hooked
on a hook that it didn't expect,
every chair in New York City that has
no arms or legs, and can't speak English,
every sofa that has ever been torn
apart by the children or the dog
and earmarked for the dump, every sheet
that was lost in the laundry, every
car that has been stripped down and
abandoned, too poor to be towed away,
too weak and humble to protest.

Listen, this song is for you even if
you can't listen to it, or join in;
even if you don't have lungs, even
if you don't know what a song is,
or want to know. This song is for
everyone who is not listening tonight
and refuses to sing. Not singing
is also an act of devotion; those
who have no voices have one tongue.

Rubin: "Not singing / is also an act of devotion. . . ." Aren't silence and speech recurring themes in your work?

Hirsch: There is a tremendous impulse for me to sing in poetry; in this particular case to sing on the behalf of places and things that don't themselves sing. For me it's a playful but political poem, probably the most explicitly political of my poems in the sense that it's the calling together of all these weak and humble objects and animals, which are, after all, metaphors for people too. I want to speak for them—which may be presumptuous. Paradoxically, it's a song for those who are not listening and not singing. I was also beginning to feel, in writing what became *For the Sleepwalkers*, that many of the people that I cared about most didn't ready poetry at all. Not only was poetry not about them, as I had read it, but it didn't answer to them and they didn't read it either. I began to feel this enormous split between where I had come from and what I was committing myself to.

Rubin: What made you choose the title, *For the Sleepwalkers*, for that collection?

Hirsch: It grew out of the poem, "For the Sleepwalkers." Once again, it's a kind of community of people who have been driven by forces that they're not entirely aware of and who find themselves suffering as a result.

Rubin: Do you have a sense of audience as you write?

Hirsch: Not initially, I guess. I try to get it right for myself—to make something from the deeper aspects of the self and then to send it out into the world where hopefully it finds some readers. I do believe that we don't write for other poets. It is a hard fate to be a poet in America because there is such a small readership and often our readership may be other poets; but I don't believe that's who we direct our poems to or speak for. You try to answer and live in your time and your place. Who the poems find is something else.

Rubin: If there's anything that defines what we've been talking about as the post-confessional impulse in contemporary poetry, it's the kind of split you're indicating here: the lyric impulse and the sense that we're responsible to history, not just to ourselves. But what really can we do with that responsibility? Your poems do come back to this sense of history, most strikingly perhaps in "Leningrad." On the other hand, there is so much delicate and affirming personal experience. Is it an impossible split?

Hirsch: To some extent it is, but we live as multiple selves, and we want to bring these things into poetry. I love poetry that has a personal risk, poetry where there is a lot at stake, but I dislike the activity of centering your own suffering above the suffering of all others. We do have to speak about our deeper, inner lives; at the same time, I think we want to be representative voices and speak about our place and our culture. That means that in writing a post-confessional poetry we can learn from confessional poetry the subjects that have been circumscribed, and ways to write about them so that we can write about our deeper and darker selves without being grounded or limited to that material. I myself believe that we don't live in a transcendental realm: we live inside of history, and we live inside of a place, and I'm going to write about that. The poet who showed me the way in that regard was the early Auden, who combined such a wonderful personal voice with a sense of speaking to history, and about history, and about politics in the world we live in. That's another kind of experience for us.

Rubin: Would you close with the poem, "The Skokie Theatre," which is that very personal voice you've been speaking of.

Hirsch: My pleasure.

The Skokie Theatre

Twelve years old and lovesick, bumbling
and terrified for the first time in my life,
but strangely hopeful, too, and stunned,
definitely stunned—I wanted to cry,
I almost started to sob when Chris Klein
actually touched me—oh God—below the belt
in the back row of the Skokie Theatre.
Our knees bumped helplessly, our mouths
were glued together like flypaper, our lips
were grinding in a hysterical grimace
while the most handsome man in the world
twitched his hips on the flickering screen
and the girls began to scream in the dark.
I didn't know one thing about the body yet,
about the deep foam filling my bones,
but I wanted to cry out in desolation
when she touched me again, when the lights

flooded on in the crowded theatre
and the other kids started to file
into the narrow aisles, into a lobby
of faded purple splendor, into the last
Saturday in August before she moved away.
I never wanted to move again, but suddenly
we were being lifted toward the sidewalk
in a crush of bodies, blinking, shy,
unprepared for the ringing familiar voices
and the harsh glare of sunlight, the brightness
of an afternoon that left us gripping
each other's hands, trembling and changed.

"Whatever Is At Hand"
A CONVERSATION WITH LINDA PASTAN

Linda Pastan

Linda Pastan is a native of the Bronx, and was educated at Radcliffe and Brandeis. Beginning with A *Perfect Circle of Sun* (1971), Linda Pastan has published six books of poetry, including *Aspects of Eve, The Five Stages of Grief, Waiting for My Life, PM/AM: New and Selected Poems, A Fraction of Darkness* (Norton, 1985) and, most recently, *The Imperfect Paradise*. She has received a fellowship from the National Endowment for the Arts, the Dylan Thomas Poetry Award, the di Castagnola Award, the Bess Hoken Prize, and the Maurice English Award.

Ms. Pastan's work has received the attention of critics, and also of other poets. Among the many who have publicly admired her work are Josephine Jacobsen, May Sarton, Maxine Kumin, Mona Van Duyn, and William Stafford. Her work has been nominated for the American Book Award and has been widely anthologized.

Linda Pastan lives in Potomac, Maryland, with her husband. Her children have grown up since the initial interview and are now graduated. Each summer, Ms. Pastan serves on the faculty of the Breadloaf Writers Conference.

The following conversation took place on 4 November 1976. Interviewer was Stan Sanvel Rubin. Ms. Pastan began the interview by reading two poems, "Go Gentle" and "Short Story." NOTE: Several additional questions were added in September 1987, in order to update the original interview, which was the oldest in this collection. In the thirteen-year interim, four new books of Linda Pastan's poetry were published.

Go Gentle

You have grown wings of pain
and flap around the bed like a wounded gull

calling for water, calling for tea, for grapes
whose skins you cannot penetrate.
Remember when you taught me
how to swim? Let go, you said,
the lake will hold you up.
I long to say, Father let go
and death will hold you up.
Outside the fall goes on without us.
How easily the leaves give in,
I hear them on the last breath of wind,
passing this disappearing place.

Short Story

In the short story
that is my life
the mother and the father
who were there from the beginning
have started to disappear.
Now the lover repeats
his one line, and the plot
instead of thickening
as it might, thins
almost to blank paper.
There is no epiphany.
Even an animal whose cry
seemed symbolic
has lapped its milk
and gone quietly
to sleep. And though
there is room for a brief
descriptive passage (perhaps
a snowfall, some
stiffening of the weather)
already
it is dark
on the other side
of the page.

Rubin: Linda, you seem to write a lot about death.
Pastan: Yes, I know. Maybe you could say that I use death as a way of
learning about life, a way of underlining the possibility of loss. I don't like

to think of them as being specifically depressing, gloomy poems about death.

Rubin: Certainly all poets write about death, but in those two poems, for example, there's a quality of "going gentle." Of yielding. Of acceptance. Where does that come from?

Pastan: Well, I guess it's partly wishful thinking. That particular poem ("Go Gentle") I did write at the time my father really was dying, resisting every inch of the way, and I was shocked to find out how angry I was at him for not doing it more easily. I think I probably won't do it easily either, but that's a way of dealing with it, at least with language.

Rubin: In the second poem, "Short Story," you end with imagery of poetry itself—of words on the blank page.

Pastan: It's a temptation that writers fall into often—to use tools of their craft as metaphor for other things. A lot of people don't approve of doing that, but I refuse to be told what I can't do. You're not supposed to be able to write about writing, and I think some of my best poems are about just that.

Rubin: You do it very well. Is writing a kind of death?

Pastan: No, I think not at all. I think the opposite.

Rubin: So, the blank page is an image of death.

Pastan: The blank page would be, hopefully, resisted.

Rubin: The reason I'm asking that is because, in your essay "Roots," in William Heyen's *American Poets in 1976*, you've written about the hiatus or block for a period of fourteen years during which you didn't write and couldn't write. I see that that imagery occasionally appears in your poetry and that you were having to struggle with language. What accounted for that period?

Pastan: Well, I don't think that period had anything to do with what I now think of as writer's block (something that all writers worry about, and which we're all prone to from time to time). That was more or less a decision, a decision of what to do with my life during those years—or perhaps a nondecision. I was very young when I married and started having children, and it didn't seem to me possible to do the sort of job I felt was expected of me as a woman and to give myself a really serious commitment to writing. I was, after all, a product of the fifties.

Rubin: Did you stop writing altogether?

Pastan: I stopped writing virtually altogether during that time, and felt enormous guilt about it. There was guilt in not writing, but there would have been more guilt in writing. It was a very very difficult period of my life.

Rubin: What brought you out of it?

Pastan: Well, I guess just being so unhappy for so long. I decided that I was going to sit down and give writing a try—see if I could organize things so that it would be possible to have four or five hours a day to myself. We reorganized our whole life—my family did—my husband took more responsibilities around the house and I started locking myself into the study every morning in a really disciplined way. And I've been doing that ever since. I need an imposed discipline or I probably would drift into silence.

Rubin: It sounds as if it might have been a frightening to suddenly find yourself with a commitment to write in a regimen.

Pastan: Oh, it was a huge relief. I mean it wasn't really frightening. It was as if I had been carrying around this burden, this idea of what I should be doing, and as soon as I started doing it I didn't have to carry it around any more.

Rubin: Your husband readily accepted this new aspect of you?

Pastan: Well, I was so impossible to live with before, I really was, that I think he was willing to try anything. I don't think I knew how unhappy I was. From reading books, I thought that real life was supposed to be unhappy. I thought it was okay to feel that way all the time—that I was real, that I was grown up. Looking back now, I don't know how I stood it for so long.

Rubin: I was getting to your feeling for language and this seems to have to do with that. I was thinking of images in poems such as "Artificer," where you talk about being surrounded by the "barbed wire of my own alphabet," and in "Soundings" ("I drown in the loosed wave of language"). I suppose that's my earlier question about writing and the connection. Where does that kind of imagery come from?

Pastan: I don't know. I really have thought about the blank sheet of paper, which appears in quite a few of my poems as also being the final sheet, a poem that's not in my book; the blank page is equated with the final sheet that goes over the dead face. But I don't think that drowning in language is a kind of death. It's more like being overwhelmed, really, in a good sense.

Rubin: There's a terrific sense, I think, in your poems, that the words are holding everything together. You don't waste words. You're not sloppy with language. You have a real urge for the precise and lucid and meaningful word. The word is there almost against the silence of this other pressure, and it's fascinating to me when the two things come together in this sort of imagery.

Pastan: Mmm.

Rubin: Sometimes, at the end of a poem which starts out perhaps being very personal or social in its concern, it comes back to language. Who are the poets who matter to you and who have mattered to you?

Pastan: One nice thing about my education at Radcliffe (the not nice thing was that I didn't get a chance to do any writing myself) but the really good thing was that I spent a lot of time really studying poetry in the old sense of studying—something I don't see a lot of students willing to do these days. I read all the great poets and don't think I'm consciously influenced by them in my writing in a specific way, but just sort of as a general standard to have. I guess my favorite poets then were Yeats and Emily Dickinson and Eliot, whom nobody seems to like any more, but who was very important to me. But in terms of poets writing now, I'm not sure about influence. When I'm going through a difficult period there are certain poets who, if I read them enough, will start me wanting to write again. Some of those are Charles Simic, and James Wright, and some of Kinnell's *The Book of Nightmares*. If I read some of those poems I get so involved in the rhythms that I can just sort of take off on my own. I read a lot of poetry and I guess one gets to a point where one doesn't really want to be influenced. You have to be careful, if you use a poet to help you get over a dry period, not to find yourself writing in his or her voice, but I think that my own voice is developed enough now so that that isn't really a danger any more.

Rubin: You just mentioned rhythms. These things matter perhaps somewhat more to you than to some other contemporary poets.

Pastan: That may be true. But I really think of myself as more of a visual poet than a poet of rhythms and sound. Although of course both are important to me. But in terms of starting a poem, or getting into a poem, it's usually a specific visual image that I need.

Rubin: What do you feel about poetry that is essentially narrative—the kind of poetry you don't write?

Pastan: I have a lot of trouble writing long things of any sort. I once tried to write a novel and it turned into a novella and then a sort of a short story. I keep cutting and condensing and polishing everything until it's nonexistent. Some of the poems in the books which look like rather short poems might have been as long as four pages at one point, but I just really keep chiseling away until only the essentials are left. I'm not really interested in narrative and in story. If I were, I think I'd probably try writing fiction. Not that I think that narrative doesn't have a place in poetry; it just isn't something that really interests me.

Rubin: You wrote, in the essay "Roots," about the poem as self-discoverer. About following the poem, and about how you learned, at some point, or came to understand that this was what the poet could do—follow the poem.

Pastan: Well, I really learned that from Bill Stafford, whom I got to know when he was poet-in-residence at the Library of Congress, and who really made me start looking at writing in a different way. It loosened me up a lot, I think. I used to think that a poem had its shape before you even began, and I knew ahead of time what I wanted to say. I'd come to the blank page with a specific idea. After talking a lot to Bill Stafford and hearing him talk, I really tried to follow a different path so that I wouldn't have any idea where I was going to end when I began—and that was really intoxicating. I mean, you really make discoveries that way—about yourself—and I think it leads to better poetry.

Rubin: How do you know when a poem has ended?

Pastan: Ah, you just know.

Rubin: How do you know when you've begun a poem, when you have one? That is, what happens to you before a poem comes? Do they come easily?

Pastan: No. They come very hard. I work for weeks. I go through at least a hundred drafts of each poem, use boxes and boxes of typing paper because I really like each new version—even if there's just a comma change—to be on a virgin sheet of typing paper. I generally start, as I said, with some kind of a visual image or a metaphor and then follow it, seeing where it wants to take me.

Rubin: Yes, in the essay you call it "velocity." The secret force of poetry is velocity. You almost think of it as a movement from you rushing onto the page.

Pastan: Yes, and then comes craft. I'm at the point in my life when I trust my craft enough to know that if I get a certain amount of raw material on the page I can make it into a poem. It's that mysterious rush of images and metaphors that I always have the fear will stop, and if it does I don't know what I'll do. Larry McMurtry, who's a novelist, gave a lecture that I heard last year and he said that writers only have fifteen years of real writing in them, and so I keep thinking what will I do after those fifteen years. Maybe I'll learn a new language and translate because I don't think the craft will ever go away. But I'm not sure about the other part—that part that I consider as given as in "you have a gift."

Rubin: In another area—that I think is still related to that period of silence—you say, "I have come late to the woman's movement, if at all." Could you elaborate on that?

Pastan: Well, I don't know. I feel that if there had been a woman's movement when I was in high school and college there wouldn't have been those fourteen years of silence. I would have known better than to lead the sort of life that I led. We lived in Boston, I was getting a Master's at Brandeis and would have liked to continue there for a doctorate. My husband graduated from medical school and there were a couple of internships, and one of them was in New Haven. That was the best internship he was offered and it never occurred to either of us that we wouldn't take that one, even though the ones in Boston were okay. They just weren't quite as good as the one at Yale, and so we just, without question, left. I mean it wasn't even anything to discuss. That's what women did automatically. They went where their husbands' careers called, and so we went to New Haven, where I couldn't go to graduate school. I had a child and Yale wouldn't take students part-time. I don't think that could happen to a young woman today—it couldn't happen to my daughter. I'm very grateful to the woman's movement for that, and I feel strongly about options both for women and for men. . . . When I say "if at all" I guess I mean that in a defensive way. My book [*Aspects of Eve*] has been attacked by feminists occasionally because it deals often with domestic kinds of things—children, and a happy marriage, and one reviewer read a poem of mine—"You Are Odysseus"—which I thought was a poem about a woman finding her answer through art (it ends with "only my weaving is real") and this critic went into a huge denunciation of women who are still willing to sit home and weave. So I guess I have that kind of defensive feeling, but I really do think that when feminists argue with my book it's a misreading. I think it really is basically a feminist kind of a book.

Rubin: Why don't you read that poem that you just mentioned?

You Are Odysseus

You are Odysseus
returning home each evening
tentative, a little angry.
And I who thought to be
one of the Sirens (cast up
on strewn sheets
at dawn)
hide my song
under my tongue—
merely Penelope after all.
Meanwhile the old wars
go on, their dim music
can be heard even at night.
You leave each morning,
soon our son will follow.
Only my weaving is real.

Rubin: That introduces something that runs through the book—mythology. The simplest kind of domestic moments with imagery, particularly from women, from the Greek myths. Why in this book?
Pastan: Well, there are some in the other book too. I think Penelope has always been someone who's interested me enormously. She seems to me to be the ultimate symbol of the women left behind. Her husband gets to

voyage all over the world, but she tries to make something of her life stranded back in Ithaca. That really has interested me. My other Penelope poem is much more passive, and as I've grown out of just the domestic scene in my own life I've sort of changed how I use Penelope and some of the other mythological characters that are in the book. When I was, oh, back in the fifth and sixth grade I had a wonderful teacher who did *The Iliad* and *The Odyssey* with us at an age where it became a part of my life, and so those people all seem like people that I almost know.

Rubin: The book is divided into three sections. The poem you read is the first poem in the section entitled, "But Eve Must Spin as Adam Delves." The leading theme that you mentioned—and the first section—is "Space within Its Time Revolves" and the last is "Because Our Exile Is Ourselves." What are these?

Pastan: Those three lines are a stanza in an Archibald MacLeish poem, "Eve's Exile."

> Space within its time revolves
> But Eve must spin as Adam delves
> Because our exile is ourselves.

When I came across that stanza, I was really excited because it helped me put a book together. I had all these poems and I wasn't sure how to place them. I wanted the whole to be greater than the sum of its parts in some mysterious way. And the way I did it was that in the first section ("Space within Its Time Revolves") the poems are mainly poems that encompass a small space and are very temporal. They have to do more specifically with death and with family in "But Eve Must Spin as Adam Delves"—the poems are about a woman dealing with the problems of women in our time, or perhaps in any time. Then "Because Our Exile Is Ourselves" tries to move back a step. These poems deal with exile—not just as a problem of women, but again as everyone's problem.

Rubin: Could you read a short poem from the first section which will enable use to discuss one of the major themes in your poetry—namely your children and the fact of motherhood. How about the short poem, "To a Daughter"?

Pastan: That poem appeared on a thousand New York City busses.

To a Daughter

> Knit two, purl two.
> I make of small boredoms

a fabric
to keep you warm.
Is it my own image
I love so
in your face?
I lean over your sleep,
Narcissus over
his clear pool,
ready to fall in—
to drown for you,
if necessary.

I was thinking that one of the things that I've been accused of by feminists—besides having knitting again, after weaving—is the domesticity of the poems. I feel that this isn't a poem about family; it's a poem about loss and the fear of loss, which I think is the central subject in all of my work.

Rubin: A lot of it has generational context in terms of your poems about your father, your family, and your own children. Is a poet continually trying to place himself or herself in time in that way?

Pastan: To some degree. I guess I feel danger from both directions—the potential loss of parents and children.

Rubin: Do you feel as close to your earliest poetry as you do to your most recent?

Pastan: Oh, I think every poet is always irrationally and passionately in love with his newest poem. It's what I'm working on now that really interests me. I don't lose all contact with the older poems, but it's somehow like having grown children. One doesn't feel quite as responsible for them any more, so that it's what I finished yesterday that I'm excited about. On the other hand, I have no way of rationally judging my newest work because I'm too attached to it. So I feel safer with things that have aged a bit.

Rubin: How much time went into *Aspects of Eve*?

Pastan: The first book came out in 1971 and that was about nine or ten years' worth of poems. This one came out in 1975 so there were four years in between. I write about twenty-five poems a year, which makes about a hundred poems in four years, and the books each contain about fifty. That means I like about half of my total production well enough to want to see in a permanent collection. I think fifty poems is a good size for a book. I like a book that one can sit down with and maybe read the whole book at one long sitting without getting exhausted.

Rubin: Would you say something about the themes a woman poet has to deal with? You deal with aspects of femininity, motherhood.

Pastan: Well, I think that any poet can write about absolutely anything. My subjects aren't deliberately chosen, they just happen to be what my life is full of. It's full of children, and we live in the woods so it's full of trees. Whatever is at hand I write about. If we should move and my life should change entirely, I would probably choose very different subjects.

Rubin: Would you read a short poem, "Aspects of Eve," from the collection?

Aspects of Eve

> To have been one
> of many ribs
> and to be chosen.
> To grow into something
> quite different
> knocking finally
> as a bone knocks
> on the closed gates of the garden—
> which unexpectedly
> open.

That's a poem that came very easily. That's one of the few that didn't take weeks of revision. Though I'm not sure why. The title of the poem came before the title of the book. I guess it's partly about the fact that when I did finally decide to go back to writing it was easier than I had expected.

Rubin: Is that where the affirmation at the ending comes?

Pastan: "Unexpectedly open"?

Rubin: It has to do with your own coming back . . .

Pastan: Right. And that the world really is there for women. It isn't so hard. You just have to decide that you're going to go and enter it.

Rubin: In the essay ("Roots"), you mention having named your first child after a character in James Joyce and your last child Rachel—a name you say your grandfather might have chosen. You were just talking about the rebellion and movement from family. Maybe that silent period had to do with that in some way, because a lot of your poetry beautifully comes to terms with one's position in terms of one's roots, one's family, one's origins. I wonder if you could say something about that.

Pastan: Well, when I had my first child, I was barely out of college. I was very young and I was at a time of life when one is trying to cut one's roots and to escape. Rachel I had in early middle age and had come to terms with my family in seeing my own children grow up. In any case, I didn't have any kind of strict Jewish upbringing of any sort. My only real connections were a generation removed—with my grandparents. My parents had both rebelled from that kind of thing so that I had never even been inside a synagogue until I was grown and went to somebody's wedding. Anything in the books that deals with Jewish themes really was from going all the way back to grandparents. But it's something that does interest me.

Rubin: I'm wondering what one leaves behind in a poem and what one comes to. Another of your themes has to do with your husband's scientific career and your difficulty coming to terms with science.

Pastan: Well, I suppose "Hurricane Watch" is a poem more about fear and loss and danger than about science. I am with scientists constantly. My son is going to be a scientist (my first son) and I do borrow a lot of images and ideas to use them in poems, although the subject of science itself only comes in occasionally. I have a real antiscientist poem in my first book. But in general it's just a question of stealing metaphors. I happen to be terrified of thunderstorms. I live in a place where there were thunderstorms almost nightly in the summertime, so that began the metaphor for this poem. As soon as I would hear on the television that the barometer was falling, I knew a thunderstorm was coming and I would be in a state of total anxiety. That's the sort of bare fact that was the germ for a poem which, I hope, is about broader things than being afraid of thunderstorms.

Rubin: "Geneticist," for example, is directly an address to your husband.

Pastan: Yes.

Rubin: You recall C. P. Snow's "two worlds." Is it something a poet has to confront, or is it just your personal vision that forces you to confront it?

Pastan: I've watched my son confronting it. He is a fine writer and all through college has taken writing courses and really has done some terrific things, mostly with the short story. And he's also premed, and it's a hard combination. My father was a surgeon and wanted me to be a doctor, and I totally rebelled from that, so it hasn't been a real issue for me. The scientists that I know are very interested in art of all sorts, and culture of all sorts. They're not at all isolated in their laboratories. They're among the most literate people that I know, and are the most interested in humanistic things. They are much more open than the writers I know are open to anything scientific.

Rubin: I think of some of the ways you describe Adam in your poems. It's almost a kind of antipoet figure in your poetry, if not quite a scientist, a nonpoet. But you seem to accept that Adam has his place.

Pastan: Right.

Rubin: Your poems tend to start, I think, quietly and precisely and open sometimes to vistas of great unease and *dis*ease. But I'd like us to close by asking if you'd read a poem that moves to a very still point, maybe with some of that unease on the periphery. I think it ties together some of these things that we've said. Would you say something first about when you wrote it?

Pastan: This poem is called "Eclipse" and I wrote it, I'm not sure what year it was when the last total eclipse came, it was maybe nine or ten years ago? I don't remember, but we were all told what we had to do to see the eclipse safely. You had to get the cardboard box and make the hole and the whole complicated thing, and I'm so bad at arts and crafts—I couldn't do it properly. I mean, we all were very very busy with the eclipse, and it did excite me and here, here particularly, might be the dichotomy between the writer and the scientist.

Rubin: It has to do with your feeling for nature, too, which often seems to be part of that process of time and generation, never standing still.

Pastan: Right.

Eclipse

A few minutes past noon:
the birds begin their evening songs
and break for the tree;
the horse nods in its dimming stall.
Afraid of a truth that could blind
I turn my cold shoulder to the sun
and catch its shadow in a cardboard box
as though it were some rare bug
about to be effaced by the moon's
slow thumb. To catalog is not enough.
What did Adam know, naming the apple?
What do the astronomers suspect?
The sun like a swallowed sword
comes blazing back.
It is not chaos
I fear in this strange dusk
but the inexplicable order of things.

*　　*　　*

The following questions were submitted to Linda Pastan in September 1987, as an update to the preceding 1976 interview. During this time, Linda Pastan published four major collections, *The Five Stages of Grief* (1978), *Waiting for My Life* (1981), *PM/AM: New and Selected Poems*

(1982), and A *Fraction of Darkness* (1985). A fifth, *The Imperfect Paradise*, came out in April 1988. She has become widely regarded as one of our most important poets.

* * *

Rubin: Linda, you still seem to write a lot about death. It's certainly present in many of the poems as well as in the title of your most recent book, A *Fraction of Darkness*. In the poem, "In the Middle of a Life" (*PM/AM*), the speaker says, "Tonight I understand/ for the first time/ how a woman might choose/ her own death." Has your understanding of, approach to, death changed in any way?

Pastan: In the years since our first interview, a number of people who were very important to me have died. So yes, my understanding of death has unfortunately deepened.

Rubin: The discussion of death points to the fact that what might be termed the main thematic concerns of your poems seem to have remained remarkably consistent over the years: family relationship—especially being a daughter, wife, and mother; death and loss; the "war between desire and dailiness." Would you care to comment on this?

Pastan: Human relationships. Death and loss. The seasons as they change. Is there anything else? These, at least, like atoms are the building blocks.

Rubin: There's also, of course, a continuing concern with language itself, and the role of the poet. *PM/AM* begins with "Instructions to the Reader." How would you describe your current attitude toward poetry and being a poet? Has your sense of *audience* altered with the increasing success of your work?

Pastan: Whenever anyone asks me why I am a poet I think of that wonderful scene in the movie *The Red Shoes* when the young ballerina is asked, "Why do you dance?" and she answers, "Why do you breathe?" I'd love to be able to give an answer like that, because writing sometimes does feel as natural and necessary as breathing. But even more often it's hard, isolating work. I don't think I've ever had much sense of an audience, certainly not when I'm actually working.

Rubin: That same poem, "Instructions to the Reader," concludes with the lines: "Evil is simply/ a grammatical error:/ a failure to leap/ the precipice/ between 'he'/ and 'I'." In the past decade there's been quite a lot written about the use of the pronoun in poetry, as if a poet's commitment to others could be measured by whether he/she uses "I." Your work still seems intensely personal; what distance, if any, is there between Linda Pastan and the "I" of her poems?

Pastan: I've always thought that the poetic "I" is more like a fraternal than an identical twin.

Rubin: When you visited the Forum in 1976, you read from the then-unpublished manuscript of *The Five Stages of Grief.* That was, in the end, a very successful book. Was that collection and the attention it received any sort of a watershed in your career? If not, has there been one?

Pastan: No, I don't think I've had a watershed yet. In fact, I think I've given up expecting one.

Rubin: How have your working methods altered—or remained the same?

Pastan: They are exactly the same. I spend all possible mornings at my desk.

Rubin: Your later poems (for example, "Ethics") seem more discursive than your earlier work, which tended to be image-centered. Does this, in fact, indicate some change in your aesthetic, in what you're trying for? A *Fraction of Darkness* ends with a villanelle, "Shadows." What are your feelings now about issues of *form*?

Pastan: Perhaps the proportion of so-called discursive poems is larger, but images are always there, always central. As for the question of form, my new book will have seven sonnets and a pantoum, so I do write formal verse from time to time. I think of it as a way of refreshing myself.

Rubin: You are a senior member of the Bread Loaf faculty, where you've taught for years. How has this experience affected your work, if it has?

Pastan: I don't think Bread Loaf has affected my work, but it has certainly affected my life. It has made me feel a part of a community of writers, and since I live and write in a pretty isolated place, that communal experience has been very nourishing.

Rubin: Rereading the earlier interview, what strikes you as the clearest difference between the poet you were then and the one you are now? What is the most significant continuity?

Pastan: I think this is the kind of question my readers and/or critics will have to answer for me.

Rubin: In the 1976 interview, you cite a Larry McMurtry comment that writers only have fifteen years of "real writing" in them. What do you think of that now? Are the eighties a good time for poetry in America?

Pastan: I've been seriously writing for some twenty-two years, and I still worry that every poem will be my last poem. And yes, I do think the eighties are a good time for poetry in America, though which poems will survive I don't think we'll know for years.

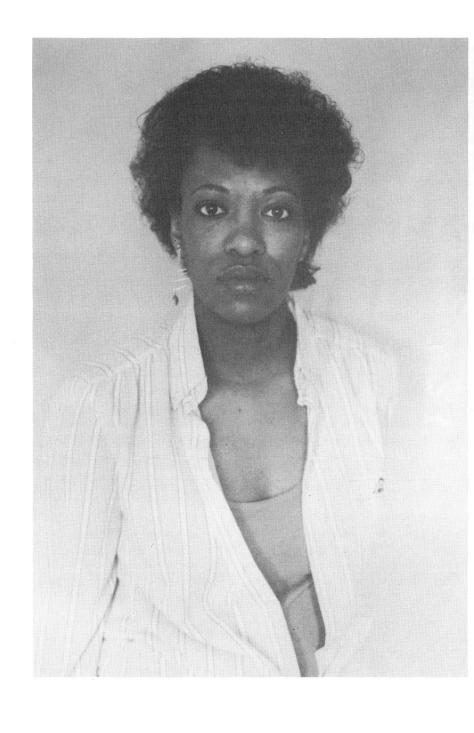

"The Underside of the Story"
A CONVERSATION WITH RITA DOVE

Rita Dove

Rita Dove, born in Akron, Ohio, in 1952, is a graduate of Miami University (Oxford, Ohio) and the University of Iowa. Her three collections of poetry are *The Yellow House on the Corner* (1980), *Museum* (1983), and *Thomas and Beulah* (1986), all with Carnegie-Mellon University Press. *Fifth Sunday*, a book of short stories, was published in 1985 by the Callaloo Fiction Series.

When *Thomas and Beulah* earned Rita Dove the 1987 Pulitzer Prize for Poetry, a prophecy came true made by Robert Penn Warren just half a year earlier when he, predicting "higher awards" for "impressive achievement," chose her for the Lavan Prize of the Academy of American Poets. Besides the Pulitzer Prize and the Lavan Award, she has received numerous other honors. They include a Fulbright Fellowship to West Germany, a National Endowment for the Arts Creative Writing Grant, a Portia Pittman Fellowship at Tuskegee Institute, and a Guggenheim Fellowship.

Rita Dove, who served as president of the Associated Writing Programs for 1986/87, is a member of the editorial board of *National Forum* (the Phi Kappa Phi Journal), poetry editor of the Afro-American literary magazine *Callaloo* and associate editor of the *Gettysburg Review*. Her work has been widely reviewed by such critics as Peter Stitt and Helen Vendler. A professor of English at Arizona State University, she lives in Tempe, Arizona, with her husband, the German novelist Fred Viebahn, and their daughter Aviva.

The following conversation took place 7 March 1985. Interviewers were Stan Sanvel Rubin and Judith Kitchen. Ms. Dove began by reading her poem "Parsley."

Parsley

1. *The Cane Fields*

151

There is a parrot imitating spring
in the palace, its feathers parsley green.
Out of the swamp the cane appears

to haunt us, and we cut it down. El General
searches for a word; he is all the world
there is. Like a parrot imitating spring,

we lie down screaming as rain punches through
and we come up green. We cannot speak an R—
out of the swamp, the cane appears

and then the mountain we call in whispers *Katalina*.
The children gnaw their teeth to arrowheads.
There is a parrot imitating spring.

El General has found his word: *perejil*.
Who says it, lives. He laughs, teeth shining
out of the swamp. The cane appears

in our dreams, lashed by wind and streaming.
And we lie down. For every drop of blood
there is a parrot imitating spring.
Out of the swamp the cane appears.

2. *The Palace*

The word the general's chosen is parsley.
It is fall, when thoughts turn
to love and death; the general thinks
of his mother, how she died in the fall
and he planted her walking cane at the grave
and it flowered, each spring stolidly forming
four-star blossoms. The general
pulls on his boots, he stomps to
her room in the palace, the one without
curtains, the one with a parrot
in a brass ring. As he paces he wonders
Who can I kill today. And for a moment
the little knot of screams
is still. The parrot, who has traveled

all the way from Australia in an ivory
cage, is, coy as a widow, practising
spring. Ever since the morning
his mother collapsed in the kitchen
while baking skull-shaped candies
for the Day of the Dead, the general
has hated sweets. He orders pastries

brought up for the bird; they arrive

dusted with sugar on a bed of lace.
The knot in his throat starts to twitch;
he sees his boots the first day in battle
splashed with mud and urine
as a soldier falls at his feet amazed—
how stupid he looked!—at the sound
of artillery. *I never thought it would sing*
the soldier said, and died. Now

the general sees the fields of sugar
cane, lashed by rain and streaming.
He sees his mother's smile, the teeth
gnawed to arrowheads. He hears
the Haitians sing without R's
as they swing the great machetes:
Katalina, they sing, *Katalina*,

mi madle, mi amol en muelte. God knows
his mother was no stupid woman; she
could roll an R like a queen. Even
a parrot can roll an R! In the bare room
the bright feathers arch in a parody
of greenery, as the last pale crumbs
disappear under the blackened tongue. Someone

calls out his name in a voice
so like his mother's, a startled tear
splashes the tip of his right boot.
My mother, my love in death.
The general remembers the tiny green sprigs
men of his village wore in their capes
to honor the birth of a son. He will
order many, this time, to be killed

for a single, beautiful word.

Rubin: I'd like to begin by talking about that long, powerful poem, "Parsley," which you just read. The poem is based on a real incident concerning the Dominican dictator Trujillo, isn't it?
Dove: Yes, that's right. In 1957, Trujillo ordered 20,000 Black Haitians killed because they couldn't roll their "r." And he chose the Spanish word for "parsley" in order to test this. It was an act of arbitrary cruelty. But it fascinated me, not only for its political implications but for the way

language enters into history at that point—that there's a word that determines whether you live or die.

Rubin: You say they died for the sake of a "single, beautiful word." Do you really believe the word creates history in that kind of tragic sweep?

Dove: Well, in a certain sense. In this case certainly the word or their ability to pronounce it was something that created history. But also history is the way we perceive it, and we do perceive it through words in a way that it's presented to us in books. And language does shape our perceptions. So I wouldn't go so far as to say that history is language or anything like that, but the way we perceive things is, of course, circumscribed by our ability to express those things.

Rubin: There's a lot of things in the poem that are expressive of your work generally, and one of them is the trade-off between fact and imagination. It's based on this historical incident, but you get as imaginative as a novelist, if I might say so. You have Trujillo's mother die baking "skull-shaped candies" on the Day of the Dead. Is this, in fact, a product of research?

Dove: No, it isn't. In fact, the only thing in that poem which is a product of research is the actual fact that Trujillo made this happen and that the Haitians worked in the cane fields. And then the fact that when someone can not roll an "r," it usually comes out as an "l"; hence, you get "Katalina," instead of "Katarina." But the rest of it—what goes through Trujillo's mind as he tries to find a way to kill someone—is my own invention. It fascinated me that this man would think of such an imaginative way to kill someone, to kill lots of people, that, in fact, he must have gotten some kind of perverse joy out of finding a way to do it so that people would speak their own death sentences.

Rubin: It's fascinating, the way you created him as a character, through flashbacks, to his mother's death, his memories of the battlefield and the knot in his own throat before battle. It becomes totally alive, even with the sense of psychopathology, going back to the mother for the reasons why he did this. It's a fascinating way of working. Do you find your imagination compelled by historical events, by fact, very frequently?

Dove: I do, especially in *Museum*. When I started *Museum*, I was in Europe and I had a way of looking back on America and distancing myself from my experience. I could look at history, at the world, in a different way because I had another mindset. I found historical events fascinating for looking underneath—not for what we always see or what's always said about an historical event, but for the things that can't be related in a dry historical sense.

Kitchen: Let's look at the way in which the poem unfolds. Could you comment on the lyric moments of the poem and the formal aspects of the poem, the repetitions?

Dove: That poem took a long time to write! I started with the facts and that in a certain way almost inhibited me: the very action, the fact that he thought up this word, was already so amazing that I had a hard time trying to figure out how to deal with it. So when I wrote the poem I tried it in many different ways. I tried a sestina, particularly in the second part, "The Palace," simply because the obsessiveness of the sestina, the repeated words, was something I wanted to get—that driven quality—in the poem. I gave up the sestina very early. It was too playful for the poem. A lot of the words stayed—the key words like *parrot* and *spring* and, of course, *parsley.* The first part was a villanelle. I thought I was only going to do the entire poem from the Haitians' point of view. And that wasn't enough. I had this villanelle, but it wasn't enough. And there was a lot more that I hadn't said, so I tried the sestina and gave that up. I think part of that driven quality remains in that second part.

Kitchen: Well, it doesn't seem accidental to me. Every line seems to have two or three words with an "r" prominent in the English language. It seems that "parody / of greenery" is a good example of something you seem to be playing with throughout the poem. Was it to call our attention?

Dove: I didn't think of it consciously, but I was very conscious of sound in the poem. And I didn't think consciously, "I'm going to get American 'r's and Spanish 'r's in it." But the "r" has a kind of a growl to it even in English, a subdued growl I suppose in American English, that was essential to the sound cage of the poem. It's all there.

Rubin: You're very aware of sound power as you write. The word *parrot* in the opening has that "r" movement Judith was talking about. So in a sense, when you keep repeating the parrot, it's always an acoustic image as much as it's a visual image, and a kind of symbol. Very interesting.

Are you worried at all that you create a Trujillo so fully that even though he's a monster he's not beyond us, but in fact becomes human on some level, with thoughts and memories?

Dove: No, I'm not really afraid. I'm not quite sure what you mean by "afraid"—afraid of bringing that out in me, or afraid of making him too human? But either way, I believe all of us have inside us the capacity for violence and cruelty. You see it even in children, and it's something we have to deal with. If you ignore it, it's far too easy to be seduced into it later. And I frankly don't believe anyone who says that they've never felt any evil, that they cannot understand that process of evil. It was important to me to try to understand that arbitrary quality of his cruelty. And I'm not afraid that I'm making him too human. I don't believe anyone's going to like him after reading my poem. Making us get into his head may shock us all into seeing what the human being is capable of, and what in fact we're capable of, because if we can go that far into his head we're halfway there ourselves.

Kitchen: That's the final poem of this second book *Museum,* and it seems to encapsulate some of the other aspects of the book. The book as a whole seems to deal with this same aspect of looking back, looking into something either historical or artistic. It becomes a museum. Could you talk about that a little bit?

Dove: Sure. *Museum* was very carefully thought out in terms of a book, and the impression it would make. I suppose what I was trying to do in *Museum* was to deal with certain artifacts that we have in life, not the ordinary artifacts, the ones that you'd expect to find in a museum, but anything that becomes frozen by memory, or by circumstance or by history. There are some things which in fact are ideal museum objects—the fish in the stone, for instance, the fossil that we observe; but there are also people who become frozen or lifted out and set on a pedestal, a mental pedestal—like poems about Boccaccio's idealized love, Fiammetta, who becomes an object of admiration. There's a whole section on my father; in a way that's the memory, childhood focusing on a father, what he seemed like to me then.

The other thing was to get the underside of the story, not to tell the big historical events, but in fact to talk about things which no one will remember but which are just as important in shaping our concept of ourselves and the world we live in, as the biggies, so to speak. So, that's why the dedication to the book is "for nobody who made us possible" and it's really for the Haitians and it's for Fiammetta, who isn't anybody really because she's not treated as real.

Kitchen: Were you able to write this because, having at that point moved to another country, you had that slight sense of displacement which seems to be underneath each of these poems? Do you think that had a bearing?

Dove: I think it really had a lot of bearing. When I went to Europe the first time—that was in 1974, way before I had thought of this book—it was mind-boggling to see how blind I'd been in my own little world of America. It had never dawned on me that there was a world out there. It was really quite shocking to see that there was another way of looking at things. And when I went back in 1980–81 to spend a lot of time, I got a different angle on the way things are, the way things happen in the world and the importance they take. Also as a *person* going to Europe I was treated differently because I was American. I was Black, but they treated me differently than people treat me here because I'm Black. And in fact, I often felt a little like Fiammetta; I became an object. I was a Black American, and therefore I became a representative for all of that. And I sometimes felt like a ghost. I mean, people would ask me questions, but I had a feeling that they weren't seeing *me*, but a shell. So there was that sense of being there and not being there, you know. Then because you are there you can see things a little clearer sometimes. That certainly was something, I think, that informed the spirit of *Museum*.

Rubin: Because the book is, as you both said, so carefully structured, I wonder if I could just go back through it for the subtitles for its sections, and just have you say something about each of them. The first is "The Hill Has Something to Say."

Dove: That comes from the title of one of the poems in the first section. A narrow way of looking at that title would be simply that every hill contained things which made it a hill, speaking specifically of Europe where practically every hill has ruins underneath it. So it has its history, if we would just listen, if we could look at what is very obvious—a hill—and imagine the layers of time. There's an archaeological sense and a magic that I was trying to get at in that title. But also I was trying to get at the inability of that hill to say anything. It's an inarticulate object. We have to dig into it, which is why at the end of that section, there are lots of characters, individuals from history who can't speak to us anymore, like the two saints Catherine of Alexandria and Catherine of Siena, and Boccaccio's Fiammetta, or Tou Wan, the Chinese. They unearthed Tou Wan and Liu Sheng's bodies and all of the artifacts, but they can't speak to us anymore. We have to go through what they've left behind and fashion it.

Rubin: Your second is "In the Bulrush."

Dove: "In the Bulrush." God, I never really thought about this one. That, too, comes from a poem, "In the Bulrush," and it has obvious religious connotations of Moses, but also the idea about becoming a chosen one from the weeds, an unlikely place to be lifted out of and to make an impact. The first poem is called "November for Beginners," and it talks about waiting for rain or that horrible weather in November to change. But that has more to do with the reedy quality of bulrushes than it does with being discovered. But then there are several people in that section who become objects for consideration like Champion Jack Dupree, the blues singer, who seems out of place on the stage, put on the spot, made a hero. Or, Banneker who was a Black from Maryland who made the first almanac and helped to survey the grounds for Washington, D.C. So, there are those kinds of things happening in that section.

Also I hate to give people what they expect, so often I try to play off on those titles. They would reflect back on the section before. I didn't want "In the Bulrush" to be the title of the first section because there were some poems in it that dealt with saints and religion. I didn't want the *obvious* connection, right? So that's why it also became the title for the second section.

Rubin: What about "My Father's Telescope," the third part of the book?

Dove: The title? The entire third section deals with my father. And it's also taken from a poem in that section. There are obviously sexual connotations in that title, too. But I was trying to look forward into the fourth section with the telescope so that it becomes much more; it becomes the technological age, the scientific age, the nuclear age, that I'm looking forward to. But also my father is someone that I've had a hard time understanding. And so sometimes he seemed almost like a planet, very far away. And to draw him closer was also part of the sense of that title.

Rubin: You have a poem in there called "Anti-Father." Would you talk about it and then read it?

Dove: Yes, a lot of those poems were written right at the time when the satellites were reporting all those wonderful photos of Saturn and Jupiter back, and that was just incredible to see these pictures being painted, you know, line by line. So that also informed that whole section, and "Anti-Father" came right about that time.

Anti-Father

Contrary to
tales you told us

summer nights when
the air conditioner

broke—the stars
are not far

apart. Rather
they draw

closer together
with years.

And houses
shrivel, un-lost,

and porches sag;
neighbors phone

to report cracks
in the cellar floor,

roots of the willow
coming up. Stars

speak to a child.
The past

is silent. . . .
Just between

me and you,

woman to man,

outer space is
inconceivably

intimate.

Rubin: And finally you have the "Primer for the Nuclear Age," which
extends the theme, as you said, to everything.

Dove: Yes, looking outward again after going to the father. I also didn't
want the father poems to appear too early in the book. Again, I'm trying
to keep people from thinking that they know what's coming. But after two
sections where there's nothing personal at all, I wanted to go into the
father poems and then to explode out of them to the nuclear age. And I
do believe that the kinds of events which are formed by the cruelty of
Trujillo or the carelessness of nuclear escalation nowadays start at very
personal levels. If you're careless with your thoughts and if you're careless
with your relationships to other people, you're going to be careless on a
larger level. Hence, that move from the father all the way to the nuclear
age.

Rubin: Ending with Trujillo is kind of ending with the ultimate nasty
father, or evil father. Was it hard to write those poems about your father?
Did they come naturally?

Dove: They were *hard*. They were very hard to write. But in a sense they
were the most satisfying to write, because I was helping myself, too. And
I felt closer to him afterwards. The poems helped me to understand him
a little bit better.

Rubin: Has he read them?

Dove: I don't know! My father told me at one point—he's a chemist and
he said that he didn't understand poetry—"Don't be upset if I don't read
your poems." That was when I informed him I was going to be a poet
instead of a lawyer, which is what he wanted me to be. But I don't know if
he's read them. My parents have my books, and I've seen one of my books
in their bedroom. I don't know.

Kitchen: There's one part of *Museum* that we've left out, and I think
there's a reason for that. It happens to be my favorite poem of yours,
"Dusting." I'd like you to talk about why it's here, why its placed where it
is, and where it leads to. Then I'd like you to read it.

Dove: I wrote "Dusting" in the middle of writing *Museum*; it came out of
nowhere. And I didn't realize at that point that it was going to become
part of a longer sequence. It's part of *Thomas and Beulah*, the next book.
At that time I had been working on some of the poems from *Thomas and
Beulah*, but mainly the poems were from Thomas's point of view. Maybe

I should say something about the whole structure of that before I go any further.

Thomas and Beulah is based very loosely on my grandparents' lives. My grandmother had told me a story that had happened to my grandfather when he was young, coming up on a river boat to Akron, Ohio, my hometown. But that was all I had basically. And the story so fascinated me that I tried to write about it. I started off writing stories about my grandfather and soon, because I ran out of real facts, in order to keep going, I made up facts for this character, Thomas. I was writing some of those while I was doing *Museum*.

Then this poem "Dusting" appeared, really out of nowhere. I didn't realize that this was Thomas's wife saying, "I want to talk. And you can't do his side without doing my side." So when I had finished *Museum*, this poem really didn't fit into the whole concept, or into any of the sections, but it did fit into the idea of *Museum*; that is, dusting, wiping away layers of unclarity and things like that. And that's why it's there as a first poem and also because it's a poem that deals with people. That was the way to enter *Museum*, to deal with the dusting and the memory which is a museum in itself, and then to go from that to the artifacts, which is what the first section is about, the hills, the archaeology of things. Dusting is a kind of archaeology. That's why I put it ahead of all the other poems, as a prologue.

But after I finished *Museum* and started to finish up Thomas's poems, I became aware that she's got to say her part, too. So *Thomas and Beulah* became actually two sides of the same story—the story of a Black couple growing up in the industrial Midwest from about 1900 to 1960. And, the first part is Thomas's point of view; the second part is his wife's point of view.

Dusting

Every day a wilderness—no
shade in sight. Beulah
patient among knickknacks,
the solarium a rage
of light, a grainstorm
as her gray cloth brings
dark wool to life.

Under her hand scrolls
and crests gleam
darker still. What
was his name, that

silly boy at the fair with
the rifle booth? And his kiss and
the clear bowl with one bright
fish, rippling
wound!

Not Michael—
something finer. Each dust
stroke a deep breath and
the canary in bloom.
Wavery memory: home
from a dance, the front door
blown open and the parlor
in snow, she rushed
the bowl to the stove, watched
as the locket of ice
dissolved and he
swam free.

That was years before
Father gave her up
with her name, years before
her name grew to mean
Promise, then
Desert-in-Peace.
Long before the shadow and
sun's accomplice, the tree.

Maurice.

Kitchen: You used the word *underside* before. You see these as being
undersides of each other in some sense?
Dove: I'm always fascinated with seeing a story from different angles. But
also in the two sequences I'm not interested in the *big* moments. Obviously some big things happened in those years. I wasn't interested in
portraying them, those moments. I was interested in the thoughts, the
things which were concerning these small people, these nobodies in the
course of history. For instance, there's a reference in one of the last poems
of Beulah's to the March on Washington, but it's a very oblique reference.
She's much more concerned about the picnic she's at. I've added a
chronology to the end of the book. I never thought I'd do this in my life,
but I did a chronology from 1900 to 1960. It's a very eccentric chronology, but you can see what was happening in the social structure of
Midwest America at the time this couple was growing up.

Kitchen: Does this remind you of Lowell's *Notebook*—where you play off the smaller against the larger forces of history?

Dove: Yes, it does. I didn't think of that while I was doing it, of course. I try not to think of anything else except the poem.

Kitchen: Talk about trying not to think about . . .

Dove: I think the worst thing that can happen to a poet is to be self-conscious, to think, "I'm writing a poem," the moment that you're writing a poem. When you get that moment where things begin to click in a poem and you begin to go off in a direction that you didn't know you were going in, you better just ride that current as far as it'll take you. That's such a tenuous connection for me that any self-consciousness is going to kill it right away. I try not to know what I'm doing. That may sound facetious, but I try not to clutter my head up with literary theories and critiques and stuff like that. I don't really want to know where I've been. I only follow what I need. I needed at that point, especially after *Museum*, to get back to family and more personal things. But I wanted to do it on a third-person level. I didn't know that I needed that. It was something that I wanted, and that's one reason why, I'm sure, it took me so long to figure out that this was going to be a long sequence. Probably anyone else looking at it from the outside would have seen it a long time beforehand. Each poem is a new field to enter. I wanted each one to be an epiphany, and so I had to enter each poem almost blind. I had the background of all the other poems and all that stuff behind me, but I tried to let it bubble up, rather than trying to just impose it onto the page.

Rubin: You really do combine what someone might call a novelist's kind of imagination of character and even interior monologue with the really intense lyric poet's love of language, of the individual word, of the moment of epiphany, as you said. Would you expand on this, on your feeling for language?

Dove: Language is everything. As Mallarmé said, "A poem is made of words." It's by language that I enter the poem, and that also leads me forward. That doesn't exclude perceptions and experience and emotions or anything like that. But emotion is useless if there's no way to express it. Language is just the clay we use to make our poems. It's something that a lot of people who are *not* writers take for granted. It would never dawn on someone who doesn't sculpt that they could simply walk up to a block of marble and just hack away; they know they have to acquire skills. Because all of us use language, we assume, "Well, anyone can do that. I talk everyday." But it's a different use of language; it is the sounds of the language, the way of telling something, that makes a poem for me. There's nothing new under the sun, but it's the way you *see* it. For me as a poet, language becomes an integral part of that perception, the *way* one sees it.

Rubin: Pursue that in your own working methods a little further. Do you say your poems aloud as you're creating them? Do you revise much?

Dove: I revise incessantly. Usually when I'm starting to work on a poem, I don't read it aloud—not until it gets to a certain point. You can lull yourself with your own voice; but I hear it in my head. At a certain point I do read a poem aloud to myself, because it's also got to work for me as music. I never want to lose that part of a poem. Also when I write a poem, as you probably can tell by now, I don't start out with a notion of how this is going to proceed. Often I will enter a poem through a word or a phrase that compels me. I think in "Dusting" it was the word *Maurice*. It really started with *Maurice*. I thought that this was a wonderful, romantic name, and I had it down in my notebook, but I didn't know what I was going to do with it. So I entered the poem through that last word in a way.

Rubin: You do keep a writer's notebook?

Dove: I keep a notebook, but I don't work from beginning to end. It can start in the middle. I keep everything in my notebook, though. I keep grocery lists in there. I try not to make it sacred, because I could get uptight, you know, if I thought, "Oh, this is *my notebook!*" You know, as if it only contains gems or something. Of course, it contains a lot of junk, too. But I keep a notebook because sometimes it is a word that attracts me, and I don't want to feel compelled to explain why it attracts me. So if I have a notebook, I just put it in there. I don't think about it anymore. If I overhear a conversation and there's something really wonderful about it, I put it in. I don't ask any questions; I just put it in. That way when I sit down to write, I'll leaf through my notebook and wait for something to hit me and say, "Oh, that's neat," without thinking about what I'm going to do with it. If I think it's nice, I'll start with it and see where it leads me. Of course, with "Parsley," I had the incident beforehand.

Rubin: Do you think of audience at some point?

Dove: No.

Rubin: Can you say briefly what got you started as a poet? What has been most helpful to you in finding your own language? That's a topic for another whole interview.

Dove: Yes, well, I'm trying to think what got me started. I hate to say I've always written. I think everybody's always written, but most people stop at a certain point and others just go on. I loved to write as a child. Talking about language and entering into language, something that happened to me in third grade is probably indicative of that tendency to go toward language, rather than content. We did spelling lessons in class, you know, those horrible spelling books. We had to memorize twenty words each week. And we had to do those—to me it seemed fairly idiotic—spelling lessons using the words in a sentence. I got finished early in class, and so I started writing a little novel using the words. Each week I'd write a chapter, and I made rules for myself: the words in the order they appeared; I couldn't change them by making them plural or using a different verb tense. It was really fun to have a whole world open up that I hadn't predetermined. But from an early point it was the language that intrigued me.

Kitchen: I understand that you have a collection of short fiction, *Fifth Sunday*, that will be appearing in the Callaloo Fiction Series. Could you tell us something about these tales?

Dove: *Fifth Sunday* is a collection of eight stories. Most of the protagonists are women, though one story, "Damon and Vandalia," uses alternating first-person narrators, and another, "The Spray Paint King," is the story of an adolescent male, a "brown baby" growing up in Cologne, West Germany.

Rubin: Was "The Spray Paint King" inspired by your own trips to Europe?

Dove: Oh, definitely. Cologne is really one of the most magnificent river cities in Europe, as well as an important center for art—and a few summers ago spray paintings had mysteriously appeared on the pristine walls of several public buildings. The outcry was pretty amazing—none of pictures were obscene, and several were artistically exciting; but the uptightness of the German mind-set, the insistence on neatness and order—all this was at stake. It was this friction between individual artistic protest and social regulations that prompted that story.

Rubin: Does language play as important a role in your fiction as it does in your poetry?

Dove: That's a hard one. I'd say that it does, but it's not as flamboyant. Fiction requires that sometimes the language be nearly transparent—traditional fiction, that is, Metafiction's another kettle of fish altogether. While writing stories I welcome that possibility to let the reins slacken a bit. But there are other difficulties that aren't present in poetry. Character development, passage of time, dialogue. In *Fifth Sunday*, though, I do explore the possibilities of prose language. Several pieces are fairly traditional, à la Joyce's *Dubliners*. "Zabriah" is a rhapsody or an aria; the major part of "Aunt Carrie" consists of a dramatic monologue.

Kitchen: Why did you call it *Fifth Sunday?*

Dove: "Fifth Sunday" is also the title of the lead story and refers to those occasional months where there are five Sundays. In the church I attended when I was growing up, fifth Sunday was youth Sunday, and the entire service—all except the sermon—was conducted with the church youth. Using that title for the book was an intuitive decision, one I can't really articulate—I suppose there is the sense of a fifth Sunday as something special—"once in a blue moon"—as well as the idea of being in control only occasionally, and in strict accordance with the social rules.

Rubin: Would you say that this theme—privilege enjoyed and withdrawn—is the dominant one in your book?

Dove: I'd hate to narrow it down that far. As I said, the title was chosen intuitively, and I would like to think that my subconscious was operating on many levels. Let's say "Fifth Sunday" was the most expansive title, the most effective umbrella for the book. All the stories, however, feature individuals who are trying to be recognized as human beings in a world that loves to pigeonhole and forget. Aunt Carrie is the old maid aunt, but she has a story to tell, she has had a life. Damon and Vandalia's attempts at communicating with each other keep missing, because social stereotyping has scarred both of them too deeply. Not all the tales are sad, though. "The Zulus" is an upbeat piece, I think.

Rubin: Do you plan to write more fiction, or was this a sidestep?

Dove: Oh, I hope to write more stories, even a novel. And plays. Just as it's tragic to pigeonhole individuals according to stereotypes, there's no reason to subscribe authors to particular genres, either. I'm a writer, and I write in the form that most suits what I want to say. When an idea occurs to me, I usually know if it will be a poem or a story—even before I even know the first line. Now, whether it will be a good story or good poem—*that* I can't tell. I just keep working at it, and hoping.

"Thinking of Baseball"
A CONVERSATION WITH JONATHAN HOLDEN

Jonathan Holden

Jonathan Holden was born in New Jersey in 1941 and educated at Oberlin College, San Francisco State, and the University of Colorado, where he received a Ph.D. Of Mr. Holden's four books, three have received major poetry awards. *Design for a House* won a Devins Award in 1972 and was printed by the University of Missouri Press. *Leverage* was the Associated Writing Program winner in 1982, and *The Names of the Rapids* was named winner of the 1985 Juniper Prize from the University of Massachusetts.

In addition, Mr. Holden is a widely published critic of contemporary American poetry and has completed two book-length studies, *The Rhetoric of the Contemporary Lyric,* published by Indiana University in 1980, and *Style and Authenticity in Postmodern Poetry* (University of Missouri Press, 1986), as well as several essays on poetry and aesthetics, which have appeared in such magazines as *The Georgia Review* and *American Poetry Review.*

Jonathan Holden is currently Professor of English at Kansas State University where he works in the writing program. He has also served on the faculty of the Warren Wilson M.F.A. Program for Writers. Among other honors, he recently received a National Endowment for the Arts fellowship for creative prose. He lives with his wife and two children in Manhattan, Kansas.

The following conversation took place on 26 April 1985. Interviewers were Stan Sanvel Rubin and Judith Kitchen. Mr. Holden began by reading his poem "An American Boyhood."

An American Boyhood

There was little important
to do but chew gum, or count

the ways a flipped jackknife
caught in the dirt.
One Sunday afternoon I had an idea.
We clamped the cables of Tommy
Emory's train transformer
to a steel pie plate
filled with saltwater
and drank through our fingers
the current's purr,
dialing that bird-heartbeat
higher, riding its flutter until
both hands were bucked
out of the water.

                        We knew
we were wasting our time,
though we had nothing
but time. Our parents
moved vague among their great
worries, remote
as the imperatives of weather.
And the stars appeared on schedule
to run their dim, high errands
again, leaving us lost
in the long boredom of our childhood,
flipping our knives in the dust,
waiting to find out just how
in this world we were going
to be necessary.

Rubin: I would like to begin by referring to the poem you just read. Why is it an *American* boyhood?

Holden: Part of it is because, when one is raised as a child in America, in the middle class at least, there are these tremendous acres of time on one's hands. And children—my own children too, I've noticed—are bored a heck of a lot of the time, and it seems that what Robert Lowell calls "our monotonous sublime" is part of what life in America feels like, especially for a child. But maybe for adults, too, boredom is an integral part of our culture.

Rubin: Of course, the things these boys are doing with the flipped jackknife, the cables of the train transformer clipped to the pie plate and all that, aren't these activities out of your own childhood?

Holden: Oh sure. One day Grant Howell hooked up this train transformer when we were just totally bored.

I wrote this poem several years ago. It was a Sunday—I've often thought Emily Dickinson's "There's a Certain Slant of Light" is really about the boredom and desolation of Sunday, that day to get *through*—and there were some eleven- and twelve-year-old boys outside on our street in Kansas, and they were just totally bored. They were wrestling, pushing each other around, perhaps harder than necessary, taking little risks, and the risks were getting bigger and bigger, and they began fencing with bits of scrap wood. I suddenly realized they were so bored they would do *anything* for relief from that boredom, and I remembered that was the way it was. That was the condition of our lives. I sat down almost immediately while they were still out there and began taking notes for this poem.

Kitchen: That *story* raises two issues immediately. One, of course, is the Grant Howell versus the poem's Tommy Emory, which I think we should get to. But also it is that element of risk. After all, you've chosen jackknives and all these things "skirting the edges." Is this a bit of what poetry is for you, too?

Holden: Well, it's certainly a bit of what boyhood is for me. I have another poem, which is not among these that I brought today. It's called "Fireworks," and it recalls hours and hours and hours of playing with fireworks when I was a kid—firecrackers, cherry bombs, things like that. Now I watch my son who is nine, ten, eleven years old, just as obsessed with matches and fireworks as I was. Firecrackers were illegal in New Jersey, so I used to buy Ohio bluetip matches, with the little, bright, phosphorus pimples on the end. You'd get a kitchen knife and cut them off—those were the parts that were really dangerous—and if you'd hit them with a hammer they'd go off like a cap. I was making fire bombs and stuff like that with matches. It seems endemic to American boyhood and, as you suggest, endemic to American culture, to think of guns, bombs, explosions.

Rubin: The key move in the poem is the ending: "how in this world we were going to be necessary."

Holden: That swerves the whole poem into a slightly different dimension. When I was young, everything in the world seemed to have something to do but me. It's probably still true for kids. The stars have to come out, and they do. Birds have to feed, and they go out looking for worms. And one's parents are working at their chores or their jobs. And the weather is minding its business. But *you* have nothing to do. You have no mission, and at the time I felt a deep, deep chagrin at my utter uselessness. But I think it's a chagrin perhaps that permeates the rest of our lives, too.

I was thinking recently about how much, especially for older people, eating is simply an activity. You go to somebody's house, turn on the television, have a kind of conversation, and the food is brought out; you eat in order to do something.

Or I recall, even more tellingly, a certain point in my young life, when I was a little bit older, simply driving and driving and driving and driving all weekend—driving with friends around Connecticut, driving back into New Jersey, driving into New York—as though one were actually making a product by covering distance. And there's something very American about that too, it seems to me.

I have a poem about that kind of thing; it's called "Seventeen." It's really about the same sort of boredom and desperation, the sense of nowhere to go, that's in the first poem. But this is not as good a poem. I'll read it anyway.

Back in New Jersey in the late fifties if you were a "juvenile delinquent," the judge would often give you the choice of being on probation or going to jail or joining the Marines—the Marines would shape you up. And some of the friends I hung out with were given that choice. The poem is called "Seventeen," and it describes driving and driving and driving.

Seventeen

That June before the judge gave
Rennie Dodd his choice—jail or joining
the Marines—we were already on patrol, part
of the nervous prod of traffic
along the cement tundra called U.S. 46,
observing protocol. Drunk,
swerving at oncoming cars, giving
pedestrians the finger,
we'd rake the AM tuner's roar
for bursts of action at the front, chasing
that low blaze on the horizon.
But this was 1959. There was no war.
We were invited
nowhere. We had to cross the state line
to buy beer. Our tires peeling their awkward
falsetto, we'd head out on a mission, sure
that, this time, the skyline was inviting
us, and eager to go, ready
to be recruited by the night.

Rubin: That "night" is maybe a little ominous.

Holden: There's a little *double entendre* there.

Rubin: Is this culture you're describing kind to poets? What does a poet do in this culture of boredom and driving and consumption?

Holden: Well, I think it impels people to take one kind of measure or another, to try to mine some kind of style and some kind of value out of a fairly styleless existence.

There was a movie recently, set in Baltimore, called "Diner." It gets at, cinematically, what it felt like to be raised in New Jersey, probably better than any other movie I've seen. In fact, it was so excruciatingly accurate it had almost an oppressively documentary feeling, but it wasn't documentary at all. "Diner" gets at a cinematic equivalent of the two poems I just read.

Kitchen: I'm going to belabor a point and go back to the same one. This poem as well seems to have that element of risk-taking, that sense of being alive when you're living on the edge, of violence or whatever. And to go back to Stan's question, does a poet in a culture like this take his own kinds of risks, looking into the self? I think a lot of your poems are doing this, and I sort of want to push it a little.

Holden: Well, the notion of poets taking "risks" has been so abused that I resist it. I went to poetry to look for beauty in all kinds of unlikely places. For example, even when I was a little kid listening to baseball games on the radio and later watching them on television—my parents didn't have a TV—I was trying to recreate verbally some experiences that I wanted to possess more fully with words.

There was a famous announcer, Mel Allen, who, when he was describing the great pitcher Allie Reynolds, a big right-hander for the New York Yankees, used to say, "The big right-hander wheels, deals." And I was asking myself questions back then, such as, Where would there be a verbal formula as good as "wheels, deals." And I tried "herks, jerks," "wings, swings." I was playing with little verbal equivalents like that because it seemed that if you could possess a little linguistic formula like that or make one up, then you *had* something. And you could go back and replay it like a little tape. It would add to your existence, make it a little bit richer. We all do this in various ways.

In fact, thinking of baseball, I invented an imaginary baseball team by the time I was nine, ten, eleven years old. There were elaborately differentiated players on this team. There was "Ted Grey," a southpaw, a sort of a cross between Tommy Byrne and Sal Maglie. And I played whole imaginary baseball games with these people, actually writing the text of the games myself. I was asking myself questions such as, Was a *smoking* fast ball more vivid than a *burning* fast ball or a *blazing* fast ball? And then I would try to come up with my own formula; the earliest one I remember was describing a curve ball that "curled" over the edge of the plate, or "curled" away over the outside corner. I was quite proud of that "curled."

I was critical of gunshot noises in comic books and very dissatisfied with the usual gunshot noises—the "pow-crack-bang-bam-boom"—those basic, almost generic names you find in comic books. But actual gunshot noises, which are beautiful sounds, with all their complicated echoes, were far more haunting than the ones in the comic books, and so I tried to come up with my own comic book sounds. Once a friend of mine was in Belgium and he came back with a Red Rider comic book—all in French. I eagerly raced to the shooting parts of the comic book, and the French equivalent of *bang* was *p-a-n*, which not knowing French, I couldn't appreciate at the time. But, "pan," nasalized in French, is pretty creative, it seems to me. So that's how one becomes a poet; you begin thinking about this trivia.

William Carlos Williams talks about poetry as consisting of "minutiae." You begin thinking about the minutiae of language as a way of trying to possess your experience a little bit better, especially the experience you find beautiful. You work on it and work on it, and you make a huge investment in language as a kind of a quiet resource that you take with you. It's a strange thing to do.

But to answer your question specifically, about "being on the edge": it seems pathetic that as a boy in America you look for beauty in those bleakest of materials—the sounds of guns, firecrackers, cherry bombs. And of course there's sports. That is the great aesthetic activity of American boys. It's the one place where if you're raised a boy in America you can go for beauty and not be branded a "fag" or something of that nature.

Rubin: You have a poem in *Falling from Stardom* called "The Edge." I wonder if you would consider reading it. Maybe you can show some of what we've been saying. And maybe it would get us into a discussion of this book.

Holden: I was taught to ride a bicycle by my Uncle Jim, who would run along beside the bicycle holding on to the back of the seat and then let go, and the bike would flounder around, and he would catch it just before I would crash. Then one day, he let go of the bike, and I wavered and then took off. It was an utterly sublime moment; and I had tremendous pleasure teaching my own children both times—I have two children—to ride a bike just that way. It was just as exciting to teach them each time as it was to be the pupil. And this poem describes teaching my son. What also interests me is that on the last day or so before my son Zachary finally caught on and took off, literally out of my hands, he knew something was going to happen; and he began getting excited and babbling and babbling. "Dad, look at that cloud. Boy, look at the sunset!" His whole aesthetic sensibility was extra sharp because he knew—subliminally he knew—he was about to go through this tremendous transition, a kind of transcendence, and he was sort of outside his life and looking back down in on it at the same time as he was in it. It was amazing. And so the poem begins with listening to him babble.

The Edge

High up on the bike, my son
Zack talks a blue streak
as I stride with him,
aiming him, sighting his fat
front tire wavering
along the sidewalk. We stride
through a narrow country
of sunshine, step off
into shadow, ford a bright creek
and flash through a place
of islands and sun-ponds.
We both see everything
this morning, husk of a firecracker,
wisp of cotton, rusty edges
of light on the grass-blades
as if we both knew
we would never see this country
again, we are leaving
today, moving west,
and the history of each wet
lawn is suddenly clear. We are
moving. I am trembling
with him. The bike
tips. He oo's as I catch him, scared
just enough, half rapture,
half fear as he teeters, balancing
in both countries at once,
right on the edge and
knowing it, knowing this
is important, that the next
moment he could find out
how quaint the Old World is,
be looking down, see
where its shores curl on the map
as the weight of him soars
out of my arms
for the last time
and only I will be left

> trembling as on the night
> he was born, when,
> home again, alone, I babbled
> as he is now, I was singing,
> laughing out loud with no one to hear,
> watching a cloud drift like a dune
> that I knew would never
> repeat itself, over a waning
> three-quarter moon,
> thinking, this is the last
> time this will ever
> happen, thinking only
> *god, that cloud, this night,*
> *that moon!*

Rubin: Lovely. It certainly combines—in its title as well as in what happens in the poem—the sense of beauty and the sense of loss and something of the sense of danger.

Holden: And there is a sense of danger. I have another poem about that sense of danger. It's called "Peter Rabbit," and it's about disobedience. One of the great charms of disobedience—of having a little bit of savory danger in one's life, not continuously but in nice circumscribed intervals—is that it sharpens your aesthetic perceptions again. If you remember the story *Peter Rabbit*, once Peter sneaks under the gate in Mr. McGregor's garden he suddenly begins to hear all kinds of warning noise—the "scritch-scratch" of McGregor's rake, for example. When you are sneaking around, you start to notice cover and terrain, things like that. You wouldn't notice them otherwise at all. That's what the story of *Peter Rabbit* by Beatrix Potter is all about. It's the best children's story there is about the aesthetic thrill of disobedience, about the aesthetics of crime.

Rubin: And returning safely to a nurturing mother at the end.

Holden: I suppose that's true. But actually the sense, when you finish with *Peter Rabbit,* is that it was all worth it. You recall Peter does not get any dessert. Flopsy, Mopsy, and Cottontail have a couple of sweets, but Peter goes to bed and he doesn't feel all that well. But we know it was worth it for Peter. We know it was worth it.

Rubin: I'd like to go back to this poem, "The Edge," that you just read. It's from *Falling from Stardom,* and I'd like you to say something about this collection, starting, perhaps, by commenting on the epigraph you have from George Gilder at the beginning of it.

Holden: Well, *Falling from Stardom* is an explicitly sexual-political book, and it's a bittersweet critique of American machismo—of typical American male behavior—by, I would say, an excomplicitor. Some of the poems in here seem to boast about sexual exploits. But actually they're looking back critically on them, while remembering some of the aesthetics.

Rubin: Would you read the Gilder epigraph? Was that appended, or was it in some way inspirational for the conception of the collection?

Holden: " . . . relaxed masculinity is at bottom empty, a limp nullity. While the female body is full of internal potentiality, the male is internally barren (from the Old French **bar,** meaning man.)" This is quoted from George Gilder's book *Sexual Suicide,* which is a pretty clever book. Much of it was published in *Harper's Magazine* as a long article called "The Suicide of the Sexes" and the article's argument is that, because of their biological inferiority to women, men must be given artificial prerogatives, artificial "perks," in our society. Otherwise they would just be outlaws; they would bolt what Gilder calls the "sexual contract" altogether and just be renegades having indiscriminate sexual exploits with different women without any futurity to them. It's *the* most clever antifeminist argument there is, and it's an argument I can't actually refute. But I suppose it opens me to the charge of writing a chauvinist book, when in fact the book is a *critique* of American masculinity. Let me read you one of the poems that is more explicitly a critique, and you'll see what I mean.

Rubin: Did you read Gilder before you put the collection together?

Holden: Yes, some years before.

Kitchen: So did you conceive of this book as a political statement?

Holden: Well, it's a difficult question to answer, because after I won the Devins Award ten years passed, and nobody wanted my book of poems. Finally I had two full books of poems and I, as one does, began separating them out into various piles. I took what I thought were my best poems at the time and put them into *Leverage,* and then there was a bunch of other poems that were left over, along with some fairly recent ones. I took some of those and arranged them thematically to make *Falling from Stardom.* But when I say I arranged thematically, I mean that I was just feeling around, the way one does. It's like looking at Tarot cards. You go by association and feel. Putting together a book of poems is like writing one larger poem. Instead of words, you have individual poems, and you arrange the poems intuitively, looking for cues from the poems themselves, and the poems begin whispering the cues to you. They begin to order themselves into little groups and piles like iron filings before a magnet. It's a very mysterious process, and I think it is *the* most interesting process that I've ever gone through as a poet—putting together books like that and finding out who one is, what one was about all along, by seeing the way these iron filings gravitate toward the magnet.

Rubin: Then you can share this little iron filing with us.

Holden: This is called "Junk." The poem is set along Lake Erie where I was a camp counselor for one horrendous summer back in 1962 about the time Lake Erie was totally dead. There were dead fish all over the beach, and it smelled rank, and indeed, the lake had been left for junk. The poem is about leaving things for junk, and what a bad thing that is to do. You know, people go into a motel; they take all the towels, the light bulbs and then they pack their car and drive on, away, the next day, thinking, "They'll never catch us." This is the great illusion, a particularly American one, that you can simply move from point A to point B, after doing something nasty at A, and if you drive fast enough, that's it. You don't have to face the consequences of what you did. You never did it in the first place.

And, of course, people treat people that way all the time. And men, especially, treat women that way. "Did you tell her your name?" It's shocking and disgusting. And the basic idea in this poem is that the places where people go for fast one-way, forgettable thrills are always trashed. The places where I used to park with a girl when I was in high school, there'd be little ruts where you'd turn off into the trees, and there'd be broken glass, all kinds of garbage just left there for junk. And when I started to work on this poem I realized that the outer landscape in places like this is a precise reflection of the inner landscape. That's what this poem is actually about.

Junk

Dim, heavy Ginny, whose wet mouth
which smelled like a washcloth
I joked about next morning
driving south as if
I were leaving this behind—
these words are more
to remind *me* than you:
that dusk when I drove us
to Lake Erie *did* happen.
Those bald spots linking
suggestions of a path
slithering downhill to the beach
were there, even though
that whole landscape had been
junked—scorched rocks
around abandoned campfire sites,
dead fish, tires flunked,

stranded on the beach,
the sand limp as a cold pancake.
Each can of Black Label I pried out
puckered, spit.
                              I now admit
that when I breathed
I love you in your ear,
I didn't mean it.
No wonder that by midnight
you wouldn't speak to me
but huddled there, teeth rattling,
your comb snagging, snapping
as you ripped sand from your hair
while I busied myself pissing
in the bushes, breaking
one-way bottles to keep warm.
                                        Ginny
whose face I knew I'd never see again—
now I think we can afford no more
to leave for junk our summer jobs
or any night like that
than to deny these
seedy little deaths we're party to.
On back roads, wherever
ruts turn off into the trees,
we must always come
upon this sudden evidence
of civilization,
these small, charred cities,
glass glinting in the rubble,
the places we have been.

And that's a sexual-political poem, I think. It's about more than just sexual politics, though.

Rubin: Very clearly it involves the notion of responsibility—the question of being responsible for actions. And you write about the issue of responsibility in poetry, too.

Holden: I would hope that the poem generalizes certain sexual-political issues, far beyond "boy-girl." When I look at the way our foreign policy is conducted, for example, it's always, "Come *on*. Step across that line! I *dare* you." *Bargaining chips.* It's like poker. It's like two kids in the playground who come up against each other and push each other with their chests. "What'd you say about my mu-thuh? Huh? What'd you say?" It's frightening. I mean, American machismo is the most dangerous force in the world, to put it bluntly.

Kitchen: This poem also seems to raise the issue of reality—that you can't sweep something under the rug. And that would extend obviously even into foreign policy, the way some things seem somehow never to have happened.

Holden: Right.

Kitchen: And Vietnam and the way we've treated the war, the way we treat the South American. . . .

Holden: Well, when one does bad things—unless one is perverted—one then tries to distance oneself; it's human instinct, to back off and not admit the humanity of people whom you've hurt.

Rubin: Changing the subject, Judith and I both turned to your essay, "What Makes A Good Lyric 'Work,' " which was printed a couple of years ago in *Indiana Review*. You discuss a poem by Nancy Willard. Do you consider yourself a lyric poet?

Holden: Sometimes. But I find that if one thinks too self-consciously about genre of *what* is a poem, one is apt to stop writing poems altogether. The best thing to do is to get into action and rely upon your sense of all the poems you've read for a sense of what a poem is, instead of trying *a priori* to anticipate what a poem should be. I mean, if a center fielder were to try to solve a differential equation for where a flyball would come out he—or she—would be standing there, writing a long equation while the ball plunked down thirty feet away.

Kitchen: That's a fairly accurate description of the way you approach criticism as a reader—that act of attention that you give to other poetry.

Holden: Yes.

Kitchen: Sometimes it's a *practical* criticism: it's *this* poem worked; it had *this* effect; why? And then you do something rather amazing from that moment on, in terms of taking the poems apart. Could you talk about that a little bit?

Holden: Well, there are several issues you raise there, but I'll try to take them one at a time. I'm an empiricist as a critic, not a theoretician. And I'm probably an empiricist because my father was a very good physical chemist, an empiricist. So I've always seen the work of being a critic as going out to the field, picking up a strange specimen of something, sort of sniffing it, drawing a picture of it, paying a lot of attention to individual poems to see what's there and then asking, as a botanist might, "I wonder what spawned this thing, where it came from; are there other things like that growing around here?"—observing things with a kind of sophisticated naiveté. Now, you talk about my taking poems apart and asking how they were made. Well, it's terribly important to ask that question in the right way.

Both of you are excellent poets. I've been "oohing and aahing" over your poems for the last couple of days. You yourselvs know that one can't anticipate these moves during poetic composition, that one fiddles around and feels around with the language and then something startles *you* and you make a connection and the freshness of the connection in the final poem is something that can't be faked; it has to be completely authentic. When I talk about authenticity in poetry, I'm talking about the authenticity of actual formal discovery through the process of composition. It's an existential notion of composition: writing is a form of action such that when we read a very good poem we're participating in the discoveries that were made by the poet during that action. As Robert Frost says, "No tears in the writer, no tears in the reader, no surprise for the writer, no surprise for the reader." Frost *knew*.

Rubin: To extend Judith's question very briefly because we're near the end, why do you write criticism?

Holden: Well, originally I wrote *The Rhetoric of the Contemporary Lyric* because—I shouldn't say this, but I'll say it—my books of poems weren't getting anywhere. I felt as though there was a huge club, and I was outside it. In much the same way as the middle class study the rich, I was looking through this plate glass window at people in the club who had written many poems I didn't especially care for, and I wanted to analyze the manners of that club and try to separate what was fraudulent, mere manners, from what was actually good. Much of it was fraudulent, and so the book came from this sort of jealous scrutiny of work by people that I thought weren't especially good but were members of this club.

Rubin: All right. We should say that one of them at least—Stephen Dunn, whom you scrutinized—you found to be quite a good poet.

Holden: He's a great poet, of course.

Rubin: Unfortunately, we're at the very end of our allotted time, with so much else on my mind unasked, I'm going to ask you if you would conclude by reading the title poem, "Falling from Stardom."

Holden: Sure. "Stardom" in this particular book is a metaphor for narcissism—a certain kind of male narcissism, and the whole book actually proposes love between men and women that can somehow get beyond narcissism, beyond this impulse that we might have sitting at a restaurant looking at some elegant couple at a table over there, to compare our lives to theirs, in order to feel inferior or superior. There must be a way of living life such that one simply takes one's experience as it comes and values it for what it is.

Falling from Stardom

for S.

When only the human remains,
our two human faces licked clean
of disguises like two friends,
I understand what an ex-lover meant
when she said she was tired
of fucking celebrities,
how this star director
who confessed he'd grown bored
with practicing stunts
on one trapeze at a time
turned out in the end to be
no more than his assortment of methods.
The persuasion in his hands,
even the tropical weather moving
through his melancholy eyes,
seemed to her ulterior.
On the mattress with him
she was a mirror.

I have friends who are afraid
to say something trite.
Every rejoinder must top what was just said.
Their gossip's hilarious,
it's a compost of envies. They'll tell you
the sex habits of each president.
At 50, they would still live as we did
before we gave up counting
the nervous thrills in this world
and bore our children.
But their mouths are chameleon, their faces
want definition, are composites of all
our faces, and we
are the score which they cannot stop keeping.
When they lend us themselves
they use the word *love.*
They would finish with us
as with a piece of heavy equipment.
Their motion's a form of immunity.
Loneliness gives them freedom to move.

I wake with you, now, and for the first time
that I can remember
I envy nothing.
The morning's singular,
it will not refer.
Am I naive?
Is this some child's drawing?

There's a blue brook. On it, a boat.
One cloud. One bird. The sun
faithful, always righthanded,
scatters its sticks of lemony candy.
Everything's loyal.
The boat wants only to be a boat,
the cloud a cloud,
the bird bird,
the brook.
If the word *love* means anything
it must be like this—
how two sticks of sun that fall in the brook
can shine all morning, shine
beneath fame, the water descending
without demur, filling
one place at a time.

"Embattled Celebration"
A CONVERSATION WITH PHILIP SCHULTZ

Philip Schultz was born in 1945 in Rochester, New York, and lived in San Francisco, Louisville, Kalamazoo, and Boston before settling down in Greenwich Village. His first volume of poetry, *Like Wings* (Viking, 1978), was nominated for a National Book Award and received the American Academy and Institute of Arts and Letters Award in Literature. His second book, *Deep Within the Ravine* (Viking, 1984), was awarded the Academy of American Poets' Lamont Prize. He has also received a fellowship from the National Endowment for the Arts.

The poems of Philip Schultz have recently been translated and printed in Yugoslavia and Israel and are represented in *Poetry* magazine's 75th Anniversary Issue. They have also appeared in such magazines as *The Kenyon Review, The Nation,* and *The American Poetry Review.* For the past several years, he has been working on a novel.

Mr. Schultz teaches at New York University and directs a private writing school, The Writers Studio, for fiction and poetry. He is a sports enthusiast who loves living in New York City, which has now become a major focus in his work.

The following conversation took place on 21 March 1986. Interviewers were Stan Sanvel Rubin and Judith Kitchen. Mr. Schultz began the interview by reading his poem "Ode." A few of these questions and answers are taken from an earlier (October 1981) interview.

Ode

Grandma stuffed her fur coat into the icebox.
God Himself couldn't convince her it wasn't a closet.
"God take me away this minute!" was her favorite Friday night prayer.
Nothing made sense, she said. Expect heartburn & bad teeth, not sense.
Leave a meat fork in a dairy dish & she'd break the dish & bury the fork.
"I spit on this house, on this earth & on God for putting me
in this life that spits on me night & day," she cried, forgetting the barley
in barley soup. It wasn't age. She believed she was put here to make
one unforgivable mistake after another. Thou shalt be disappointed
was God's first law. Her last words were: "Turn off the stove

before the house blows up." Listen, I'm thirty-four already
& nothing I do is done well enough. But what if disappointment
is faith & not fate? What if we never wanted anything enough to hurt over?
All I can say is spring came this year with such a wallop
the trees are still shaking. Grandma, what do we want from them?
What do we want?

Rubin: I would like to begin by noting a theme that is strong and quite obvious in your work—dealing directly with family experience. Would you say something about that source for your poetry?

Schultz: I am so much a product of that world that it's not even a matter of choice: I know I write best about those things that I feel most strongly about. And that's my past. I'm always five to ten years behind myself; it takes that long for me to assimilate what's happening to me, and to understand my experience well enough to write about it. I write best about what's oldest, the feelings that are most "vintage." My family and the past is a different world that has nothing to do with the world I'm living in now. In Randall Jarrell's words, it's a "lost world." The impulses that make me write—the grief, the nostalgia, the fascination with the past—are ways to understand the present.

Rubin: You've written poems to your father, your mother, your Uncle Jake, other family members. I wonder how these people come to you in your imagination. Do you find yourself continuing to go back to this material, or was it more of a concern in your first book?

Schultz: I think I'm dealing with family almost more now than before. One day it's my ambition to write a novel about that world. In a way, coming back to Rochester helps that; but I can only come back for a certain period of time. When I do, it just stimulates all kinds of old feelings.

I feel strongly that we live in two worlds at the same time—the lost world in which we make figures from the past into a personal mythology, and the present world. Often I project that older world onto the present. That confusion turns into a dismay that wants to express itself in poetry. I write to sort out those two worlds. They're both beautiful in their own ways, and important; but if the boundaries between them keep blurring, often we don't know where we are. Jake, my father, mother, my grandmother—the ones that are dead—are easier to write about, because like all writers I write out of a myth. We want to raise ourselves and the people around us into a kind of mythology. We like archetypes, and I try to create my own. I no longer remain faithful in any sense to who these people actually were or to their psychology. It's an emotional context out of which I see the world. I am a prisoner of my own private mythology.

Kitchen: I'd like to ask you about this new figure that has appeared in *Deep Within the Ravine*—your "guardian angel Stein." Where did he come from?

Schultz: Actually Stein appeared in two poems in my first book, *Like Wings*. As an only child, I had imaginary friends, but I didn't have a guardian angel Stein. In the poems from the first book, he just appeared. I needed an alter ego in this poem called "For the Wandering Jews." Stein was also in "Main Streets" in that book as a superego that says, "Vork, vork, vork," when the character wants to play. I heard so much about Stein from people at readings that I decided he deserved his own poem in this second book. He got it, and then I heard more about him. He's a greedy little fellow; he took over the title poem, "Deep Within the Ravine."

Rubin: But he is a guardian angel figure for you too. He knows everything about despair, doesn't he?

Schultz: He serves as comic relief; but he's also another voice. Since the poetic persona is conflicted, Stein is the happier, more stable side; at least that's his purpose in the title sequence.

Rubin: He authorizes the darker voices?

Schultz: The main character in the long poem is in despair; this is a bad winter in his life. Stein, who doesn't believe in psychoanalysis, sits out in the waiting room with him reading Spinoza, hardly tolerating the narrator's need to see a shrink. He gives the narrator advice like "Don't feel so bad about this woman who just left you. Go see a movie, have an ice cream." Stein is the more positive voice. It's hard to kid yourself or cheer yourself up in a poem when you're the voice that's speaking, even though I'm speaking of myself in third person. As the author, I can't come in and cheer this character up, even though I have some distance from him, because I'm the narrator. I needed another character to serve as ballast, a lighter side; I guess the two sides of this character really come into confrontation in a section called "The Fronts," where the two philosophies hit head-on. It's almost a Talmudic war going on.

Kitchen: But what is your focus in the sequence? Is it a going into the depths of modern city life? Is it approaching the problems of middle age? Is it real phyical infection or a spritual malaise?

Schultz: This character—who is essentially nameless, but you assume he's the poet—goes to the Metropolitan Museum of Art, where he stares at a Hans Hofmann painting, which is also called "Deep Within the Ravine." This is his way of holding himself together. He sees this very abstract painting as an explosion of sexuality, an expression of passion and freedom. He feels all locked up, frozen in time; something is struck in him, and he feels infected. He's looking at the painting as a source of inspiration, hoping to find in it a key to unlocking passion in himself. I don't think he knows what his fascination with the painting is, but every day he goes to look at this painting.

The character is unhappy, but the quality of unhappiness in New York is probably different from that of any other city. There is a way of being unhappy in New York that, on the one hand, makes it more glorious and, on the other, makes it more pathetic—there's something about being overwhelmed constantly—so New York plays a large part in the poems. It's almost a character in this narrative. He focuses a lot, as people do when they're depressed, on headlines in the *New York Post* and begins to identify with the characters in the *Post*. He's in a Dead Sea of memories.

In section two, Stein appears almost in response to the questions:

> Why does the mind destroy what it loves most,
> why must we crush our last hope of continuance?
> he wonders, roaming the streets like a blind man
> after inner vision as Stein, his guardian angel,
> overweight & unaccustomed to such devout self-loathing,
> hurries to keep pace. "You need a woman full-grown
> of heart and mind, that's remedy for self-mythification.
> Meantime, let's see a movie or have an ice cream."

There's something very basic and home-grown about Stein.

Rubin: What is the principle of movement in the poems?

Schultz: There is a story. First, I set up all the things that are wrong: his woman has left him, he feels stuck somewhere in the past and being stuck in New York adds salt to the wounds. He's trying to come out of himself, to explode like the Hofmann painting. The infection is essentially emotional, but it becomes physical and his leg goes bad. It's a mystery to him, but he ends up in the hospital with an infected foot. After he leaves, he has the confrontation with Stein. There's a kind of mysterious ending— the last poem is angry; I wanted it to be apocalyptic. I see the poem as expressive of the dark side of my nature, aspects of my personality I haven't been able to express in other poems.

Kitchen: As in a good novel, all the threads in the poem sequence come together in that last poem. There's the toy angel—not only the real imaginary angel Stein—on the Christmas tree that persists in mocking throughout the poem.

Schultz: In an earlier poem, there's a toy angel in the window of F. A. O. Schwartz, and this rather perverse clerk is clipping its wings.

I'd like to add that the last poem in the book is called "The Quality." When I was writing the title poem, I felt the need to express this more negative part; but what made it possible to write it was knowing that I wasn't going to end on such a dark note, that "The Quality" was going to be affirmative.

Kitchen: Last night you said that certain poems permit us to write other later poems. You spoke of the two grandmother poems as "companion pieces." And you seem to be finding other companion pieces in the second manuscript that mirror and return to the same source as the earlier poem. How aware are you of doing that?

Schultz: They're not companion pieces in the old sense of, say, Milton's writing a poem that would be a lead-in to another. I write very much out of obsessions: I'm trying to figure out or discover something, and whatever leads to the typewriter has to be strong, because there are other places that are more fun to be. I call later poems "companion pieces" to earlier ones in the book, because having written the earlier grandma poem, for example, permitted me to deal with the later one. Having written the early love poem, "Like Wings," gave me permission to feel more openly, to make myself more vulnerable, in a way that allowed me to deal more inclusively with that subject matter in "Ode to Desire."

Kitchen: You have a line, "Passion for distance," that I'm going to take out of context to ask you if some of that "distance" between the two poems gives them a different "passion."

Schultz: As I said before, I need a lot of time to work on a poem. It's like a sliver—inspiration is a metaphorical "sliver" that takes a long time to work its way through the system. All you need is the hint of what a poem is about. The very slightest intimation of what I feel about women in "Like Wings," or about a certain woman, allowed me to write that poem; and then more of the sliver came out and allowed me to write "Ode to Desire." If I'm lucky enough, as more of this begins to emerge, I would like to see myself getting a little smarter and discovering a little more about myself and how I feel about certain things. That's how I go after my subject matter. There are limitations to the subject matter; my writing method is obsessive, and I guess in all my books one poem will be a companion to another.

Rubin: What do you mean that your writing method is obsessive?

Schultz: I write draft after draft after draft. When I was a very young man, I showed my work to the poet George Oppen, whose comments made a deep impression on me. He said, "Until every comma has a reason for being in a poem, it isn't finished." If I applied that to myself, it wouldn't be every comma; it'd be every ampersand.

My earliest drafts are sheer prose—I let everything out. Then I hone it down, going through version after version. I'll get up in the morning and write five versions, knowing that maybe four or five words will improve. The improvement will reveal itself so slowly as to seem almost futile.

There isn't a poem in either of my books that didn't look entirely different at various stages of its development. The hardest part of the poem is when it goes through its "adolescence"; it's a matter of various, often awkward stages. Both of you saw early drafts of "Deep Within the Ravine" when it was five times as long.

Rubin: You really do labor to make the poem happen.

Schultz: I'm probably an extreme case. Because I write about my own inhibitions and conflicts, the act of writing about them causes inhibitions and conflicts. I have to overcome a real resistance to the act of writing, and I do it by muscling my way through.

Rubin: You show drafts in progress? How do you know whose response to trust?

Schultz: I have a number of people whose opinions I find very trustworthy. I know that at certain stages they are so much more objective than I am. Actually I don't show drafts until they're at a later stage. The earlier stages can last months or a year, because I can't deal with the poem and have to put it aside. My "mother poem" is a good example. I put the early drafts away for over a year, because I didn't have the emotional stamina at that point to go through the obsessive process of draft after draft.

Rubin: While you're going through this process that can involve hundreds of drafts, what is it that is leading you on? Is it the poem itself? You said that you wake up and you write a draft. Is it because you tell yourself as you're going to sleep that you'll wake up and do another draft in the morning? Or, do you wake and find that you must do it?

Schultz: It just occurred to me that it is almost sexual. It's a kind of pursuit, with the smell of the hunt. I'm fascinated by the shape that this poem is going to take, its form rather than its content. Of course, I'm very interested in what I'm going to reveal to myself; it's like going after a dream and trying to interpret it. I'm very interested in that, but the poet in me is very curious about the final shape of the poem.

I think I use the ampersand because I want momentum. After having worked on a poem so long and having gone through so many drafts, I want it to reveal itself like a player piano—I want the momentum to play itself out at its own speed, which is often fast. When I near the end, there's a kind of sexual excitement. There's pleasure in the process, but also a lot of agony, frustration, and confusion. I'm after the pleasure of having the poem finally be responsive. When the poem talks back, it's finished.

When I was a child, I felt I had to give eighty percent to get twenty percent, because of the circumstances of my family. I was an only child in a house of immigrants, and my grandmother didn't speak English. You had to work so hard to get a small response. Maybe that has carried over into my work, although I'd never thought of it until this moment. The response at the end of the journey will somehow be worth all the work.

Kitchen: You do have pleasure reading your poems to audiences. I've watched you at least three times now, laughing at some of them, as though you'd just read them for the first time. Laughter, or that sort of comic relief, seems a very important part of your poetry. Last night I heard for the first time the line, "Laughing into silence that should last." Could you talk about the laughter in your poems and the silence underneath it?

Schultz: Some part of the laughter is sheer nervousness. [*Laughter*]

Kitchen: But your audience laughs along with you.

Schultz: I'm often terrified during readings. I think if I live to be eighty, part of me always will be. You lose control. You're almost revealing too much too quickly. It's like the primitive's fear of photography—that you're giving away too much of yourself. But you're talking about something deeper, I suspect.

Kitchen: I'm talking about a poem called "Laughter," and about how your audiences laugh. In a poetry reading there is very often not very much audience response, because poetry is dead earnest. That's not to say that I don't feel yours isn't dead earnest, but you've used laughter in that silence.

Schultz: I seem very much to need audience response. When I read my "serious" poems, there isn't very much response. For the most part, people listen intently and they're quiet. That's O.K. for the last half or two-thirds of the reading. But in the beginning the response I get that is most audible and pleasurable is laughter. When I set up a reading, I begin with more amusing poems; and when they're not laughed at, I'm a little traumatized. I think that it's probably part of the process of writing. I start out lightly, hoping to win my right to an audience's serious attention.

Laughter is, of course, a wonderful defense. When I grew up, we were a poor family, and the one pleasure we had was laughter. It was the best way of letting out steam. There was all the grief and rage, but there was also laughter.

I called the book *Deep Within the Ravine* because during that period of my life I felt that's where I was taking myself, in my writing and my life, into the ravine of consciousness, emotion, and if you do it, you need a light to shine against that darkness. Humor makes the unbearable bearable. It's like matzoh, a leavening. Poets who have no humor in their poetry or who look down upon it are limited. I have my limitations in terms of the emotional ground I plow, but I don't think poetry should exclude anything which is a part of life.

Rubin: It's a kind of necessary self-mocking in that sequence. It's a means of gaining knowledge.

Schultz: When you're confronting aspects of yourself that you don't particularly like or aspects that you fear, the danger is to take yourself too seriously. You have to take yourself seriously enough to get a tone that's genuine and authentic, but the danger is crossing that line (which is in a different place for everyone) of taking yourself so seriously that it becomes self-pity or sentimentality. Salinger says, "Sentimentality is loving your character more than God does." If you make more of your problems or obsessions than someone else would—your reader, for instance—it becomes maudlin. One way of avoiding that is to add humor.

Kitchen: You seem to allow yourself the opportunity to explore feeling *knowing* that the humor is there to act as leavening.

Rubin: Would you read that short poem, "Laughter"?

Laughter

One night my father yanked a tablecloth
from under my face & plates spun like meteors
as he wrapped it over his shoulders & his bald head lit up
like a pumpkin as he waltzed my mother round our crooked house
& tears soaked my collar & my stomach jumped into my mouth
as they flew chair over sofa & the world was a moment so full of us
I think of the Samurai playing with a daisy as he waits for his enemy
& only the daisy & the bright summer sun in his smile & I ask you
if at a time like this you would wonder if there was a beginning or end
with angels gathering on the roof to fear such loud tearing
at the fiery curtain of human delight.

It's not a funny poem. I guess it's about humor, but it's a dead serious poem. That's interesting!

Rubin: Hearing it just now, I noticed how it sets up a particular relationship against time. So much of your family mythology, as you call it, is really affirmative; it draws all this beautiful energy of love and caring and passion into these moments in which we are so full of ourselves. But there is another strain in your other poetry—a kind of more "present" exploring of yourself right now. In those poems there seems to be a void, a searching for identity, while the earlier ones are full of affirmation of identity. How do your poems relate to your moods? How conscious are you of choosing the subject matter of your poems?

Schultz: Perhaps I can answer that by talking about one image in this poem—the Samurai playing with the daisy. While I was having dinner with a friend one night, she happened to mention that in the film *The Seven Samurai* the Samurai was waiting for hundreds of enemies he'd have to fight, and he was lying on the road playing with a daisy. Because of his Zen philosophy, instead of being afraid he could remove himself from his fear and concentrate on a daisy. Wouldn't it be sweet to be able to remove yourself from your own anxiety long enough to achieve that kind of concentration that opens itself into pleasure?

Writing is a process in which we have to unplug ourselves from the world, the static of the world, our own confusion, and into that impulse that leads to poetry. It's like the concentration of attention on the daisy while waiting for the enemy to come down the road; what appears or is revealed may be frightening, but you have to detach yourself and concentrate on the process. You also have to have faith, blind faith, that what comes down the road will amount to something worthwhile.

Kitchen: That same poem has only one period. I wonder if you don't have a small war with form. I'm thinking also of another poem in which you have a three-line stanza going and then a single line comes loping by itself across the page, as though you wanted to break out. But this poem breaks out in another way, to develop a speaking voice as opposed to the written voice. How do you feel about form?

Schultz: I have an intense dislike, and beyond that even fear, of recipes, roadmaps, rules. I was never good at following them. I would always mess up as a child, and I was never a good student. I love to cook, but I can't follow the simplest recipe. It's not emotionally possible for me to pour a single cup of milk into anything, or to find a place with a map. I always assume that's a kind of test which I'll fail.

Poetry is so personal and so free that I love to use content, or my feelings, as a way of discovering form. Form is the last thing I come to in a poem. When the form is right, the poem is often done. I trust that intuitively more than I trust any kind of intellectual equation. The poem is finished for me when the lines seem right and the music seems right. Form is music.

Rubin: What do you think of the current notion that there are two kinds of poets: one is a "word" or "language" poet who cares about form, and another is concerned with feeling and describing "real life"? Is my perception accurate that there is this kind of "war" in contemporary American poetry?

Schultz: I don't see it as a "war," but I'd be surprised, and even pleased, to see myself described as an intellectual poet. There *are* intellectual poets who intellectualize emotions, and their form parallels that. I don't work that way, and I have to be true to my own impulses. "In the beginning" for me there was not the word, but emotion. I'm not very interested in feuds; what is true and good remains, what isn't will be lost.

Kitchen: But aren't those ampersands a mark of rebellion against form?

Schultz: I've been told more than once that there's something perverse about me. I teach mostly adults, but I discovered a lot about myself when I taught children. There was always a lot of wild laughter, but they felt like writing and I felt like writing. There was something so unabashed about that experience that I think maybe humor in us *is* perverse. I mean by "perverse" allowing yourself the uninhibited freedom to express yourself—which is always going against the grain, usually your own. We always have some censor somewhere in us that tells us that something shouldn't be said, or even felt. But the impulse to write is liberating; you free yourself from those inhibitions.

My humor tends to be perverse. When I was working with children, I encouraged them to express that part of their nature and they loved that. There was this immediate reciprocity, because it allowed me to express a freer part of myself. Yes, that part that would express itself in form would want to take a long poem and take out all the stops and use ampersands to speed up the movement. Occasionally, as you noted, a line will break out on its own.

Rubin: You have a number of references to Russian literature, as well as painters like Picasso and Modigliani. What roles does allusion play in your work? Do you consciously seek out these allusions?

Schultz: I envy painters, especially that tactile, physical involvement with their work. I began by painting and drawing. Probably the closest art form to sheer expression, other than dance perhaps, is drawing, the natural extension of the psyche. It's so natural. What is this mysterious force that moves the hand of the drawer? When you're writing, emotions are constantly being sifted and channeled through thought patterns, through censors. When I began drawing and painting, I had this terrific love affair with color. This poem is from my "red period."

Kitchen: Would you read it?

Anemone

Once everything was blue
the faces lips blood dreams
the way emotion invades reality
& then things turned green
the floors ladders gardens
opening into fields of such lush
possibility & then the world
turned yellow the hair breath
touch of the woman who pulled him
from one dark wonder into another
& then the stars earth walls sea
he swam night after white night
the drifting through white space
there is no doubt that death

is white the blizzards he feared
would go on forever & then the feast
flaring up like a plague of locusts
yes red is what's left when everything
leaves & time is the last dinner guest
who sits with his legs on the table
toasting the anemone that springs up
like the recrudescence of hope yes
red is the first moment of appetite
opening the eye like vision

Rubin: What turned you away from drawing toward poetry?

Schultz: I never really figured it out exactly. I think it's a matter of transcendence; I need to explore something fully, and writing is more intellectual. I realize that's counter to what I was saying earlier. I want to be as explicit as possible, and drawing or painting is primarily implicit. It's representational only in the sense that it's a kind of mirror; it allows too much to go unsaid. My main obsession at the bottom of the well of obsession is to say the unsayable—which I think all poets want to do.

There's something about the intensity of poetry that leaves an imprint as no other art form does. I write to transcend all my bad feelings, confusions, fears; and a poem often isn't finished until I've transcended those things.

Rubin: You're pointing to something distinctive and particularly strong in your work—the way it comes from inside, from the self, and confronts the contradictory voices of feeling. It's as though you'd set yourself the task as poet of facing feelings and their contradictions. That's what poetry is about for you, rather than subjects.

Schultz: It's the only way I can write. I envy a great many people who can write well without a great cost to themselves. You have in your average novel or book of poems a lot of filler—very brilliant stuff technically, but still filler. You can't expect a poet to feel deeply for fifty poems in a book, especially if you're going to produce a book every two or three years. I would like to write that way and don't. I'm not exactly in love with my own method of writing. It isn't any act of bravery; it's the only way I can write. When I try to write every morning, much of it is very bad. When I'm not feeling deeply about something, often trying to heal myself in some way, then I don't write well, and it's nothing I can show anybody else. It doesn't mean that I don't have poems that other people wouldn't consider filler, or that there aren't lighter poems; but most poems for me are emotional confrontations. I can write twenty drafts of a poem on a level that won't be too expensive, but the poem won't be very good, unless I take it further and go more deeply into myself. I look at Picasso who couldn't even think about painting without doing something significant—that's a wonderful genius, but I don't have that facility. So I'm almost forced to confront myself and write something that matters and often hurts, in order to get anything worth showing to other people. Poetry can be an embattled celebration.

Rubin: You've been talking a lot about a poet's growing into his material in some sense. I agree that all poets try to say the unsayable—but the real effort is in facing the unsayable, instead of turning away from it, whatever it happens to be. In that context, how do you handle your role as a teacher? What good does it do to have a writing program, or to teach poetry-writing? As one to whom so much of his poetry has been "given," how do you approach the relationship with students?

Schultz: Almost the same as with the relationship from one poem to another—permission. What I wanted most as a young writer was the approval or permission of someone who has gone the route already. I wanted that very much, and I enjoy giving it to others. Certain people have been very generous to me, and I want to return that generosity. Writers can write despite total lack of attention or recognition, but I see young writers blossom in the classroom, with encouragement and criticism. The most important thing is permission.

Rubin: I'd like you to conclude by reading "Ode to Desire." But before you do, I'd like to know why you entitle this and other poems "odes."

Schultz: Originally, in ancient Greek, it meant "song." I can't carry a tune, but a poem isn't finished for me until it's musically worked out. This poem in particular is a form of song, not necessarily a hymn, but it is spiritual in nature.

In the poem, I'm working on a part of me that I never understood. Sexual desire is something we spend a lifetime exploring and trying to understand. There's nothing definitive about this poem; in fact, I'm not sure what it finally says. I was interested in the image of marathon dancers, because I feel in a relationship people hold each other up. There has to be an equal strength. There are times when you are weak and your partner holds you up. In the old newsreels you see that—one dancer sleeps, while the other keeps going.

Ode to Desire

Remember how we watched a hang-glider lift himself
between heaven & earth & the music in the sway
of his arms & how for a moment he was one with the light
& as perfect as the world allows—as if love were a kind

of weather where one moment there is a calm so complete
the earth rolls on its side like a woman turning
in the generous folds of her sleep & then thunder
strikes like the despair of total embrace?

Remember the newsreels of marathon dancers,
how they cling like shadows long after the music
of first passion, how they push & drag each other
like swimmers stretching toward the surface light
of their desire to continue the embrace
another quarter turn round the speckled floor?

To think that after we have given up all hope
of perfection I am still jealous of the red towel
you wrap round your raisin hair & of the photos
of you as a child who looked happy enough not to know me
& that I still cannot understand the blood's rush to give all
& the urgency that opens in my chest like an umbrella
which will not close until you take me back
into the tides of your breath!

What rage, our bodies twisted like wires
in the brain's switchboard, hurt plugged to joy,
need to desire, how it happens so quickly, this entering
of another's soul, like molecules of fire connecting
flesh & dream in the sheets of a hundred beds, spring
suddenly knocking at the window as your long female body
sprawls into full radiance, ah, such high laughter
in light-flushed rooms, our bodies so perfectly crossed!

Remember the night we read how the female whale whips
her tail out of reach as the male splits the ocean
plunging round her for whole days & nights crying
such symphony of rage birds whirl round their spindrift waltz
as the sea is shaken like a fishbowl & the sky is shredded
into ribbons of light? Yes, it is curious, the risk of such
attraction, but isn't there implanted in the anemones of her eyes
the smallest smile? for all creatures large & small must realize
that in stirring such passion the prize must be worth the promise
& yes, I am tried of this endless dancing in circles & suddenly
the light of this spring morning does not throw back its color
so splendidly as before though there is still the joy that comes
only after long pain as you slip slowly within reach & everywhere
the air burns like the stained glass in the attic window
where I sat as a boy listening to the wind with such longing
the light itself was song!

"The Rush of Language"
A CONVERSATION WITH ROBERT MORGAN

Robert Morgan

Robert Morgan was born in Hendersonville, North Carolina, in 1944. He received his B.A. in English at the University of North Carolina at Chapel Hill and his M.F.A. from the University of North Carolina at Greensboro. His eight books include *Red Owl* (W. W. Norton, 1972), *Land Diving* (LSU Press, 1976), *Groundwork* (Gnomon Press, 1979), *Bronze Age* (Iron Mountain Press, 1981), and *At the Edge of the Orchard Country* (Wesleyan University Press, 1987).

In addition to poetry, Robert Morgan writes and publishes short stories, essays, and articles on poetry. His work has been included in many anthologies, including *A Geography of Poets, The Generation of 2000, The Morrow Anthology of Younger American Poets*, and *Strong Measures.* His books have been reviewed by William Matthews and William Harmon, among others.

Robert Morgan is Professor of English at Cornell University in Ithaca, New York, where he teaches as a member of the M.F.A. and creative writing faculty. His many awards include four National Endowment for the Arts fellowships, a New York Foundation for the Arts fellowship, and Hawthornden Fellow in Poetry, International Writers Retreat, Hawthornden Castle, Scotland. He lives with his wife and three children in the country near Freeville, New York.

The following conversation took place 7 November 1985. Interviewers were Stan Sanvel Rubin and William Heyen. Mr. Morgan began by reading his poem "Buffalo Trace."

Buffalo Trace

Sometimes in the winter mountains
after a little snow has blown in the night
and nothing's alive in eye-range

but clouds
near peaks frozen clean
in the solstice sun,
the white finds a faint depression
to stick in out of wind
and makes visible for the first time
through woods and along the slopes
to where it nicks the rim
perceptibly, a ghostpath
under brush and broomsedge,
merging in the pasture with narrow
cowtrails but running on through fences
and across boundaries, under branches
in tattered sweep out to the low
gaps of the old migrations
where they browsed into the summer mountains
then ebbed back into the horizon
and back of the stars.

Heyen: I've liked the poem "Buffalo Trace" from the first time I read it. It begins with something close and then moves out, as so many of your poems do, through the collision of the buffalo and the cow all the way to the stars. I'm reminded of what you say in an essay: "The ear knows long before the mind whether a poem or passage is working." What about that idea regarding a poem like "Buffalo Trace"? I know Robert Frost said, "Watch my sentences." And I just have a feeling the way that poem works that it completed itself for you musically as much as it did intellectually or through idea.

Morgan: Poetry is in some ways a fairly primitive art. It belongs perhaps more to the Stone Age than to the twentieth century. It is primarily an art of sound. As Frost said, "The sound is the gold in the ore." I've noticed in writing and revising my own poems, and in reading the work of other poets including my students at Cornell, that I can tell whether a poem is going right first by the way it sounds; long before I figure out what's wrong with it, I can spot a weak passage because it doesn't sound right. Poetry is a miracle: it's the way we can say something that is true, that has depth, that has metaphoric resonance we don't always recognize at first, and we can say it in the fewest words possible—that's part of the poetic act also— and it's done somehow with the unconscious and the conscious working together. The sound is the testament of that; if it sounds right, it's probably saying the right things.

Heyen: Conciseness can actually lead to the poem's music.

Morgan: It can lead to the music and to new recognitions. Any number of times I've discovered in revising that I could take out a word or a short phrase and change the meaning slightly, and the new meaning would be better. It'd be a deeper poem with much greater ramifications. The art of poetry is to a great extent the art of compression and economy. Prose does not have to be so compact. Poetry is so much in the texture, in the sound, and that depends to a great extent on how quickly something is being said. As I say in my essay in your anthology, the music of poetry, especially modern poetry, is derived as much from that compression and concision as it is from the stresses. You can, after all, write something very dull in iambic pentameter; it's not necessarily poetry, even though it scans and superficially is musical. Our sense of the music is some strange fusion of the content and the quickness of the expression, with the stresses, the syllables.

Rubin: You see the music, then, as being the connection with the primitive.

Morgan: Right. It's something of the ear and of the senses, of the body as much as of the mind. I can see that especially in a poet like Eliot, whom I was teaching yesterday. Even if you don't understand "Prufrock"—and I'm not sure I understand it although I've been reading it for twenty-five years—you're still haunted by the music of it. It's like Mozart; once you're heard it, you never forget it.

Another test of poetry is memorability; that is, if you want to say it aloud, to repeat it, then it's probably good poetry.

Rubin: Does this argue in some way for the traditional approach to music and meter in poetry?

Morgan: It's very hard to get away from them. Those traditional devices of poetry were discovered and used for a good reason—they worked, they delighted the ear.

That's one reason poetry has lost its large audience. I don't think the general public has ever taken to free verse; free verse sounds like poetry to poets and literary people, but when the average person thinks of poetry, he or she thinks of Poe, who is in some ways our "poet laureate." If you ask people to repeat a line of Whitman, they probably can't do it; but if you ask them to repeat a line of Poe, everybody can say, "Once upon a midnight dreary, while I pondered, weak and weary." Those trochees just trip off in their minds.

Heyen: And there's been a flattening in general in contemporary poetry, I think, and it's ironic that much of the flattening is the result of poets trying to reach an audience; but, as you've said, plain speech sounds like poetry only to poets.

Morgan: People delight in music, and they get that kind of poetry these days from rock 'n' roll and folk songs and country music. There's a lot of poetry all around us. Poetry is not just verse; it's not just T. S. Eliot. Poetry is any imaginative use of language, of metaphor and figure: it's in prose, it's in fiction, it's in editorials. Often we feel it's not as sophisticated as the poetry we try to write.

Heyen: How did you get started? Where did poetry enter your life?

Morgan: The traditional answer for a Southern writer is to say, "Of course, I absorbed poetry from the oral tradition in the South," and that's partly true in my case. I heard a lot of storytelling around the fireplace; I grew up in a community that was still in some ways in the nineteenth century, and people talked more than they do now. They told stories, and Southerners *are* particularly good storytellers.

The other answer for a Southern writer is, "I got it from the King James version of the Bible and from preachers." There is *that* oral tradition in the South, and that's certainly true in my case. I heard a lot of great preaching, and I grew up in a very religious family—we read the Bible twice a day, prayed three or four times a day—so I was exposed to that very rich Elizabethan rhetoric of the New Testament.

The first time I read modern poetry was when I was about fifteen, and my sister had gone off to Bob Jones University where she used Cleanth Brooks's anthology of American literature in Freshman English. She brought it home one weekend, and in paging through it I came upon Whitman. I remember vividly reading the first lines of "Song of Myself": "I celebrate myself, and sing myself, / And what I assume you shall assume, / For every atom belonging to me as good belongs to you." But the line that really leapt out at me was "I loafe and invite my soul, / I lean and loafe at my ease observing a spear of summer grass." It was the contrast between "soul" and that one "spear of grass" that really struck me. I thought, My goodness, you can go from something that grand to something that precise and small. It was that juxtaposition that first started me thinking about poetry, and, of course, that's exactly the way poetry works—in the positioning of the big with the little, making the far near, and the near far.

At the same time, in flipping further, I came upon Wallace Stevens, whom I'd never heard of. I read "Domination of Black," where he talks about how the leaves turn, as the fire turned, and he looks out the window and sees the planets turn—that correspondence between the things very close and very far—and I never forgot that. I didn't know anything about poetry, never read Stevens or Whitman again for years, but I never forgot that. It seemed to have planted a seed of some sort.

It's also true that living just down the road in Flat Rock was Carl Sandburg, who had bought an antebellum mansion there. He was always in the paper—he was going to Hollywood or New York—so I had a model of somebody who was a professional poet.

But those were the "beat-the-Russians" years of the early sixties and someone from the working class like myself would never have thought of going to college to study literature or to be a writer; you were supposed to study engineering, something technical, to help us beat the Russians. They had put up their Sputnik, and you had a patriotic duty. I was pretty good at science and math, so I left high school after my junior year for Emory to study science. When I got very interested in applied mathematics and theoretical mechanics, I transferred to North Carolina State which was much cheaper and had a better program in that. I got pretty far in math; I completed a major in it, and by my sophomore year I was taking advanced courses in differential equations and calculus.

I ended up taking a course in creative writing on a fluke. I had never finished high school, and there was a requirement at N. C. State that you had to have had solid geometry, which was a high school senior course. I told my advisor that I wanted to take this graduate course in partial differential equations the next semester, and I was certainly qualified; but he said, "Since you haven't made up this deficiency in solid geometry, I'm not going to let you do it." In that time slot there just happened to be a course in creative writing, taught by Guy Owen, so I took that. Guy encouraged me, and I started writing, and I never really stopped. I kept up with math for another year, completed the major, but just couldn't quit writing. I wrote stories, pieces of novels, some pretty bad poems, but poem after poem.

Rubin: Surely there was something else besides the time slot. Had you no familiarity with Owen's work?

Morgan: Oh, in this time I had been reading some poetry and even writing some. I had never really abandoned the idea of writing poetry, even from the time I read Whitman and Stevens. But it didn't seem something I could do, a real possibility, then.

Rubin: You mentioned Sandburg, and so much of your early work is concerned with the Western Carolina mountains and the country you spent your boyhood in. Some of that poetry is suggestive of Sandburg. I wonder if you would say more about the influence of your region and your boyhood on your work.

Morgan: The irony is that Sandburg, of course, has been associated with the Midwest. It was only after World War II that he moved to North Carolina. But I did admire his work, and it gave me ideas about poetry— its vernacularity or conversational tone—a poetry aimed at ordinary people. He said that he wanted to write for the truck-driver and the waitress, and that was certainly one of my ideals early in my writing.

I think he's a very underestimated poet, actually; he's forgotten, partly as poetry has moved deeper and deeper into the academy to become something for a graduate seminar. Sandburg needs little explication;

therefore, he's not read as much. Stevens would be the perfect poet for the graduate seminar because he's so "difficult." Difficulty has become a measure of quality.

But I didn't really think of myself as a writer about the Southern mountains until I came up North. I had written some about it, but I really thought of myself as an American poet. The models I had in mind at that time were Sandburg and Gary Snyder and Robert Bly, the great influence on me in my early twenties. But I did begin to discover that I had a subject.

I decided about 1965 or 1966 that I wasn't going to write fiction for a while—I had written stories and even published a few—because Southern fiction had been "done." It was what we associated with the South and Southern writing—Faulkner, Eudora Welty, Walker Percy—but there was no such thing as "Southern poetry," and certainly very little poetry about the Southern mountains. That seemed an opportunity.

I decided *consciously* to do something different from what was thought of as traditional Southern writing—which was very colorful and highly rhetorical. I wanted to become a writer of very precise poems, concise poems. The models in American literature I found the most useful were Thoreau and, to some extent, Dickinson. As I say in my essay in *The Generation of 2000*, I wanted an almost classical concision and precision with no rhetoric, or very few rhetorical effects. I wanted something very direct, honest. The models I found that I admired most then were Thoreau's poems in *Walden*—the "Smoke" poem, the "Haze" poem— and at that time I would take the simplest and most ordinary thing and try to write a poem, about gravity or copper or a chair. I was taking Whitman literally, when he said: "If you want to find me, look for me under your boot soles." He's speaking as the spirit of American poetry—not literally as Walt Whitman, but as the American imagination. And he was right: you find the poetry wherever you are, just looking in the most unexpected places. You don't need anything grand as the subject of a poem. You find the grandeur within the poem as you write it.

Heyen: Would you talk about and maybe read "Mountain Bride"?

Morgan: After I came to Cornell, I began to get interested in two or three things that were new for me. One was writing in traditional forms, like the ballad; another was writing narrative poetry; and a third was writing some of the stories that had been told to me by my grandfather and other people—to get the folklore or the legend of a place into poetry. This is an example of one of the poems I wrote back then.

It's called "Mountain Bride." This is a story told to me by the fireplace by my grandfather when I was a kid. Scared me to death, as many of these stories did! I later found out that it is a traditional Appalachian folktale.

He told it as though it had happened just up the road; of course, that's the way folk tales should be told.

Mountain Bride

They say Revis found a flatrock
on the ridge just
perfect for a natural hearth,
and built his cabin with a stick

and clay chimney right over it.
On their wedding night he lit
the fireplace to dry away the mountain
chill of late spring, and flung on

applewood to dye
the room with molten color while
he and Martha that was a Parrish
warmed the sheets between the tick

stuffed with leaves and its feather
cover. Under that wide hearth
a nest of rattlers,
they'll knot a hundred together,

had wintered and were coming awake.
The warming rock
flushed them out early.
It was she

who wakened to their singing near
the embers and roused him to go look.
Before he reached the fire
more than a dozen struck

and he died yelling her to stay
on the big four-poster.
Her uncle coming up the hollow
with a gift bearham two days later

found her shivering there
marooned above a pool
of hungry snakes
and the body beginning to swell.

Heyen: I like that poem. In Pound's sense, it's "news that stays news," because, even though I know what's going to happen, I keep enjoying the reading of it.

You said once that you thought a poem is the closest thing you know to a perpetual motion machine. What did you mean by that?

Morgan: The poem is a verbal machine—that's Williams's definition—I like that sense of objectivism, the poem as an object. A really good poem seems to renew itself with every generation, with every reader, and I'm not sure exactly how this happens, but it's the miracle of poetry that it does. Somebody can write a *Lycidas* or the seventy-third sonnet of Shakespeare that seems to speak to each new generation of readers in a new way; it seems to have an energy of its own but also a power to transform the future into new energy. Long after the writer's gone with whatever energy he put into it, it keeps renewing itself.

Heyen: It keeps moving with that vertical audience down through time. I like that.

Morgan: It's also able somehow to assimilate the energy of whatever age it's read in, using new concepts to renew itself. Dante's a good example. No matter what happens in astronomy or psychology, Dante seems to have already been there. His image of the universe is perfectly consonant with relativity, quantum mechanics, the newest discoveries in astronomy, the notion of a circular universe. I think the reason is that the imagination is universal, and no matter where human beings look they will come up with essentially the same metaphors. As far as I'm concerned, science is just as imaginative as poetry: it's all part of the same imagination looking for metaphors and a vocabulary for explaining experience.

Heyen: And Shakespeare knew everything that Jung was to discover.

Morgan: Everything there is to know has already been known; we just keep inventing new figures of speech for it.

Rubin: Clearly you don't believe in this split between science and poetry that has been made much of in our century by Christopher Clausen and others. On the other hand, you are an exception as a poet, in having had training in science.

Morgan: I've found that most poets have an interest in science. Science *is* in a way the theology of the twentieth century; it's important to us in the way that mystic philosophy and theology were to Dante. That was for Dante the new explanation of reality. In so far as we have an authoritative new theology in our century, it is Einstein's and Darwin's. In so far as we believe in truth, it's there.

Of course, this is a great issue for modern poetry: what is truth? We are no longer as confident of the Romantic answers as people like Emerson and Whitman were. They said, "Look into the self, and whatever seems true to your self is truth." One of the great issues for us has been, What is the self? Is there a self? Can we know the self?

Eliot's answer was that truth comes from the tradition: you cannot know it on your own; you have to learn it from society, from the community. Truth is a communal act. That's true particularly for poetry and language, because language is a communal instrument. It's not something you would arrive at on your own. This has been proven. Somebody who lives in isolation doesn't develop very much in the use of language. Poetry is a thing of the community.

Heyen: You read a poem last night that held your audience—it's called "The Gift of Tongues." It goes back to the religious experience of your childhood, and it talks about language in some of the ways you've been talking about.

Morgan: As I said earlier, I was raised in a very religious household. My mother was a Southern Baptist, and my father was a Pentecostal Holiness; and I went to both kinds of services. At one service that I remember going to, my father spoke in tongues. I had heard other people speak in tongues, but it seemed different when he did it. It was terrifying!

The Gift of Tongues

The whole church got hot and vivid
with the rush of unhuman chatter
above the congregation,
and I saw my father looking at
the altar as though electrocuted.
It was a voice I'd never heard
but knew as from other centuries.
It was the voice of awful fire.
"What's he saying?" Ronald hissed
and jabbed my arm. "Probably Hebrew."
The preacher called out another
hymn, and the glissade came again,
high syllables not from my father's
lips but elsewhere, the flare of
higher language, sentences of light.
And we sang and sang again, but
no one rose as if from sleep to
be interpreter, explain the writing
on the air that still shone there like
blindness. None volunteered a gloss
or translation or receiver
of the message. My hands hurt
when pulled from the pew's varnish
they'd gripped and sweated so. Later,
standing under the high and plain-

sung pines on the mountains I clenched
my jaws like pliers, holding in
and savoring the gift of silence.

As I said last night, I think I've finally figured out what that poem is about. What was so frightening was the sense of language being used under inspiration but without control. It's important for poets to feel a sense of control at the same time they are inspired. You have the rush of language, but you're in control of it. It's conscious mind and the unconscious working together. So much of the power of poetry comes from that particular fusion of unconscious, memory, dream, with consciousness. It's that place or threshold that people in the nineteenth century called "reverie," the place where there's an intermingling, a washing back and forth between dream, sleep, and consciousness. It takes both the control of consciousness and the rush from the unconscious to write good poetry. Poets are people sensitive to that particular threshold; they can put themselves into that state of semipassivity.

After I got to college, I looked up books and articles on speaking in tongues, or glossolalia, and I found out in psychological studies that it's related to epilepsy and hypnosis. Certain cells in the brain fire off under eye contact from a charismatic leader. It's a very primitive, ancient kind of thing, and it was always seen as a visitation of some sort, back into the Stone Age. Remember that in earliest recorded history epileptics were considered gifted people, inhabited by good demons.

Rubin: This is a very rich area you've opened up here. One is the issue of control. You're suggesting that this kind of energy and power is close to what the poet feels, but without the control it isn't poetry.

Morgan: My favorite line in all of Emerson's poetry is in his poem "Bacchus," the Dionysian poem of the pair, "Merlin" and "Bacchus"— "Merlin" is wisdom; "Bacchus," drunkenness. Of course, he means drunkenness in the spiritual sense; he talks about the wine that doesn't come from the grape. He says that in that state of blessed drunkenness or intoxication, he'll "hear far Chaos talk with me." That's it! You're close enough to hear chaos, but you're not in it. If you were *in* chaos, you couldn't write it; it'd be pure turbulence. Poets are people who can get close enough to chaos to feel the rush of energy, that primordial power of the imagination, but they can control it within a form.

Rubin: They are not just the vehicles or mediums for it; they have the requirement of craft and, as you're suggesting, conscious awareness of tradition.

Morgan: They're makers, craftsmen or craftswomen, as well as mediums.

Rubin: In a related area, I'd like to ask you about your language. The poem you just read, which is recent, uses terms like "glissade" and phrases like "sentences of light," which are by no means vernacular; yet you, like so many contemporary poets, come out of that tradition of being in touch with the vernacular. It's very clear that you transform American speech, that you won't render just the looseness of overheard speech. I wonder if there is a tension or even a paradox somewhere at the heart of American poetry that we must all contend with: namely, fulfilling the commitment to being vernacular, populist, and yet maintaining a special obligation to language. Have I said too much?

Morgan: No, I'm very concerned with that, and I've never settled that issue for myself. I'm beginning to suspect that vernacularity in poetry is one of the myths of Romanticism we love. We want to give the impression that we are writing in the vernacular.

The man who articulated this theory was Wordsworth, and he was never able to live up to the theory. The next man to articulate it was Whitman, and if you know Whitman, you know that whatever he's doing it's not the vernacular, the spoken language of America. It's very elevated language that gives the impression of an oratorio, or an Italian *bel canto* opera.

It's a part of our democratic heritage: we want to believe that everything we do is for everybody. But sophisticated poetry, in fact, is probably not going to be read by everybody.

There's a long, painful history for me in that. I started out wanting to write for everybody, and I've gradually come to realize that really good poets probably don't. You're writing for people who are pretty literate. In that sense, I am not a "folk poet," even though I've been called one. You use words like "glissade," and it shows you know something about ballet. It's based on a cultural tradition, as well as a folk tradition. I don't think it's important, finally, what kind of language you use as long as you accomplish aesthetically what you want to in a poem. A theory of poetry is much less important than the poem itself.

In fact, what really good American writers do is give a plausible *impression* of vernacularity. Look at Hemingway's dialogue, which seems realistic, but, of course, it's not. It's highly compressed. We want to give that impression because we are the inheritors of that myth of the common man and the myth that poetry is common speech. Even somebody like Sandburg who tried hard to write ordinary speech does it only in bits and pieces, gists of slang here and there to give the impression. The "local color" writers of the turn of the century experimented with this, and they're mostly bad writers because they were trying to be true to the native speech of Maine or Georgia more than the art of storytelling; they rendered the speech but they didn't write very good stories or poems for the most part.

Rubin: As teachers we've all encountered the motivation students have sometimes in starting this business of poetry—wanting to be prophet figures, or to have that connection to the mass they don't otherwise feel. That often seems to come from this wrong image of Whitman we've perpetuated—that he wandered around, speaking the speech of common people and naming everything, and that's all they have to do to become poets.

Morgan: He wanted to give that impression; that was part of his legend.

Rubin: Maybe because poetry has lacked a clear place in our culture from the beginning, American poets have been particularly afraid of the isolation and loneliness and inwardness that poetry comes out of and they have been particularly defensive, proclaiming our poetry gets its justification from its important themes and cultural statements. But in actuality poetry comes out of language, and what touches us in Whitman or any great poet is language. Maybe we need to acknowledge that we are in some sense unwillingly an elite, or at least a minority, in responding to language in that way.

Morgan: The other danger in that area is going too far toward specialization in vocabulary. In academia this is particularly a problem of a priestcraft evolving a jargon for ourselves that nobody else understands. You see that priestcraft particularly in critics who have a magic language, and graduate students who come to them to learn it.

I'm not interested in being that specialized. I would like to see poetry achieve a classic balance between sophistication and precision, in a vocabulary that can say with great subtlety exactly what you want to say. I would not like to go to either extreme—poems that anybody can understand on the first hearing or poems that are completely hermetic.

Rubin: You are not, I gather, particularly enamored of Ashbery's work.

Morgan: He interests me a great deal—especially before he was canonized as the great Romantic poet. Back in the sixties I read his Dada poems; they're a lot of fun. But he doesn't interest me as much as somebody like Geoffrey Hill or T. S. Eliot, somebody whose difficulty is part of the complexity of what he's trying to say. It's not difficulty for the sake of difficulty.

I have a recent poem that deals with my interest in language. I'd like to read "Writing Spider."

Writing Spider

When Uncle Wass had found the spider's
W woven between the limbs
of a dead chestnut over on

the Squirrel Hill, he said he knew
there would be war. But even before
Pearl Harbor he was gone himself
and my Grandpa, his brother, told
how the writing spider's runes could spell
a message to the world, or warn
of the individual reader's own
end with an initial. That web
was strung significant as lines
in a palm and the little webster,
spinning out its monogram like
the fates, put the whole dictionary
of a life in one elaborate
letter to be abstracted from
the jacob's ladder of floss and dew
in the eye of the beholder,
a lifetime's work for it and all.

This poem is related to an idea I keep going back to—the way we find writing in nature. Science is really doing that. It's decoding one kind of writing everywhere it looks. Everything is language.

Heyen: What about in the suburbs, "at the edge of the orchard country"? Where, then, is the nature?

Morgan: That's one of the problems for contemporary, and perhaps future, American poets. American poetry starts with Emerson whose first book is called *Nature*. Our first poets evolved a tradition of celebrating nature and reading nature as a mirror of the self, as an image or a language of the self.

The best clue to what can be done in the suburbs is probably William Carlos Williams. There's someone who confronted this issue way back in the twenties.

The problem is that the suburbs are a world in between. There's great poetry of the city, in Whitman and Hart Crane, Ginsberg, and great poetry of nature. How do you make a poetry of the middle landscape, the middle range of experience, the bedroom towns? No one has done that very well, except Williams. It violates the grain of American poetry.

"Accumulating Observations"
A CONVERSATION WITH STEPHEN DUNN

Stephen Dunn

Stephen Dunn was educated at Hofstra University, the New School for Social Research, and Syracuse University and is the author of six collections of poetry, including *Local Time* (William Morrow, 1986), winner of the National Poetry Series Open Competition. His previous books are *Not Dancing, Work and Love, A Circus of Needs, Full of Lust and Good Usage* (all from Carnegie-Mellon University Press), and *Looking for Holes in the Ceiling* (University of Massachusetts Press).

His awards include a Guggenheim Fellowship, two NEA Creative Writing Fellowships, two Fellowships from the New Jersey State Council on the Arts, the Theodore Roethke Prize from *Poetry Northwest*, and many others. His work has appeared in *The New Yorker, The Nation, The Atlantic*, and *The Georgia Review*, to name just a few.

He is Professor of creative writing at Stockton State College and teaches in the M.F.A. Creative Writing Program at Columbia University. In the summer he is on the faculty of the Bennington Writing Workshops at Bennington College.

The following conversation took place on 2 November 1984. Interviewers were Stan Sanvel Rubin and Judith Kitchen. Mr. Dunn began by reading his poem "Essay on the Personal."

Essay on the Personal

Because finally the personal
is all that matters,
we spend years describing stones,
chairs, abandoned farm houses—
until we're ready. Always
it's a matter of precision,
what it feels like
to kiss someone or to walk

out the door. How good it was
to practice on stones
which were things we could love
without weeping over. How good
someone else abandoned the farm house,
bankrupt and desperate.
Now we can bring a fine edge
to our parents. We can hold hurt
up to the sun for examination.
But just when we think we have it,
the personal goes the way of
belief. What seemed so deep
begins to seem naive, something
that could be trusted
because we hadn't read Plato
or held two contradictory ideas
or women in the same day.
Love, then, becomes an old movie.
Loss seems so common
it belongs to the air,
to breath itself, anyone's.
We're left with style, a particular
way of standing and saying,
the idiosyncratic look
at the frown which means nothing
until we say it does. Years later,
long after we believed it peculiar
to ourselves, we return to love.
We return to everything
strange, inchoate, like living
with someone, like living alone,
settling for the partial, the almost
satisfactory sense of it.

Rubin: I'd like to begin by asking about the poem you just read, "Essay on the Personal." As the poem says, the personal finally is all that matters, and that seems to be the central project of your own poetry, but the poem sets the personal against style in an interesting way. Would you say something about that?

Dunn: Well, the impulse to set pen to paper is always personal in some way. The question is how directly and from what distance does one confront experience. The closer you attempt to get to your own experience the more the dangers are clear—solipsism, self-congratulation, all the perils of the "I" voice. So whenever I can deal with the personal somewhat directly and make it available in larger terms for others, the personal being overheard, rather than that kind of private impulse of the personal, then I'm pleased. But I don't think of the personal as something that is at odds with style in any way. Style, in fact, is what's most personal. The details of our lives are what's most communal in a poem. Thus, content should be communal. People have similar experiences, however interior they may be. But, as my poem says, "We're left with style." It's how we speak about our experiences that distinguishes us one from another.

Rubin: It's interesting that a poem about the personal uses the plural pronoun "we" throughout.

Dunn: It *is* risky to do that, to speak in a collective voice. But I thought of the poem as about poets, or certain poets, more than just about myself.

Kitchen: Let's push that a little in terms of pronouns. Jonathan Holden recently labeled you the master of the second person. And yet I looked hard and found not too many poems in the second person. What makes you choose to move suddenly into a "you"?

Dunn: I don't know. I really haven't done it that much. And I know the dangers of the impersonal, where you can't locate a definite person in the "you." And I don't even remember what he said any more about how I got away with it.

Kitchen: Well, you don't substitute a "you" for an "I." You turn it into something larger, and I wondered if as a writer coming through the poem somehow there was a moment when you realized that the "I" would not suffice.

Dunn: I'm sure that was the case, but I can't even remember the poem any more that he singled out. In fact, it was a poem that I don't think I ever collected. He found it in a journal some years back, and after he did the little exegesis I wished I'd collected it; it seemed like a good poem. But I don't even remember what it was now.

Rubin: To get back to the personal for a moment, do you feel that there's been a turning away from the personal, almost ideologically, in American poetry for the last decade or so, with post-confessional poets?

Dunn: Only in a few instances. Maybe under the notable Ashbery influence. People abuse the confessional impulse, but it is still very much with us. When personal poems don't work, you feel like calling them confessional poems because they make you feel like a voyeur. Many poems that others call confessional, such as Snodgrass's "Heart's Needle," I'd simply call good poems. That poem, for example, is concerned with more than speaking about the author's personal life. It's also examining its subject. When personal poems don't examine and evaluate their subject matter, then the confessional label makes sense. How to make the personal poem work and not seem confessional—that's the hard part. The writer has to have some philosophical disposition toward himself and his subject. I don't think there can be a strategy for it. You may have to believe that the circumstances of your life finally are not that important. The people who write the poems about the personal and actually believe their lives are very interesting often don't "make" the poem enough; they don't create it; they actually offer their lives. That always seems a little boring to me; I'm not interested. Really you're making poems for others, as opposed to the person who writes out of just the impulse to cover some terrain of his life for his own sake.

Kitchen: You seem to be concerned about man's relationship to man, as opposed to his relationship to nature. Does this lend itself to the personal?

Dunn: Yes, I guess so. I've been taken to task for that too. Somebody said that Dunn has no feeling for nature. I do, but it's mostly for human nature; that's what I pay attention to. When I walk down the street, I rarely notice all the things that everyone else notices, but I almost always can tell you what is going on between people. A friend of mine who is a Jungian analyst gave me the Jungian personality test. It determines your dominant qualities, but the people who give the test are really interested in your deficient qualities. I came out as an intuitive, thinking type, which I thought he was going to congratulate me for, but he just wanted to point out that I was weak in sensation, in perceiving things around me, which I realize is true. Occasionally this deficiency helps my poetry. When I actually do see things in the natural world, and of course I do, I get rather excited. Say, a goose, or a certain flower. Jesus Christ, a goose! Other people seem to notice those things as a matter of course, but I'm usually startled when I finally discover myself paying attention to the natural world. Still, it's the human and social dynamic which interests me most.

Rubin: At that point, may I ask you to read "Corners," the first poem in *Not Dancing?* I think that it maybe makes that point poetically.

Corners

I've sought out corner bars, lived in corner houses;
　　like everyone else I've reserved
corner tables, thinking they'd be sufficient.
　　I've met at corners
perceived as crossroads, loved to find love
　　leaning against a lamp post
but have known the abruptness of corners too,
　　the pivot, the silence.

I've sat in corners at parties hoping for someone
  who knew the virtue
of both distance and close quarters, someone with a
  corner person's taste
for intimacy, hard won, rising out of shyness
  and desire.
I've turned corners there was no going back to,
  corners
in the middle of a room that led
  to Spain or solitude.
And always the thin line between corner
  and cornered,
the good corners of bodies and those severe bodies
  that permit no repose,
the places we retreat to, the places we can't bear
  to be found.

Rubin: That certainly is a poem noticeably devoid of sensory imagery. And it's discursive, like a lot of your work, tightly controlled but discursive. Would you say something about how that particular poem came to be? Maybe that will tell us something about your sources.

Dunn: I don't remember exactly. You can manufacture answers, and they're always at least half-true. The poem draws on a lot of experience over many years, but I don't remember what was the immediate impulse to write it. I will say something about the discursive, if that's all right.

Rubin: All right.

Dunn: I think it has to do with just the way I was taught to write poetry, the way people of my generation were, if in fact we were really taught. But the emphasis on the tightness, on the image, all the things I've paid attention to in my first book, finally seems very restrictive. I probably didn't fully free myself of those constrictions until the *Work and Love* book. It had to do with the notion of the image that was so prevalent: the image had to be that little nugget. I was never very comfortable thinking of an image that way.

I came upon an essay by Pavese which defined the image in a way that was soothing to me. He said, "Why not think of the image as something that a whole poem might give you?" The image may not be finished until the poem is over—one image. And that's kind of what I do. Or, in many of my poems I do that. Ever since then I really haven't worried about making images in poems. I do now and then, but it is not a concern, and it allows me to talk in poems the way I feel comfortable.

Kitchen: It's interesting, then, the way the reader of "Corners" does a mental adjustment finally and allows for all your various corners to come together. That doesn't happen until you make your play on "corners" and "cornered," and then suddenly there's a sort of readjustment all the way back through the poem.

Dunn: Well, the poem has been accumulating observations about what it means to be a corner person all the way through. I would hope that each advance the poem makes enlarges the issue and that each assertion plays off of a previous assertion, both in terms of sense and texture. In other words, that the poem's language is cooperative while being surprising.

Rubin: The contemporary critic and poet Jonathan Holden, who thinks so highly of your work in his book *The Rhetoric of the Contemporary Lyric*, says that you're the master of the realist lyric. He describes your voice as that of a "single man using it to himself, aware that the process of his inner life is being overheard." I think that fits "Corners." How do you respond to that and to the "realist lyric" designation?

Dunn: That's fine. I think my poems end up offering a kind of realism, if by that you mean that they move us closer to the real. I've always been suspicious of realism, at least as I understood it, which seemed like some direct rendering of experience. Mine is always reconstructed, and that it ends up feeling realistic, where people would think it conforms to the real, seems a very high goal indeed. That's one of the reasons I write—to make those connections between people, to have people at least *believe* what I say. I think we're always making illusions, and when my illusion is right and I think it constitutes the real, in a small way, the way Stevens meant belief—poems are "credible truths," things we can believe for a little while—while I've done that, if somebody else would say that's realistic, I think that's fine. How the real gets made, though, or gets believed to be real, is a fascinating subject.

In *The New Yorker* recently, the painter Frank Stella talked about his work as a "constant negation of impulses." That seems to me how I make at least my personal poems. I try to resist everything my conventional mind can say about my experience, which I assume is not very interesting until it's made interesting. And I assume that the first thing I'm going to say is the wrong thing, and that the next thing might be a little better, a little truer, resisting that even. In the "Essay on the Personal," the dialectic is constantly resisting what I've just said. I offer something, and then I doubt it, and then it goes on to the next thing.

Rubin: Another thing that Holden has said about you, notoriously perhaps, is that you're the "Woody Allen" of contemporary American poetry. But Holden did go on to make clear what he meant, mainly that whereas humor reduces everything to one emotion, your poetry, he says, is "overflowing with a range of complex emotions." He seems to feel that you have set yourself almost a project to describe what he calls the "unlived life of America." To what extent do you feel that this is accurate, that America is your subject or this "unlived life of America"?

Dunn: He was writing about *Full of Lust and Good Usage*, and my handling of subject matter has changed a lot since then. In my last two or three books, I think even Jonathan would agree that the allusion to Woody Allen is not apt, even though I like Woody Allen. But what he goes on to say after that is insightful.

I think if you set out to write about America or anything grand, you're obviously going to write some kind of public jargon. I never begin with such intentions. I'm writing just—the way most people do—out of certain imperatives of subject or concern at any given time. Obviously, when you put together a book, patterns form, and it might then be accurate to say I'm writing about the "unlived life of America." Since most of my poems deal with middle-class life which is my life—it's very tempting to make the connection between middle-class life and the unlived life in which most of us think about doing something and then don't; it's a natural conclusion. I thought it was a nice one. But being writers yourselves, you know that you can't think thematically like that when you write, or if you do it's probably injurious.

Rubin: Yes, you might argue that writers shouldn't have that kind of consciousness. But what about the humor aspect? One other striking thing about your work, that very pleasant thing about it at readings, is how entertaining it is on the surface level, how much wit and irony are at work. It's a very accessible wit or irony, and yet there's so much happening. Are you conscious of that? Does it come naturally to you to be a humorous, on-the-surface poet at times?

Dunn: Most of my poems are not humorous, as you probably know, but any time I can be humorous in the way that I like to be, which is arising out of a seriousness peculiar to a particular situation—humor is a large part of how we deal with the unlived life, with the difficulties of being unable to do the things we would like to do—when I can be humorous without lapsing into jokes, I like it.

This summer on CBS there was a special on dwarfs. It was wonderful, especially one little line I've remembered because it's the kind of humor that comes out of a serious situation that I would always keep in my poems if I could be as good as this. One of the dwarfs was having a discussion with a Black man, and the Black man was saying, "You know, my people have been oppressed for two hundred years," which was, of course, correct and right. The dwarf listened for a while, and he said, "Yeah, I understand, but my people for a thousand years have been given away as gifts." He said it with absolute seriousness. It was an insight, it was even historical, and it was funny—all those things. It would be wonderful if one could do that in a poem.

Rubin: This kind of humor in poetry implies to me a social setting, a communal quality, and yet your poetry really is the man overhearing himself, I think, as Holden suggested. Would you say something about your feeling for audience? Does it enter into your composing process, or is it different when you are writing as opposed to when you're reading? What is your feeling for audience?

Dunn: I'm always aware there's an audience. I never write for it. You write to satisfy some editor in yourself, the demands of the poem as the poem unfolds—those are the things that I'm conscious of, mostly. But I always know that the poem is going to be read or heard, or I wish it would be. That matters a great deal, because poems are for others and *should* be for others, and I know that. But I don't have a particular audience in mind.

Kitchen: It would be nice to hear a poem that has that element of humor in it. Last night you read "The Substitute," and that might be the one that would demonstrate . . .

The Substitute

When the substitute asked my eighth-grade daughter
  to read out loud,
She read in cockney, an accent she'd mastered

listening to rock music. Her classmates laughed
  of course, and she kept on,
straightfaced, until the merciful bell.

Thus began the week my daughter learned
  it takes more than style
to be successfully disobedient.

Next day her regular teacher didn't return;
  she had to do it again.
She was from Liverpool, her parents worked

in a mill, had sent her to America to live
  with relatives.
At night she read about England, looked at her map

to place and remember exactly where she lived.
  Soon her classmates
became used to it—just a titter from Robert

who'd laugh at anything. Friday morning,
  exhausted from learning
the manners and industry of modern England,

she had a stomach ache, her ears hurt, there were
  pains, she said,
all over. We pointed her toward the door.

She left bent over like a charwoman, but near
   the end of the driveway
we saw her right herself, become the girl

who had to be another girl, a substitute
   of sorts,
in it now for the duration.

Rubin: A marvelous poem. I presume that it is drawn on an actual anecdote, an incident.

Dunn: Yes, it was. Of course, my daughter thinks I falsified the entire experience. And, in part, I did. That is, it's much more valuable to come up with the made-up *right* detail than to have any allegiance to fact. And certainly this poem has a lot of fictive elements.

Rubin: Let's talk about revising. Do you write every day? Do you have a ritual to help you do it? Do you revise a lot?

Dunn: I revise a lot. I used to write every day. I sit down to try to write every day I'm able to. In the past, I'd actually *write* every day. Now things seem to take longer. I always have to be saved from myself in case of revision. My editor says, "No more!" at a certain point, because, especially when a book is near to coming out, my tendency to change is high, and I'm constantly revising.

The father poem that's in *Not Dancing*, "The Legacy," was begun eleven years ago and was in many versions, many of which I thought were fine, were finished versions. A year later or so, it always seemed I had falsified the emotional situation, hadn't gotten it right, hadn't known enough about it yet, and finally I ended up with that version which seems, to me at least, the truest of all the versions. That's an extreme case—working eleven years on a poem. I always think I have it right right away, you know, and then I don't.

Kitchen: Let's talk about *Not Dancing* as a book, both as a concept of a book and the way in which you came to its title, its sort of working concerns.

Dunn: The poem bearing the title "Festivals after Dark" was the title of the manuscript, very close to the publication date. The poem now called "Afloat" which contains the words "not dancing" was "Festivals after Dark," but it had an entirely different thrust. It was a poem I obviously liked well enough to allow to be a title poem. Then I read it over one day about three months before publication and found myself not only liking it very well but disagreeing with it and thinking it politically naive and being terrified because this was such a central piece in the book. I went about rewriting it; in about a week's time, I got it by resisting the whole notion of the festivals after dark. It originally had the speaker observing these poor people in the mountains going home at night and his imagining for them festivals after dark, which is probably true enough in a way but very romantic and politically silly in this age. What finally got the rewrite for me was the discovery that they would likely be planning something; in a political sense, not "dancing." And that allowed the poem to come forward as it now stands.

Kitchen: And then it became an informing spirit somehow for the rest of the book.

Dunn: Yes. Then the hard thing was deciding what to call the book. I had written the "not dancing" line, and I spent a while looking through the book. What would be right to call it? "Festivals after dark" was now a line in the poem. It seemed totally wrong as a title for the book. I looked at the poem "Enough Time," which also seemed to mention "not dancing," and then in the "Wavelengths" poem there's a mention of "not dancing." And yes, finally the spirit of the book seemed to cooperate with "not dancing" too.

Rubin: Where did this knowledge come from that made you realize you had it emotionally correct?

Dunn: I don't know. I think my politics were the same as they are now. In the act of composing the first poem, I suppose I wanted things to be better, which is the Romantic fallacy. You know, when you caution your students not to be romantic, it's essentially saying, "Don't tell lies; don't be sentimental about the world." And I had allowed myself to be that for whatever reason.

Kitchen: Was it in the face of a certain powerlessness? It seems that the "not dancing" comes up under those circumstances.

Dunn: Maybe. I don't know. I thought the book tonally was my most melancholy, if not negative, book. And that was because of personal things going on in my life. I simply wasn't "dancing," in the spiritual sense, for a couple of years. I guess when the phrase arrived, it felt right, cooperated with some things that I'd been feeling on an unconscious level. That's all I really know.

Rubin: Was *Work and Love* the first collection in which you really consciously gathered thematically similar material, organized the book as a book?

Dunn: Yes, in that sense, but in *Full of Lust and Good Usage*, I knew the principle of organization too; they were poems about and against landscape.

Rubin: This comes partly from your experience teaching in Minnesota?

Dunn: Yes.

Rubin: You said in one of those poems that mood invests landscape.

Would you elaborate on that and how that comes from your Minnesota experience?

Dunn: When I went to Minnesota, I had an adversary relationship with the landscape. Its flatness, sameness. For as long as I was uncomfortable with it, the landscape was colored by my feelings about it. And then the more the landscape won me over, and the people, the more I was able to relate to it as it was, in fact very beautiful and varied. I lost my need to beat it up. But it proved to be a very useful tension for me. In fact, the better poems in the book *Full of Lust and Good Usage* came about when I did feel the adversary relationship with it. It was a working out. And it was essentially about being in the middle of America, with a certain kind of Eastern superiority, thinking I was special, and maybe on some level knowing I wasn't, the way we are when we're insecure. So a lot of poems were formed with that kind of tension and discovery of self in the middle.

Rubin: But you definitely are cutting against the grain of certain American poetry workshop truisms, by not being a poet who tries to fashion the sensory image, or "deep image," or even to respond to landscape as if it were your soul, your raison d'être. You've felt a kind of individualism of voice, a loneliness.

Dunn: Well, I was willing to trust it. I was only writing the poems that I could write. I had no program for them and had not raised it to any philosophical principle. It was simply what I was doing. There's always a degree of loneliness involved in writing poems. If you're doing it right, you're off entirely on your own. They're simply the poems I had to write at that time.

Rubin: Another aspect of your work is a number of really wonderful poems about—as you said in your reading—the fact that you like women. And I wonder if we could ask you to read one. I'm toying with asking you to read "Eggs" or "Desire." I'll leave it up to you.

Dunn: I'll read "Desire." It's shorter.

Rubin: O.K. "Desire" does comment on your changing relationship to desire and, as you said, the fact that you appreciate women. I wonder if you'd comment on that after you read.

Desire

I remember how it used to be
at noon, springtime, the city streets
full of office workers like myself
let loose from the cold
glass buildings on Park and Lex,

the dull swaddling of winter cast off,
almost everyone wanting
everyone else. It was amazing
how most of us contained ourselves,
bringing desire back up
to the office where it existed anyway,
quiet, like a good engine.
I'd linger a bit
with the receptionist,
knock on someone else's open door,
ease myself, by increments,
into the seriousness they paid me for.
Desire was everywhere those years,
so enormous it couldn't be reduced
one person at a time.
I don't remember when it was,
though closer to now than then,
I walked the streets desireless,
my eyes fixed on destination alone.
The beautiful person across from me
on the bus or train
looked like effort, work.
I translated her into pain.
For months I had the clarity
the cynical survive with,
their world so safely small.
Today, walking 57th toward 3rd,
it's all come back,
the interesting, the various,
the conjured life suggested by a glance.
I praise how the body heals itself.
I praise how, finally, it never learns.

Kitchen: This seems, if not a new concern, at least an inviting concern, the relationship between men and women, and especially the relationship as we age—how one lives with someone, as you say. Would you talk about that?

Dunn: As I mentioned the other day, I used to write those poems out of some degree of certainty that I knew what I was talking about. Now it just all seems mysterious and fascinating. I don't know how people stay together, though I know there are rituals involved, and I've been interested in those rituals. I've been trying in the new book to get at some of them. I have maybe five of them. This one is a midlife desire poem, and it interests me in that way. The desire poems you write in your twenties are full of unmitigated desire—I want, I want—and how nice it is, or how frustrating it is.

There's always a moment in a poem where the poem suddenly becomes mine, the moment I startle myself, the moment when I discover something. And that occurred in the poem as I was walking the streets, desireless. I had been teaching at Columbia, hadn't been in the city regularly in fifteen years, and just seeing all these things that you see in New York, enormously attractive people, and finding myself not interested—that was interesting to me. But the whole notion of having desire after you know a lot about it, after you know the cost of desire, even in the sense that one decides these things, deciding to be desirous, deciding to fall in love—all these things that you never could have truly entertained when you were younger. So it's that kind of desire poem, and to the extent I got a little of it right, I'm pleased.

Rubin: How did you come to be a poet? Why are you a poet? You're one whose poetry so closely reflects your changing inner life, as we've been discussing. And were there a couple of significant events, moments, or influences that turned you to poetry?

Dunn: The real motivation was—this is always somewhat of a half-truth—that I wanted to change my life. I didn't like my life at all. I was working for the National Biscuit Company in New York, getting promoted, getting terrified by doing well in a job I never took seriously, and I needed a way out. I quit after getting a big promotion, quit right away, and went to Spain to see if I could write. I had been writing fiction at the time. It was taking a chance—one of those things that in somewhat romantic terms you're really at the point where you can lose your soul, or what you consider your soul. And I was very close to that, not happy at all. The fiction and then the poetry were a way to recover it, though I didn't really know that then; I was just taking a chance that I could write. By trying to write a novel, I discovered that I was much more of a poet than a fiction writer, much more interested in language than in plot and character, for example. I was around twenty-seven at the time.

My friend Sam Toperoff was very important to me. He was the only literary—and one of the few intelligent people—I knew at that time. He came to visit, he and his wife, in Spain, and he actually liked my poetry. It was one of those lucky things, and I don't know, if I hadn't gotten that kind of reinforcement then, what would have happened. I never, ever, thought of going to graduate school, but Faith Toperoff persuaded me to go and told me that there were such things as M.F.A. programs, which I never had heard of. I was totally removed from all that. So, I had some good friends, a little ability perhaps, the need to alter my life.

Rubin: In a birthday poem you wrote to yourself, you say that there are two or three things that you do well, and they're going to have to do. I wonder, What are those two or three things that a poet needs to be able to do well?

Dunn: The two or three I was thinking of, not necessarily confined to being a poet, were probably writing, playing tennis, and loving well, being good at receiving love too, which more and more seems to be maybe the best of all things. The danger of *hubris* in saying these things out loud is very great, and of course I've failed at each of those things many times. But what I was really saying in the poem was the importance of being satisfied with the few things you can do well, given how many things there are that most of us don't do well. And that, after a while, after a certain age, self-help groups aside, you're pretty much who you are. That was my birthday gift to myself. I wasn't to worry any more about improving myself.

"Passionate Midnights in the Museum Basement"

A CONVERSATION WITH KATHA POLLITT

Katha Pollitt

Katha Pollitt was born in Manhattan in 1949 and grew up in Brooklyn. She was educated at Radcliffe and Columbia. Her book of poetry, *Antarctic Traveller* (Knopf), received the 1983 award in poetry from the National Book Critics Circle.

Katha Pollitt has taught at Princeton, The New School for Social Research, and the Poetry Center of the 92nd Street Y. In 1987, she won a Guggenheim Fellowship. She has also received National Endowment for the Arts and Ingram Merrill fellowships and a CAPS grant. Her work has been reviewed in such places as *American Poetry Review*, *The New York Times Book Review*, the *Hudson Review*, and was cited by critic Roberta Berke in her book on American and British poetry. Ms. Pollitt is also a literary critic and a contributing editor to *The Nation*, where she writes regularly on feminist issues. She lives in New York City with her husband, the writer Randy Cohen.

The following conversation took place on 8 July 1986. Interviewer was Stan Sanvel Rubin. Ms. Pollitt began by reading her poem "Archaeology."

Archaeology

"Our real poems are already in us
and all we can do is dig."—Jonathan Galassi

You knew the odds on failure from the start,
that morning you first saw, or thought you saw
beneath the heatstruck plains of a second-rate country
the outline of buried cities. A thousand to one
you'd turn up nothing more than the rubbish heap

225

of a poor Near Eastern backwater:
a few chipped beads,
splinters of glass and pottery, broken tablets
whose secret lore, laboriously deciphered,
would prove to be only a collection of ancient grocery lists.
Still, the train moved away from the station without you.

How many lives ago
was that? How many choices?
Now that you've got your bushelful of shards
do you say, *give me back my years*
or wrap yourself in the distant
glitter of desert stars,
telling yourself it was foolish after all
to have dreamed of uncovering
some fluent vessel, the bronze head of a god?
Pack up your fragments. Let the simoom
flatten the digging site. Now come
the passionate midnights in the museum basement
when out of that random rubble you'll invent
the dusty market smelling of sheep and spices,
streets, palmy gardens, courtyards set with wells
to which, in the blue of evening, one by one
come strong veiled women, bearing their perfect jars.

Rubin: The poem you just read, "Archaeology," seems to be a whole little theory of poetry, or even creativity, in a small package. Is it?
Pollitt: Yes, it is, and the funny thing about it is that I'm not sure I believe it any more. This poem was written in response to a poem that my friend Jonathan Galassi wrote to me. Both poems came out of a discussion we had years ago in which I said that I was dissatisfied with my work and wanted to write a different kind of poetry than I had been writing. Jon said to me, "Look, you can only write what is within you to write." He wrote a poem called "To Katha Pollitt" which had as its theme the notion that "our real poems are already in us / and all we can do is dig" to recover them. Since I couldn't agree that we're stuck with our material, I wrote "Archaeology" as a kind of riposte, trumpeting the transforming powers of the imagination and the will. Later, he wrote another poem, which he published in *The Paris Review*, in which I really think he got the better of the argument. I've come around to believing that one *is* stuck with a lot of one's material, but perhaps it's not as depressing a fact as it seemed at the time.

Rubin: So what about these "passionate midnights in the museum basement" when you invent? The role of invention isn't as critical?

Pollitt: Oh, it is, but you're not inventing out of nothing. You're inventing out of rubble and shards that you were given by your history. We don't create ourselves out of thin air. Jon put the emphasis on the rubble, and I put it on the museum basement.

Rubin: In the poem, the poet seems to have had some prior experience with the real, exotic landscape which is then reinvented.

Pollitt: Yes, the poet has been this "archaeologist."

Rubin: Let's go back to the book. The language is so precise and evocative that it seems very polished work. I'm wondering about the genesis of the book: what period of work does it represent? How hard was the "birthing"?

Pollitt: I wrote these poems over a shamefully long period of time. There are a few poems in the collection that I wrote in my early twenties. So it represents about a decade of work.

I find it hard to say how long a poem is going to take. There are poems in the collection that came very quickly—a day or two—and others that just went on forever. There are poems that I thought I had given up on, but I would go back to them a year later and completely transform them, and other poems that were basically finished except for a particular word or phrase or transition that caused endless trouble to get right. In fact, scattered throughout the book—and I hope that only I can see them—are words that still bother me. Sometimes I like to think that before I die the right word will come to me.

Rubin: So you're like Yeats, continually rewriting your poems?

Pollitt: If you look at history, that's usually such an unhappy experience. John Crowe Ransom is a good example of a poet who, as an older man, went back to some of the wonderful poems of his youth, and I don't think any of his later revisions were in a happy direction. At a certain point, you have to say, "That was me then, I did my best, and I'm not going to potchky with it any more."

Rubin: When did you feel you had a book, that these poems belonged together?

Pollitt: I'm not a poet who thinks a whole lot about that kind of thing. I felt I had a book when I had written enough poems that I was pleased with. I didn't think, Oh, I need to go a little more in this direction to balance that, or maybe there's too much of this. I wrote them pretty much as they came to me and watched the folder get thicker over the years. I can't say that I arranged them in a particularly becoming order.

Rubin: The question was partly motivated by the fact that the book is organized in three parts. Was that your arrangement?

Pollitt: Yes. I had a theory at the time, but I don't really remember now what it was. I put the Japanese poems together, of course, and I wanted to end with the poem from which the title is drawn. You want to have a certain balance of short and long poems, and you want to separate poems that are too similar. But beyond that, I can't remember any principle of organization I had in mind.

Rubin: Let me ask you what was going on in your life during this period of ten or twelve years.

Pollitt: I had jobs all over the publishing world. I went to graduate school. I've always written book reviews and literary criticism. I fell in love, I fell out of love. A lot happened.

Rubin: And all the time you were writing poetry regularly? Or was there a break in there?

Pollitt: I think there were many breaks.

Rubin: When did you discover that you were a poet?

Pollitt: I started writing poetry when I was in grade school, and I know that by seventh or eighth grade I took it very seriously. I remember saying, "Oh my goodness, I haven't written a poem all week." Now I think that to write a poem a week would be something.

Rubin: Were there some poets who mattered particularly to you?

Pollitt: The earliest poets I can remember caring about were Shakespeare, Keats, and Tennyson. I loved Tennyson when I was a kid, because of his lush sound effects—very overblown and Victorian, sort of rotted Keats. Also, Tennyson is not one of the profounder minds of his century, so I could understand him. I don't know what I got out of Shakespeare's sonnets, but I loved them very much.

Rubin: Did you take writing courses as an undergraduate?

Pollitt: I made a conscious decision not to major in English, as all my advisors were telling me, but in philosophy. I figured I'd take something hard, where you really needed help. And I think I made a good decision, because I would never have read the books that I did, if I hadn't majored in philosophy.

Rubin: Were you sending out poems for publication?

Pollitt: I sent poems out to the *Mademoiselle* college competition, and I won; but I didn't send poems out for publication until I graduated.

Rubin: So you weren't writing with publication in mind?

Pollitt: What do you mean by that?

Rubin: Earlier, you said that you don't write poems with the thought of a book in the future.

Pollitt: No, what I said was I didn't consider the overall structure of a book when I was writing the individual poems. Some poets, like Sylvia Plath, do a great deal of thinking about the structure of their books. Her plan for her book *Ariel* was quite elaborate; it began with the word *love* and ended with the word *spring*. It had a real theme of regeneration, which was unfortunately not preserved when the book was published after her death. I can't imagine writing a poem that I really loved and saying, "But this just doesn't fit in with the thirty-five other poems; I'll leave it out."

Rubin: Plath is a poet who matters to you.

Pollitt: I admire Sylvia Plath's poems. She has been put to some unfortunate uses, and she has unfortunately given credence to the Romantic notion of the union of poetry and death—and behind that, the notion that a gifted woman must destroy herself. But her poems are brilliant, and she has meant a great deal to me over the years, although we haven't much in common in our ways of seeing the world.

Rubin: Do you think of your poetry as very personal?

Pollitt: I think of it as "personal" in the sense that I would like to believe only I could have written these poems: I hope that the stamp of my character and my sense of the world is on them. They are obviously not personal in the sense that Anne Sexton's poems are—I was just watching that videotape in the Forum Library. She gives you a great deal of information about the private aspects of her life, and my poems are not like that.

Rubin: Your book *Antarctic Traveller* has a wide range of subject matter, but the poems seem to coalesce around a moment of insight or perception, which is the justification for the poem. Would you agree with that assessment of your work?

Pollitt: Poets have their own metaphors for the way they see a poem, such as a field of energy. Richard Wilbur said that a poem is a window, not a door; Anne Sexton cited that distinction and said that her poems were doors. I've always had this notion of my poems as condensed little packages. You start with a draft which is a big mess full of irrelevant lumps and dangling strings, and you pare it down until everything coheres in a verbal pattern that is very tight. Then the poem stands up by itself like a little Christmas package.

Rubin: That stress upon "closure" is sometimes derided as not giving enough due to time, temporality, and flow, to allowing the poem to become part of our ongoing experience. Instead, you opt for the kind of poem that insists on a moment of reverie, a self-contained moment of perception or thought.

Pollitt: I think of poems as little arguments; they're not like ongoing conversations that you could have more of the next day. I enjoy poems that don't have that sense of closure—Roethke and Whitman, for example—but I don't write that way.

Rubin: One theme in the book is memory and time. Memory becomes obscure for you, and there's a strong focus on the moment of crystalized perception in these poems.

Pollitt: I'm very conscious, as we all are, of the passage of time, mortality, death—you were you in the past, but where is that you now? That's been a poetic platitude ever since there were poems. Poets have always talked about immortality as the goal of their verse—"Not marble nor the gilded monuments / Of princes shall outlive this pow'rful rhyme." It's an attempt to make a shape in language that will hold, what Frost calls "a momentary stay against confusion."

Rubin: Would you read a poem that has this theme—"In Memory"? I notice that this one also has a philosophical epigraph, reflecting your background in philosophy again.

Pollitt: At Harvard we read Wittgenstein's *Philosophical Investigations* once a semester, every year I was there, for every course. It's one of the most mysterious books ever written—it's like reading runic inscriptions. It's a beautifully poetic book in its sense of language and its images. I don't think I understood the book at all, but I did carry away some phrases that have stayed with me.

In Memory

"But can we not sometimes speak of a darkening
(for example) of our memory-image?"—Wittgenstein

Over the years, they've darkened, like old paintings
or wainscotting in a damp house in the country,
until now the streets where you roller-skated brim with twilight,
your mother drinks morning coffee from a cup of shadows,
and out in the garden, the hardest August noon
is washed with a tender, retrospective blue—
like woodsmoke, or the shade of an unseen lilac.
Upstairs, you can hardly make yourself out, a child
peering out the window, speechless with happiness,
reciting your future in an endless summer dusk.

At first, this maddened you. You wanted to see
your life as a rope of diamonds: permanent, flashing.
Strange, then, how lately this darkening of memory moves you,
as though what it claimed it also made more true,
the way discoloring varnish on a portrait
little by little engulfs the ornate background—
the overstuffed sofa, the velvet-and-gold festoons
framing an elegant vista—but only deepens
the calm and serious face. The speaking eyes.

Rubin: What memory comes down to there is the focusing upon one memorable image. We can't rely on memory itself to provide any clarity or coherence.

Pollitt: It's about the way our childhood memories are transformed by our later experience and become darker in the light of knowledge.

Rubin: We invent our memories, in a sense.

Pollitt: No. But we color them. Or life colors them for us.

Rubin: The middle section of the book has five poems on Japanese paintings. Would you like to say something about why they're there?

Pollitt: I wrote those poems after seeing an exhibit of Japanese art at the Metropolitan Museum. I thought the paintings were tremendous because they were so reticent and yet so opulent and vivid. Reticence was a quality that appealed to me at that time. Much more than it does now, I must say, although I still love Japanese art.

Rubin: The third and final section of the book starts out with what you call "vegetable poems." You've got "Potatoes," "Tomato," "Onion," "Eggplant," "Nettles." There is some thematizing in that short series of poems of maleness and femaleness. I suppose vegetables suggest the traditional notion of women as food-providers, and you play with that. You have a poem in that section called "Metaphors of Women." Now, although your work is in no way polemical, you seem in the book very conscious of being a female poet.

Pollitt: I would say that I am a feminist. I must say that I don't see images of women as food-providers in the vegetable poems.

Rubin: Yes, but those images are easily evoked by the poems.

Pollitt: Not in my house! I don't do too much providing of food.

Rubin: What about the first line of "Tomato?"

Pollitt: Well, that's the image of the female sexual organ. And potatoes are sort of male sexual organs.

Rubin: Say something about "Metaphors of Women."

Pollitt: "Metaphors of Women" is a poem I wrote because of all the people that have ever lived upon this planet the one I hate most—leaving aside people like Hitler—is Carl Jung. His notions are very appealing to lazy minds; you know, that there is an archetypal male and an archetypal female, that certain images attach themselves naturally to one or the other—the moon is a woman, the sun is a man, et cetera. I hate all that, because what you end up with is, Yes, a woman can be rational, but that's a male quality. A man can be kind and tender, but that's the female in him. That is not at all true to our human selves, which are much more complex. I don't believe that reason or feeling has a gender. Also I think that way of seeing humanity is very boring. That's what this poem is about—the boredom of sex-typed imagery. I was just proposing that we think of some new things.

Rubin: The poem starts, "What if the moon / was never a beautiful woman?" You're playing with those sex-specific archetypes.

You're now working on another manuscript, and you've said that it takes a while before enough poems gather themselves into a collection. Could you describe what you're doing now and how it's different from what you were doing in the earlier book?

Pollitt: My newer poems are perhaps less tightly constructed; they're a little more rough, even when they're in form.

Two poets interest me greatly right now. One is Philip Larkin, whose death this year made me tremendously sad, because it made me realize it isn't often in reading of a writer's death that your first thought is, Oh no, no more poems from that person. The other, and I know it's a strange juxtaposition, is Bertolt Brecht. In both poets, I like the combination of formality and roughness, real colloquialness along with a highness or largeness of spirit and sense of society.

Rubin: Let me ask about your working method. Has that changed over the years? Are you down in that metaphoric "museum basement" sweating away?

Pollitt: Yes. Sometimes, as I said, I can finish a poem quite quickly. But I have written one hundred drafts of a single poem—never fewer than ten. But then I like to write the poem out whole, even if I make only a little change. I like to type, it makes me feel that I'm making progress.

Rubin: Are you constantly throwing away the old drafts, or do you stick them away somewhere?

Pollitt: I save them, because I never know whether I will want to go back to an earlier draft to see if it's better. I'm a pack rat, so I save them all.

Rubin: Do you say your poems aloud at some point? How important is the oral dimension?

Pollitt: It's immensely important to me. The sound of a poem is *the* thing. I'm not interested in the visual pattern the words make on the page. Theories of line breaks put me right to sleep. But I am extremely interested in vowels and consonants and echoes and patterns of words. I spend a lot of my writing time on that kind of thing.

Rubin: Your poems are really intended, then, to be read aloud?

Pollitt: There's a way of reading silently in which you're hearing the poem. But, yes, they're meant to be read aloud, but not as a performance poet means that phrase. I hope they're more complicated than can be grasped just by hearing them once; but that is an element.

Rubin: Are you more concerned in this new manuscript with form and metrical work?

Pollitt: No, I go back and forth between using formal structure and trying to have a sense of formality in free verse. I know that there is the ongoing American "war" between the two, but I think that's sort of silly.

Rubin: How do you relate to the sense of an American tradition in poetry?

Pollitt: I read mostly American poetry, but not exclusively, and some of the poets who have meant a great deal to me are not American—for example, Brecht and Cavafy, Vasko Popa, the Yugoslav poet, and Cesare Pavese, my new hero.

Rubin: Your work is not particularly polemical, but you have described yourself as a feminist.

Pollitt: Absolutely!

Rubin: And your poetry doesn't seem particularly political. It is what it is. I gather that's the final statement you're going to leave us with.

Pollitt: Well, no. There's politics and politics. I doubt that I'd sit down and write a poem against nuclear war or in favor of the ERA, because there isn't much to say on those subjects that can't be said in a magazine article. But politics is more than newspaper headlines. It's how you see the human condition in our time, your view of life. For me, feminism is bound up with notions of democracy, individual worth, reason, justice, and skepticism toward authority. With a sense that people make their own history, and that just because something has been done a certain way doesn't mean it has to stay that way. Which is, come to think of it, what "Archaeology" says, too.

"A Poet of Eyesight"
A CONVERSATION WITH MICHAEL WATERS

Michael Waters

Michael Waters was born in New York City in 1949 and attended SUNY College at Brockport. He received his M.F.A. from the University of Iowa and his Ph.D. from Ohio University. He is the author of *Fish Light* (1975), *Not Just Any Death* (BOA Editions, 1979), *Anniversary of the Air* (Carnegie-Mellon University Press, 1985), and *The Burden Lifters* (Carnegie-Mellon, 1988). He is also the editor of *Dissolve to Island: On the Poetry of John Logan* (1984). He has been anthologized in such books as *The Morrow Anthology of Younger American Poets* and *The Generation of 2000*.

Mr. Waters has been the recipient of a Fellowship in Creative Writing from the National Endowment for the Arts and has taught at Ohio University, the University of Athens (Greece), and Salisbury State College. He has been Banister Writer-in-Residence at Sweet Briar College during 1987–89. His work has been cited by such critics as Ralph J. Mills and Joseph Parisi.

During the past few years Michael Waters has spent extended periods in Greece, Costa Rica, and Thailand. In 1986, he participated in the Al-Merbid Poetry Festival in Baghdad, Iraq.

The following conversation took place on 27 February 1986. Interviewers were Stan Sanvel Rubin and Gregory Fitz Gerald. Mr. Waters began the interview by reading two poems, "The Mystery of the Caves" and "Singles."

The Mystery of the Caves

I don't remember the name of the story,
but the hero, a boy, was lost,
wandering a labyrinth of caverns
filling stratum by stratum with water.

235

I was wondering what might happen:
would he float upward toward light?
or would he somersault forever
in an underground black river?

I couldn't stop reading the book
because I had to know the answer,
because my mother was leaving again—
the lid of the trunk thrown open,

blouses torn from their hangers,
the crazy shouting among rooms.
The boy found it impossible to see
which passage led to safety.

One yellow finger of flame
wavered on his last match.
There was a blur of perfume—
mother breaking miniature bottles,

then my father gripping her,
but too tightly, by both arms.
The boy wasn't able to breathe.
I think he wanted me to help,

but I was small, and it was late.
And my mother was sobbing now,
no longer cursing her life,
repeating my father's name

among bright islands of skirts
circling the rim of the bed.
I can't recall the whole story,
what happened at the end . . .

Sometimes I worry that the boy
is still searching below the earth
for a thin pencil of light,
that I can almost hear him

through great volumes of water,
through centuries of stone,
crying my name among blind fish,
wanting so much to come home.

Singles

I don't know anyone more lonely
than the woman listening

to the late news, memorizing
baseball scores for coffee break.

She must undress so carefully,
folding her beige blouse
as if for the last time,
not wanting to be found unkempt

by detectives in the morning.
Sometimes I hear her talking
as she roams from room to room
watering her plumeria,

the only splash of color.
She sets two places at the table
though no one ever comes,
then turns to the boredom of bed

thinking *Indians 7–Yankees 3,*
Cardinals 11–Mets 2
until she rises before dawn
and drives crosstown to work.

Could anyone be more lonely?
She doesn't acknowledge, again,
the man in the toll-booth
who's spent the whole night there,

not even a magazine before him,
grateful now to be making change
and touching fingers, briefly,
with such a beautiful stranger.

Rubin: I'd like to begin by asking about the poems that you just read from your new collection, *Anniversary of the Air.* As you noted, they have the theme of loneliness. Is this something that ties the collection together for you?

Waters: I think so. These poems explore different types of loneliness and offer definitions for those types that the word itself doesn't denote. There is a loneliness we feel when we're by ourselves; there's a loneliness that two people feel together, et cetera. There are several characters moving through these poems whose lives I imagine as lonely, projecting, I guess, some of my own loneliness.

Fitz Gerald: Does loneliness have anything to do with the development of the writer?

Waters: I'm not sure what that connection is, but, yes, I do think that it's there. Certainly when you decide to commit yourself to writing—or at least in my case—there is an immediate fear, because you're divorcing yourself right away from "the common lot of humanity." I don't mean to over-romanticize here, but writing, of course, is always done in solitude. When the writing is not actually going on, the creative process is still at work. You are always receptive, and there's an accompanying loneliness—that constant introspection, the examination of the self—how am I feeling about this? what does this mean to me? why has this trivial event or particular word or musical phrase affected me in such a way? One of the reasons that I write is to try to understand these emotions and what triggers them. The task for every writer becomes a lonely one.

Fitz Gerald: Many people are ceaselessly interested in the creative process, why the writer engages in it. Could you tell us how and why you became a writer?

Waters: That's never an easy question, and I'm not sure there is an answer. I think I became a writer because I have a love for the language; for some reason, words have always attracted me—their sound, the texture of each syllable on the tongue, their meanings, what they can suggest in different contexts. I love the possibilities and promise inherent in using our language to express an emotion with some precision.

Another reason is the desire simply to talk with people. I've always been one—I hope this doesn't sound too sentimental—whose heart is touched by strangers. Someone I see on the street in New York, or while walking over here to the studio this morning, might move me, and I need to share and try to explain that. Writing does that for me. Other people might express this desire through dance, painting, or another art form.

Another factor, more personal, is that I am an only child, and both my parents worked. My father was a New York City fireman, who moonlighted as a bartender in the Starlight Lounge on Long Island. My mother was a full-time secretary, and I was cared for by my grandparents, who weren't very talkative. I think having no one to talk with, then, sent me to books and got me talking with myself. The writing was a natural extension of that.

Rubin: Who were the first poets whose work spoke to you?

Waters: I can remember, when I was very young, my father reading to me the poems of Robert Service—"The Cremation of Sam Magee." I found it very easy to memorize, of course, because of all those clanking rhymes. That singing and storytelling was a means of communication between father and son. Later, as a teenager in the late sixties with the Vietnam War raging, I discovered the poems of Allen Ginsberg and Lawrence Ferlinghetti. I can remember reading them in high school, and my own very early poems were attempts to imitate them—to rhapsodize about masturbation or to express the adolescent anger swirling inside me.

Rubin: Were these poems actually written in high school?

Waters: Yes, in notebooks. They were just poor imitations of Ginsberg and the songs of Bob Dylan. It wasn't until I took a course in college that I was introduced to a broader range of American poets—Richard Wilbur and W. D. Snodgrass, for example—and the possibilities of craft and precision. Then the real work began.

Fitz Gerald: During 1972–74, you were a member of the Iowa Writers Workshop. Do you think that workshop experience has had any marked effect on your work?

Waters: Definitely. I don't believe it affects everyone's work, and there are some real pitfalls to the workshop experience. But one of the advantages of the Workshop was that it gave me time to work on poems. I'd already earned the M.A. degree before going to Iowa—the Workshop offered time to write. It also introduced me to a community of other writers. That became very important for me.

At the same time, the problem with any workshop seems to be twofold. Sometimes you're in a situation where you don't have anything to say, and it seems to me that when you don't have anything to say, you should be quiet! Instead, a workshop encourages you to write even when you've nothing to say. The other problem, because workshops have proliferated, is that we have so many writers of my generation with *exactly* the same background: they've gone to school all their lives, then begun teaching; they have no experience outside the university. The only work they know is a sort of *literary* work. Because of this, so many poets of my generation are writing the same type of poem, using the same style.

Rubin: There is such a thing as the "workshop poem."

Waters: Yes, and one needn't have been in a workshop in order to write it. A "workshop poem" is one that is well crafted, employs irony, a couple of nice enjambments, but finally says nothing and didn't need to be written. Nothing compelled the poet to put those words on paper.

Fitz Gerald: Implicit in what you're saying is the suggestion to young poets to get out there and get a job in a hashhouse or driving a truck, and *live* a little. Is that what you're saying?

Waters: Who knows what's best for a writer? Certainly it would be good not to have so many writers in the academy. But I don't know what alternative to offer. If you want to be a writer, you're not going to be able to make a living at it, so in many ways you're protected by staying in the university.

Fitz Gerald: Still, in the past we had Oxford and Cambridge dons writing poems.

Waters: Yes, but remember that William Carlos Williams was a doctor and Wallace Stevens an insurance executive. T. S. Eliot worked in a bank. That's something we no longer have—poets aren't members of any community except the academic community.

Fitz Gerald: And you feel that keeps them out of touch with the rest of the world?

Waters: That's part of it, yes. But also there is no longer any sense of discovery. One of the reasons Ezra Pound went abroad was to locate something extraordinary, to translate, for example, Troubadour poets; he was gathering information—that terrific desire to learn. What we have now is a professor saying, "You should read Rilke, Anna Akhmatova, and don't forget Chekhov's stories!" So everyone of my generation has read the same books.

Rubin: Also, perhaps by default, what we can call "careerism" has taken over for discovery—building your career, getting your grants at the right time, and so forth. When you refer to Pound and the kind of risks he took, it almost seems as though they're no longer possible. Do you advise your students to do something else and not go on for an M.F.A. degree?

Waters: I don't make any general rules, but I do encourage them to discover on their own and not to depend entirely on me to tell them what to read. They need to be a little more aggressive in forging their own habits, creating their own backgrounds.

One of my true pleasures in the past five years was being able to spend half that time out of the country. What a feeling of liberation to be on the Caribbean coast of Costa Rica or on the Greek island of Ios where the mail service is poor-to-nonexistent, and not to think about sending out poems and not to be getting magazines and books, not to be knowing who was receiving awards, but simply to be writing poems!

Rubin: Let's go back and look at your work a little more specifically. You did *Fish Light* soon after you left Brockport with your M.A. in 1972. What kind of movement was there in your poetic and thematic preoccupations between that collection and *Not Just Any Death* in 1979?

Waters: *Fish Light* was finished when I was twenty-four and published when I was twenty-five. I enjoy those poems still, but they're very different from the work that I've been doing in the past decade. Those poems seem a bit wild: they depend to some extent on an associative imagery; people have told me that some of the poems simply don't make any sense to them. They make sense to me, but I wasn't communicating the way I'd like to. I've always wanted in poetry to speak directly and say something true. I'm not sure I was doing that in *Fish Light*—I simply had not developed the craft. I was thinking not in terms of the poetic line, but the sentence, the image, something flashy. Having gotten that out of my system, I began writing poems with a calm voice, poems that weren't clamoring for attention. With *Not Just Any Death*, the poems show a surer sense of craft. The tone seems more conversational, perhaps a bit more serious than the tone of the early work.

Rubin: You're more conscious of wanting to communicate to an audience?

Waters: Not to an audience so much, no. It's not as if I picture a reader out there; John Logan has said, "The first audience is the listening part of yourself." It's just a sense of saying something very clearly and concisely and precisely. That's for myself as much as it's for anybody else.

Fitz Gerald: You seem to be saying, along with others, that it's the process itself that gives the deepest satisfaction.

Waters: It *is* a process. Beginning writers often think of it in terms of poems, of what you're left with; but finally the poem is less important than the actual process of writing it which is a process of discovery. The "creative process" we talk about is a learning experience. It's the writing of the poem, sitting down not quite knowing what it is I have to say, working with one word or a musical phrase that's attracted me and letting it develop—that seems to me to be pure pleasure.

Rubin: Picking up on your working methods, have they changed significantly over the years?

Waters: Yes. The poems in *Fish Light*, for example, came very quickly. I'd been reading Robert Bly, particularly his short poems, and relied upon the white heat of inspiration. And Bly, of course, had been writing and rewriting those little poems—I couldn't see that. Now I'm less concerned with getting finished quickly.

I still work on only one poem at a time. Sometimes I go through 120 drafts, and what a wonderful feeling it is when it's finally finished, Yeats's box clicking shut. The process can take as short a time as three or four days of six to eight hours a day; other times I've worked on a poem over a period of two months—looking at the poem every day, carrying it around with me. I remember going into movie theaters with a poem and waiting for the light from the screen to be bright enough so I could change a word because I could not get my mind off that poem. I like that feeling!

Fitz Gerald: I'm pleased to hear about your process of revision. I remember Ginsberg saying that he never revised. Richard Wilbur said that maybe Ginsberg should have!

Waters: That's a misconception about Ginsberg, isn't it, based on these "white lies" he tells? If you look closely at a poem like "Howl," it's beautifully crafted, and almost any poetic device you want to teach to students is there. I couldn't see this when I was first reading him. And there's such a rich, interior life triggering those poems. But he likes the image of himself as always divinely inspired.

Rubin: I'd like to bring you back to your poetic progress. You're up to *Not*

Just Any Death. What had you learned, or what did that collection represent to you?

Waters: It's a short book—twenty-five or thirty poems—and during the six years following my first collection I may have written fifty. In addition, there were, of course, many false starts, poems that were never finished. In terms of being conscious of any developing themes, that's not something I was thinking of while working on the book. Once I got to the point where the book was almost ready, I began to think about an arrangement, how the poems spoke and offered support to each other.

Rubin: The book is beautifully arranged. The first poem, "Apples," is dedicated to your father. The book does take up the looking back to childhood as one of its themes, doesn't it? The last poem is "If I Die," which picks up the apple imagery in an affirmative way.

Waters: I was thinking about death constantly—not in any suicidal way, but it was bordering on obsession. I needed to think less about death, and one of the ways of dealing with it was through writing. I think that death-consciousness comes to us at a very early age when we first think, "My father's not going to be around forever," or "My mother is not going to be around forever." The next immediate thought must be, *"I'm* not going to be around forever," and we have that fear of death that we have to begin to work through. "I had a terror since September," Emily Dickinson wrote, "I could tell none, and so I sing, as the boy does by the burying ground, because I am afraid." It must be a stunning moment, that arrival of death-consciousness, but few people can remember exactly when it occurred.

"Apples" is a dreamlike poem, a way of talking with my father, finally saying things to him that I can't say in general conversation partly because of the relationship of men in our society. So it's a love poem, finally.

Apples

for my father

I was the clumsy child
who stole apples
from your favorite tree
to toss them into the lake.

I have no excuse, but
those apples were never lost.
Each night, while you slept,

as apples bobbed in moonlight,

I waited in shallow water
until the apples washed ashore.
Each night I gave you an apple.
Sometimes I remember that desire

to take whatever belongs to you
so I can return it.
Now, on windless nights,
when the lake lies still,

I have another dream:
I gather you in my arms,
after death, and ease you
like a basketful of apples

into the moonlit water,
and we float home,
with an awkward grace,
to a continent dark with apples.

The poem for my mother is very different. My mother is Jewish—she converted to Catholicism when she married my father. I was raised as a Catholic. It wasn't until years later that I began to wonder about that side of my heritage—how much of it was my mother's and therefore mine. So "In Memory of Smoke" touches upon the Holocaust.

In Memory of Smoke

I found her again this morning,
my mother, sleeping
with her head in the oven,
on a pillow of human hair.

On her knees, exhausted,
wanting the oven forever clean,
she might have been praying
in memory of smoke.

I don't know her reasons.
I guess something simple
as cleaning the oven
becomes a compulsion for those

who have been lost in snow,
in childhood, wandering
from town to burning town

in search of a family

I guess you might recognize
the family as smoke
billowing over black trees.
So I let my mother sleep.

I know she would never shut
her eyes, place her cheek
on the burning pillow each night,
without a prayer for her family,

giving thanks
for the work she manages daily,
in memory of smoke,
in fear of the coming snow.

Rubin: Both poems catch the tone of this elegiac, meditative collection, which is very strongly held together. Clearly you've achieved something internally with this book. What happened between *Not Just Any Death* and *Anniversary of the Air?*

Waters: The poems became less self-centered. So many poems in the earlier book are *I, I,* and try to make sense of my childhood, of my relationship with my parents, and my coming to terms with death. *Anniversary of the Air* broadens out a bit: there are characters in that book, people I've seen on the streets of New York and whose lives I imagine. It's a reaching out. Some of the poems are more extended pieces.

Rubin: You're still conversational, but you seem to have a renewed or new interest in form in some of these poems—even in the way they are arranged on the page and stanzaic patterns.

Waters: For some reason over the past decade I've become very comfortable with unrhymed quatrains. That form seemed useful in finding a natural voice, but recently I needed to see what else I could do. In fact, the title poem, "Anniversary of the Air," was written not long after I finished *Not Just Any Death*, and I wanted very much to wrench myself away from forms in that book. I lengthened the lines and just generally tried to give myself a little more room to breathe. For that particular poem, it seemed to work. In some of the others, I went back often to four-line stanzas, but I think they've tightened up. There's more concern for each word in its place. But this sort of talk makes me uncomfortable— often the poet is the last one, finally, to have anything useful to say about his own work. Roethke was blunt: "Frankly, I don't think what the instrument says about his tune (or sperm) is very important."

Rubin: I hate to have to ask a question that has to do with notions of truth, so I won't. But as you say, you've been publishing poems that catch the life of the moment glimpsed in New York and elsewhere. To what extent can you describe the mix of fantasy or imagination with real observation? Are these poems provoked by something which you've seen in most instances?

Waters: My poems are always triggered by something I've seen—I'm a poet of eyesight rather than a poet of vision. I keep journals and I'm constantly jotting things down. Driving along the Bowery one afternoon, for example, getting ready to make that left onto Houston, and seeing all those bums on the traffic island, I happened to notice one pair of women's shoes. That stayed with me, and several months later I began the poem "Green Shoes." Or, I can remember walking through an ethnic neighborhood in Pittsburgh and seeing blood sausages hanging in the grocer's window. That stayed with me and triggered, to some extent, "Anniversary of the Air." The character in that poem is named Anna, and I have another poem now, "Romance in the Old Folks' Home," that makes use of that same character. I think it's a way of talking about my Jewish grandmother, who was spoken of in several poems in *Not Just Any Death*. I need to have something trigger this creative process; I can't just sit there and invent.

Rubin: Your mentioning your grandmother reminds me how much women matter in your poetry. That's not entirely unusual for a male poet, but I was wondering if you'd say something about it. There's a line that comes to mind from the film critic Molly Haskell writing about Charlie Chaplin; she says, "Women were traumatically crucial to his art." Certainly that line somehow fits many of the poems in *Anniversary of the Air.*

Waters: I'm not sure how to respond. Obviously I love women very much. There's a poem, "The Stories in the Light," that's triggered just by seeing a schoolgirl walking across Fifth Avenue on a windy afternoon. There are several poems, like "The Auction," in praise of older women. Certainly women seem to me always lovely and mysterious. My relationships with and responses to women always interest me. I think about them very often—how I'm touched by a woman when I meet her, for whatever characteristic it might be—certainly not always a physical attribute, but something particularly tender and feminine that men simply do not possess. I try to explore that in some of these poems.

Rubin: You do both. You write about women—seen, desired, observed, remembered—and you take a risk, as in the poem "Singles," of that "negative capability," of putting yourself into the situation of the woman, assuming the persona of the woman. Could you say something briefly about that kind of imagining?

Waters: That's unusual for me—not so much "Singles," but there are several poems like "Bonwit Teller" spoken by an older woman. Now in the new manuscript I have two poems spoken by very young women. That's not something I set out consciously to do; I'm not trying to create a dramatic monologue after Robert Browning. But there's a sense in writing these poems that sometimes the woman herself insists on speaking. I think that through writing I come into touch with that feminine side of myself, and sometimes that's drawn out so much that side might want to speak for herself.

Rubin: In the last few moments remaining, could you talk very briefly about the manuscript you're working on now [*The Burden Lifters*]?

Waters: These are poems that again talk about my Brooklyn boyhood, but I don't think they're quite so personal. They're concerned with the notion of becoming a writer. Many literary figures walk through these poems, even back in Brooklyn in the 1950s. The book functions as a *Bildungsroman* of sorts. Also, a number of the poems are based on my travels in the past few years; they're triggered by scenes in Greece, Italy, and Costa Rica. But they're not travel poems in the sense of "I did this, I saw that." Rather, they mean to convey and ease, to some extent, the burden of humanity we bear wherever this world might lead us.

Rubin: Could you end by reading a fairly recent poem?

Waters: I'll read "Lipstick" which, I think, touches on much of what we've just been saying.

Lipstick

Who can hurry past the five-and-dime,
the cardboard Max Factor ad

fading in the yellow light
of the abandoned, fly-littered window,

without recognizing the miniature skyline—
spires, smokestacks, the blinking red antennae—

his mother's lipsticks etched
on the powdered, greenhouse air of her bedroom?

Only God or someone taller could count them!
I wanted to explore that foreign city,

hold her hand across the cinnabar avenues,
whisper in libraries of peach frost and ruby.

Grey school-mornings in the railroad flat,
pretending to be still asleep,

I'd watch my mother dress

for the subway ride into Manhattan.

She'd sit in her bra and half-slip,
elbows propped on the vanity top,

brushing the flames across her lips,
first one flavor, then another—

forbidden strawberry, crushed orange, cafe au lait—
then close her lips on a tissue.

I'd steal the paper from the wicker
basket to taste the exotic

spices, the delicious
mocha, creme caramel, glazed papaya,

and when I was older, ten or twelve,
I'd wrap tissue after tissue

around my small, preening member,
smudging the lipstick on my flesh.

I never wrestled any desire
to smear the lipstick on my face,

touch the tubes
to my own parched lips,

but was touched by the story of Rilke,
poor Rainer, whose suffocating mother

painted the lips of her dear Maria!
O the poems! His problems with women!

Was his mother drawing out,
as she layered shade upon shade,

the lovely woman who lived inside him,
or was she blotting out,

dyeing his lips a deeper red, deeper
till almost black,

the boy who peeked
from behind his eyelids, feverish and weak?

"At the Border"
A CONVERSATION WITH BRUCE BENNETT

Bruce Bennett

Bruce Bennett grew up in Philadelphia and was educated at Harvard University, where he received his Ph.D. in 1967. His books include three chapbooks of poetry (Bits Press, 1980, and State Street Press, 1981, 1987) and a full-length collection, *Straw into Gold* (Cleveland State University Press, 1984). His work has appeared in numerous magazines and journals, including *Poetry*, *The Nation*, and *Pequod*.

Mr. Bennett is a founding editor of the magazines *Field* and *Ploughshares* and has recently become an associate editor for State Street Press. He has performed as a member of Three For All, a trio which performs poetry, music, and dance. From 1983 to 1986, he served as a member of the Literature Panel of the New York State Council on the Arts.

In addition, Bruce Bennett was written numerous reviews for such places as *The New York Times Book Review*, *American Book Review*, and *The Nation*. He is currently Professor of English and Director of Creative Writing at Wells College in Aurora, New York. He is married to an art historian who teaches at the University of Rochester. They spend the summer in Florence, Italy, with their two children and a dog who still barks at the name of Nixon.

The following conversation took place on 5 October 1984. Interviewers were Stan Sanvel Rubin and Judith Kitchen. Mr. Bennett began by reading his poem "The Storyteller."

The Storyteller

They were with him from the beginning: The
Lost Cloud, The Lonely Caterpillar, Voice From the River
. . . His alone, to be guarded and hoarded.

Then, he told one. And faces gathered:

beautiful faces. He'd never seen such faces. He told more. And more.

He stepped out of the shadows, into a place of light. There was music; laughter. Someone offered her arm. They whirled.

He forgot words . . . voices . . .

When, at last, he returned, it was like waking. Or, like finding, and trying on, a miraculous coat.

He began telling new ones: The Man Who Bartered His Name; The Fever; The Old Coat . . .

Rubin: I'd like to begin by asking you about the poem you just read, "The Storyteller," which underscores your interest in narrative. It seems to focus on what storytelling does for the storyteller. Would you comment on that?

Bennett: I'm not sure what the poem came out of, but I think I was remembering that I had written earlier poems with titles perhaps a little like those at the beginning of the poem. Also behind the poem are *Songs of Innocence* and *Songs of Experience*. What I've been doing in these little prose poems, which sometimes are only a paragraph or two long, is to see how much of a story I can tell just by implication or suggestion. Another poem, "The Bad Apple," for example, will refer to just one detail—"the peasant with the black tooth," for example—in the hope that that one detail will set up the story within the mind of the reader. In this one there is the passage from innocence to experience as well as the response of the audience—those who listen to the story of the storyteller for whom this may be the only way to communicate.

Kitchen: Could you talk about the prose poem as such? Has that form allowed you to tell your own stories?

Bennett: Yes. Actually I came to the prose poem rather late. I started writing at the age of eight, and I always thought of myself as somebody who wanted to write poems, but it wasn't until what could be considered a rather late date that I stumbled upon the prose poem, luckily, through the series of visiting writers in the program that I direct at Wells College, especially Russell Edson and Robert Francis. The summer that I was preparing for their visit and reading their work, I began to write prose poems; it was also during that time that I began to write more than I ever had. Before that, I had written a few poems that I treasured as the basis for my claim that I was a writer, but about that time something happened through writing that kind of poem that set something free in me as a writer. Perhaps now I write too much! I write in other forms, but it seems that the kind of storytelling I wanted to do could only come out in this form.

Rubin: What kind of needs are met personally by the prose poem form?

Bennett: A student asked me after the reading last night what advice I could give a young writer, and I said that I feel it's very important just to trust your imagination. Somebody else asked whether the idea comes first and then you write the poem, and I could say that the poem always comes first for me, that I never write to any kind of preconceived idea. I have used in class William Stafford's essay, "A Way of Writing," in which he stresses writing as process. That is, we don't know what we're going to say until we say it, but as we talk, things will always come to us. I've found that writing is an adventure; it's very exciting to sit down and not know where you're going to go. A phrase will come to you, or a snatch of dialogue or an image, and a story will grow out of that for me.

The other thing Stafford stresses is that the critical part of you should be held in abeyance until you actually get something down on paper. I keep what I write, but I regard it as something that I can build on; if I show it to other people it's with the understanding that it's not a finished work. Instead of working a lot on a few things, I will simply take what will come. I have a poem from this summer's work that is called, "Take What Comes." If you're not responsible to anybody else for what you write, then writing can become a genuine adventure, and it can lead to who knows what.

I might send out for publication or use in a reading or try to get into a book only ten or fifteen poems from a couple of hundred pages. But I could not have gotten those ten or fifteen poems if I hadn't been writing constantly.

For me, first of all, the poems in form come as naturally as the prose poems. When I sit down to write, it might be a poem in set form or a free-verse poem or a prose poem. I think that there is something in not sitting down to write a particular kind of poem that allows for that kind of freedom.

Rubin: It's certainly true that a lot of poets have worked in the prose poem form in the last decade—Robert Bly comes to mind—but they have tended to use the prose poem as a slightly more expansive way to capture some of the experience that they get in other poetic forms. But you do something quite different that has much more affinity to the traditional narrative. You draw on fairy tale, legend, myth, and classical fable. Is there any conscious attempt on your part to draw upon these sources?

Bennett: No, I think it comes down to what a poet is trying to do—and this may be largely unconscious—in his or her work in relationship to an audience. And the audience is a very important part of it—one doesn't tell stories to oneself. I'm interested in a kind of accessibility. Someone asked last night whether I'd mind if she said that she found the reading I gave "entertaining." I said that I was delighted. For me that's very important: I want poetry to be enjoyable at the level that children gather to hear a story.

Kitchen: It's worth mentioning, then, that you are involved in a group called "Three For All," performing with a pianist and a dancer. Would you talk about that performance experience?

Bennett: I find it very satisfying to perform or to read directly to a particular audience. Everybody says it, and it's certainly true, writing is a solitary act; but part of the pleasure of writing is showing it to other people and having them respond. An extension of that is reading directly to an audience. You can sense when an audience is really listening, just as you can in a classroom, and the audience is responding to you. One of my goals in reading has been to work toward a feeling of direct communication with an audience, and it has affected the kind of poems I have written.

Our goal in "Three For All" is to interweave the three art forms at a level that will not be so esoteric that it will be just for a trained, sophisticated, intellectual audience. Of course, we hope that that kind of audience will also find something in our performance, but, as you know, we perform for groups of children too. For me, storytelling is important because it's a way of talking person-to-person on a very human level. What a poem is "saying" is less important than the fact and act of communication.

Rubin: "Three For All" has been a very successful collaboration. Did the blending of the three art forms come easily? Did it seem natural to you as a poet to blend your words with music and dance?

Bennett: Yes, it did, in the sense that the other two do all the work. The poems already exist, so it's relatively easy for me to get up and recite them. The other two often tease me, because the dancer has to warm up for a half hour, and the pianist has to get ready, but I can just walk out and start reading. Since the poems already existed, the dancer and pianist were able to turn their practiced eyes to what they could use. Although I don't write poems with "Three For All" in mind, the collaboration has affected some of my work. In fact, once I had written "The Storyteller," it seemed immediately appropriate for the group.

Kitchen: One of your most successful poems, from the point of view of performance, though, is not a storytelling poem but a sestina. How do you explain that?

Bennett: I don't find any conflict between the uses of any kinds of form. I have written form poems, free verse, and prose poems all in the same day. Maybe that kind of facility isn't particularly good. I admire Auden, but sometimes I think he wrote too much or too easily. On the other hand, it comes very naturally to me to write in whatever form the poem begins in. I realize also that I've never really said goodbye to any particular form. I thought I would never write another sonnet after I wrote one called "The True Story of Snow White," when I was twenty-one, but I have. It is however, a sonnet about writing a sonnet. I do find that I write set-form poems as comments about poetry—poems about poems. It's difficult to write formal poetry now without the awareness that most people don't write formal poetry and feel that they've moved on to something else. These really are, I hope in a good sense, "self-conscious poems" *about* the form they're in.

Rubin: Could you say something about the particular challenge of writing a sestina?

Bennett: I teach modern American poetry so I had taught Pound's sestina, but I wrote the poem in Italy, and it was only after I had finished it that I discovered I hadn't followed the pattern. Since I knew I couldn't rewrite the poem, I decided to call it "Sort of a Sestina," with a subtitle familiar to those who have written dissertations: "In Partial Fulfillment of the Requirements."

Sort of a Sestina:

In Partial Fulfillment
of the Requirements

"What? You've never written a sestina?"
You gazed incredulous across your coffee.
"But I should think you'd take it as a challenge;
I mean, with all your fancy-work in form
Well, if you ever write one, let me see it."
"I will," I promised. Here. I've kept my promise.

The thing is, I don't write things for the challenge.
Of course, when something's done I like to see it,
And once I start, it's sort of like a promise:
For instance, if I said, "We'll meet for coffee,"
We'd meet for coffee. It's like that with form,
And that's the way it is with this "sestina".

Don't get me wrong. I love to play with form,
And there's a certain pleasure in a challenge.
Again for instance, I've included "coffee",
A word that doesn't have a lot of promise,
To say the least, for use in a sestina.

Once having used it, I'm obliged to see it

Through. Okay. Let's say I'm stuck with "coffee".
I need a spot to stick it, then I see it
And bang! (as right above) I've met that challenge.
That's what you've got to do with a sestina.
You pounce on any opening with promise
And score your piddling points against the form.

But having seized those openings with promise
And being well along in one's sestina
And every time it comes around to coffee
Sneaking another by to beat the form
's not such a grand achievement, as I see it.
Suppose you prove you're equal to the challenge—

The point is, what's the point? Who's going to see it
As anything but diddling with a form?
That's *why* I've never written a sestina.
It's always seemed a wholly senseless challenge.
But I remembered what you said at coffee;
And also, since a promise is a promise

(Even when it takes form as a sestina),
I'm hoping you may see it as a challenge
To promise we will meet again for coffee.

Rubin: As a poet you've obviously mastered forms along the way in your development, and you've come to your own most congenial style, which departs from those forms. Must a poet come to terms at some point with traditional metrics, or isn't that necessary in American free verse?
Bennett: Poets individually have to find their own ways. But it does seem artificial for a teacher to ask a student to write a sonnet. On the other hand, I've been teaching writing since I was at Oberlin in the late sixties, and I continue to find students come to the writing of poetry without a background in forms. I think it would definitely be to their advantage to know something about them, which would of course include trying to write in them.
Rubin: How do you feel about the question of voice? The interesting thing about the sestina you just read is that you have, on the surface at least, a colloquial voice; but the pleasure is for the eye in this very challenging form.
Bennett: Something I've noticed in my poems for a very long time is that they always involve people talking; even if it's not actually dialogue between two or more people, there is usually a colloquial narrative voice. I have admired Frost very much, and his capturing of the speaking voice

in poetry has been behind much of what I do. You asked about the colloquial voice within the set form, and that's really Frost's "sentence sounds" and "sound of sense." And that ties into the role of the story-teller.

Kitchen: I was going to ask you about the tension in your work between the prose and the set form; but I see the tension as between an obvious humor and a current of seriousness underneath it—something which I see getting stronger in your work.

Bennett: It's easy to misread poems that are lighter or humorous on the surface, and anyone who writes poems that are "enjoyable" must feel occasionally that readers aren't connecting with what's really happening in the poem. I have written poems that other people—and I—find funny, but I don't set out merely to be funny.

The element of tone is extremely important, and voice is crucial. When I say ideas aren't important in my poems, I mean simply that what is being said is less important than the voice of who's saying it. Therefore, irony is very important. So many people see my poems as "whimsical," but Mary Elsie Robertson just said something about *The Strange Animal* that I wish more people would recognize about my poems generally; she said, "Beneath the surface they're frightening and very dark." That tension is crucial to my work. Often in poems like "There Are Lies" and "Irony" what is meant is literally the opposite of what is said.

Kitchen: Would you read "There Are Lies"?

There Are Lies

There are lies, which,
repeated often enough,
come to seem the truth.

So-and-so is an honest
man. Such-and-such didn't
happen like that. Believe
what you want, these are
the facts.

Bit by bit, conviction
is chipped away. Perhaps
you didn't see what you
recall. Are you certain
you heard what you thought?

You never claimed
infallibility. Others may

be, as they insist, in
a position to know. In
any case, one must keep
an open mind.

Besides, there's
your personal history.

To be painfully, indeed
brutally, frank, isn't it
likely, given your experience,
it's you who are mistaken?
Isn't it quite probable?

Face up to it. And
then, ask yourself this:
what is "the truth", anyway?

Rubin: I'd like to get back to the question of the stories in your storytelling poems. There are so many transformations going on that I suppose the reader can feel after a while that there is no stable reality, that the poet is not giving us any place to plant our feet. Is that the way you look at things?

Bennett: In *The Strange Animal* some of the poems are story poems, and some are about the storyteller or the act of storytelling. But the poems toward the end of the collection, like "The Stick" or "The Return," *are* questioning the basis of reality. Any storytelling is involved with imagination, and the stronger the imagination is, the less one is sure finally of what is real and what is merely imagined; or, as Wallace Stevens puts it, "Nothing is only real, or only imagined, but an admixture of the two."

There was no conscious effort to do it, but in certain poems like "The Boy Who Cried 'Wolf!'" the imagination creates the wolf to such a point that it actually frightens the boy to death. I suppose that Nabokov's fiction is behind the story—the idea that "reality" is the only word you should never use without quotation marks. That probably has been in the background for some time, but it may be more in the foreground now, and I'm more conscious of it.

The first section of my new book, *Straw into Gold*, is a section called "At the Border." Many of those poems are at the border of reality and imagination. Many come out of dreams and attempt to create or evoke a dream atmosphere. Curiously, these prose-poem forms are melding into set forms, and on the page they look like short-line poems. My editor was a little puzzled because I couldn't really tell him how I wanted the poems on the page. Those poems, it occurred to me later, are also on the border between set forms and prose.

Rubin: What has the experience of putting together your first full-length collection meant to you?

Bennett: It was a long process. I first sent out a full manuscript in 1972, before I began teaching at Wells. Each year after, I was adding new poems so that the manuscript got completely revised and reshaped. I enlisted the help of anyone who was willing to read it. One writer who was visiting from Oberlin said she liked the poems but I had several chapbooks rather than a coherent, complete collection. She suggested that I take one of them and expand it. Also, I had the problem of figuring out what editors were looking for and the fact that you may have to read a number of my poems to get acquainted with the voice and tone before you know how to deal with them.

Rubin: Before we conclude this discussion, would you read the title poem, "Straw into Gold," and talk about how you came to this material?

Bennett: When my son was four or five, I was reading him an edition of *Rumplestiltskin* with illustrations by Edward Gorey which are pretty sinister. The more I looked at the story, the more the motivation of everybody in it seemed questionable. Out of that came "Straw into Gold," which is essentially the voices of the four main characters speaking their parts.

Straw into Gold

The Miller's Daughter

It was my father who claimed I could spin straw
into gold, I who can barely thread a needle.

Since then it's one damned room after another,
with the attentions of a midget.

If I'm lucky, they say, I'll marry the King, a bore
who'd just as soon kill me.

Why didn't he brag I'm beautiful and a virgin?
At least I'd have had a night on the town.

Rumplestiltskin

If I play this right, I'll get her and the baby both.
She'll have to tell how she turned all that straw into
gold, and he'll boot them out. That's the sort of pig he
is. Call me runt, will he? And she's another. Two of a
kind, they are. Games? She doesn't know what

games are. Just wait till she and the kid are in my house in the woods. Then they'll see games.

The King

Gold, gold, glorious gold! Heaps and heaps turned into gold! I'll build them high as mountains. I'll impound the harvest. I'll have straw imported! Death to anyone who touches a piece of straw!

The Miller

That little slut! Imagine keeping a secret like that! From her father! I'd'a whipped her good. And I'd'a kept my mouth shut; you can bet on that! She'd'a spun night and day. In a couple months, I'd'a been King.

Imagine!

That little slut!

"The Holy Words"
A CONVERSATION WITH PAUL ZIMMER

Paul Zimmer

Paul Zimmer was born and raised in Ohio. He has worked as a warehouseman, shoe salesman, technical writer, stockbroker clerk, steel mill electrician, college teacher, bookstore manager, and reporter. Beginning with A *Seed on the Wind* (1960), Paul Zimmer has published nine books of poetry, including *The Zimmer Poems, With Wanda: Town and Country Poems*, and most recently, *Family Reunion, Selected and New Poems* from the University of Pittsburgh Press. He has read widely across America, recorded his poetry for the Library of Congress and won numerous awards, including an American Academy and Institute of Arts and Letters Literary Award in 1985. His most recent book, *The Great Bird of Love*, was chosen for the 1988 National Poetry Series by William Stafford and is forthcoming.

In 1986, a book of writings on the poetry of Mr. Zimmer was published by Ford-Brown, entitled *Poet as Zimmer: Zimmer as Poet*, edited by Jan Susina. His work has been praised by X. J. Kennedy, Michael S. Harper, and Hayden Carruth, who calls him "consistently entertaining." For the past three years, Mr. Zimmer has been director of the University of Iowa Press, after having served as director of the University of Georgia Press and, before that, as associate director of the University of Pittsburgh Press. He now lives in Iowa City.

The following conversation took place on 11 October 1984. Interviewer was Stan Sanvel Rubin. Mr. Zimmer began by reading his poem "The Eisenhower Years."

The Eisenhower Years

Flunked out and laid-off,
Zimmer works for his father
At Zimmer's Shoes for Women.
The feet of old women awaken
From dreams, they groan and rub
Their hacked-up corns together.

261

At last they stand and walk in agony
Downtown to Zimmer's fitting stool
Where he talks to the feet
Reassures and fits them with
Blissful ties in medium heels.

Home from work he checks the mail
For greetings from his draft board.
After supper he listens to Brubeck,
Lays out with a tumbler of Thunderbird,
Cigarettes and *From Here to Eternity.*

That evening he goes out to the bars,
Drinks three pitchers of Stroh's,
Ends up in the wee hours leaning
On a lamp post, his tie loosened,
Fedora pushed back on his head,
A Chesterfield stuck to his lips.

All of complacent America
Spreads around him in the night.
Nothing is moving in this void,
Only the feet of old women,
Twitching and shuffling in pain.
Zimmer sighs and takes a drag,
Exhales through his nostrils.
He knows nothing and feels little.
He has never been anywhere
And fears where he is going.

for my father

Rubin: I'd like to ask you about this poem. I presume it was written during the Eisenhower years. Were you "flunked out and laid off"?
Zimmer: No, I wrote it some years after the Eisenhower years. Yes, I did it all. It wasn't easy.
Rubin: Like many of your poems, it draws on your own life very directly and it makes yourself, Zimmer, a character in a kind of small drama. It is from *The Zimmer Poems* originally?
Zimmer: No, it was originally published in a chapbook called *The Ancient Wars.*
Rubin: Would you say something about how you came to this character Zimmer and the freedom with which you use him in poetry, starting with your earliest work?
Zimmer: I had a very difficult time when I was a young person and was

reeling around after having flunked out of college. I went to work in a steel mill, and the steel mill went on strike after ten days, and then I was drafted. So there was a succession of blows, and I really didn't know who I was. I obviously felt I was a failure, that I didn't really have a lot on the ball. I went into the army and got interested in reading, especially poetry, and I went out and bought a tweed coat and pipe and told everybody I was a poet. But it took a while.

When I first started writing poems, I didn't think I was a very interesting person, so I made people up. I wrote poems through them—famous people like Joseph Conrad, Juan Belmonte, or Johnny Blood, the football player. Then I decided to make up my own characters, and they all took on names like Imbellis, Peregrine, Cecil, and Wanda, and I spoke through them. Finally I decided that I was interesting enough to write about myself. I began making Zimmer poems.

Rubin: You're still writing them?

Zimmer: Oh, yes, I still do.

Rubin: I noted that, in your book *The Republic of Many Voices* (1969), the Zimmer poems are the fifth section and all these other voices occupy four-fifths of the book. Then your next book is *The Zimmer Poems*. Does this imply that all of these other personae came to you in the same period of time?

Zimmer: It developed over maybe a five- or ten-year period. Actually David Way, the editor from October House who published *The Republic of Many Voices*, when I gave him the manuscript with the first four parts, said, "Something is missing." I said, "I don't understand." And he said, "You. You are missing from it. Who are you?" I said, "I am Zimmer." That started the whole thing.

Rubin: How honest are these poems?

Zimmer: Well, they're poetry. They're as honest as poetry is.

Rubin: Do you feel that little anecdote implies that all the many other voices were ways of creative evasion? Did you feel something different in coming to the Zimmer character?

Zimmer: I felt a new energy, a tremendous release, and I had to devise ways of restraining myself from writing too many Zimmer poems. It was a neat way to start, writing through other voices. I didn't have the problem of worrying about how honest I was being or anything like that. I could do anything I wanted with these people. It was marvelous. I still do that.

Rubin: Poets really shouldn't have to worry about that. But I guess my point is, did it feel different to start to handle Zimmer? Or, did he just take his place rather naturally in your imagination?

Zimmer: It was exhilarating, but it was rather natural.

Rubin: The first books you published were with October House and

Dryad. Could you say something about your early publishing history—how you came to collect and publish these poems? Were they written with the intention of publishing?

Zimmer: Of course. I don't believe people who say that they write for themselves. When you write, it's implicit in the act that you want to share. Of course, I wanted to publish. But it took me years to be able to publish. I didn't have a poem in a magazine until I was in my early thirties, and I had been writing for many years. I never attended a writing workshop and, like most young poets, I kept recasting the manuscript and working on it. Finally I sent it to the right editor on the right day when his stomach wasn't sour and he liked the poems and it worked. It was a miracle. It was wonderful.

Rubin: Are you telling us something about the editing profession?

Zimmer: In some ways maybe I am. You do have to catch the editor on the right day. There's no question about it.

Rubin: Did you feel initially that these poems were different from what was being written? Was there something out there that was inspiring you or serving as an early model?

Zimmer: Oh, there are a lot of peole I read for energy. I've loved Yeats, Theodore Roethke, James Wright, Galway Kinnell, and people like that. And the old poets I love them—John Skelton, Sir Thomas Wyatt, Chaucer, Shakespeare, Emily Dickinson, Walt Whitman, John Clare. I get energy from them. I've never tried to imitate them. I did when I was younger, I guess. That's the way you begin. Yeah, I felt I was doing something a little different.

Rubin: These poems are generally so liberating for a reader. I'm sure I'm not alone in that response. Yet I wonder if you didn't feel kind of odd. What was the first of these many voices that came to you? Do you recall the first of these personae?

Zimmer: It was a long time ago. It was a poem about a witch. There was a woman that I created in my mind—I was interested in the occult at the time—and I realized that I had made something rather different. I don't think the poem was ever published. But I knew that I had done something. I had made a major breakthrough for myself, and I felt at long last I knew what I was doing. It went on from there.

Rubin: You weren't in a writing program of any kind. Did you have someone who was important early on in sharing or critiquing your work?

Zimmer: My wife has always been my first and best reader. I never really met any poets until I was in my late twenties or early thirties.

Rubin: As you've gone through your career, have some of your voices become more important or less important? Do you find them being useful for a short time psychically and then others take their place, or do you consciously reach for these different strains of yourself and try to see where they're going?

Zimmer: They all have different meanings for me. I guess two voices have really come to the center for me; one is Imbellis, who has been my adversary throughout and still gives me fits. And then I made a whole book about Wanda. She's the kind of Everywoman figure for me, based on women that I've known and women that I've wished that I'd known. She is my way of writing about women; I've always wanted to be able to do that. I'm very pleased about the reception of that book. I was worried that women were not going to like it, but I've had really wonderful reactions from women, even ardent feminists. I'm very glad about that.

Rubin: I was going to ask you particularly when Wanda entered the "republic," when and why she came into being. Do you recall the first Wanda poem?

Zimmer: There were Wanda poems in my very first book, *The Ribs of Death*, many years ago. It was just that I wanted to write about women, and it was a way I devised of doing it.

Rubin: In the book *With Wanda*, which was published in 1980 by Dryad Press, you really run through just about all the possible permutations of the female archetype from the most revered woman on the Romantic pedestal, to the images of the fallen woman as well as every kind of male-female relationship. And you run through every kind of form too. You've got a miracle play in there. You've got romantic poetry and parodies, such as "Lost Poem From Sir Thomas Wyatt's Egerton Manuscript." Wanda is eternal and recurring, and she runs up against these other characters, Gus and some others. Would you say something about the book *With Wanda*? Were these poems written over a particular period of time? Did you conceptualize them belonging together?

Zimmer: After a while I realized they were all going to go together. I was just writing, and suddenly I realized what direction I was headed in.

The poems are divided into two parts. The first part is rural poems I worked on when I was staying in my cabin in the woods and farmland of Northwestern Pennsylvania. Most of those were conceived while talking to people who lived around there and the voices and tones of those people come into the poems. The second part was the other half of my life that I was living right in the middle of Pittsburgh. They are very urban poems. There's one in which Wanda goes from the country into the city, and men talk about her, rural men at first and then city men talk about her.

Rubin: I wonder if we could have a taste of these. I'm going to ask you to read one of the letters to Wanda that was written by one of these characters because it will give us an idea of your unique style—the one where she becomes Emily Dickinson. This catches up something that runs through your work. I hesitate to call it parody, but I guess strictly speaking it's parody of all sorts of other literary forms, and even of specific poems. Here, you have your character Wanda being written to by another of your voices, and she's writing a poem as if she were Emily Dickinson in your character's dream. It's one of the most complex poems, dramaturgically speaking, I've ever seen in such a short space.

Zimmer: This is in the form of a letter that I have written, Zimmer had written, to Wanda:

> Dear Wanda,
>
> Last night I dreamt you were Emily Dickinson.
> I waited for you, uneasy in your parlour.
> After many hours you came into the room.
> You were ill, your temples sunken,
> A light sweat stippled your upper lip.
> Still, you made me nervous. You handed
> This poem to me and left again:
>
>> This was my letter to a Moor
>> Writ in mad divinest sense—
>> From a life closed twice before
>> That made my lines so lean and tense
>>
>> The words I chose were hard and few—
>> Of liquor, heather, snake and claw
>> Of other things I never knew
>> And did not see—but saw
>
> Wanda, I have remembered
> Every line. The cadence has
> Frightened me, the rhymes leer
> At my uneasiness. Please do not
> Come into my dreams again.
>
>> Love,
>>
>> Zimmer

Rubin: Somehow I don't think he's sincere, that he doesn't want her to come into his dreams again; or, at least I know she will. That's a very complex poem.

Let's get down to your working methods. How would a poem like that be composed?

Zimmer: I work like most poets. It's a very difficult and laborious process. I think I wrote the parody first and then I decided I would "stud" the parody into a letter and other things in the book. It seemed to come together in that way for me.

Rubin: Is this something that you've done for quite a while and it comes naturally to you to parody great or less-than-great poems by great poets of the past?

Zimmer: I enjoy it very much.

Rubin: You don't pick on the second-rate a lot. How do you feel about doing that? It must come a little easier to you than it would to many other poets at this point to pick up a Keats poem or a poem by Shakespeare and do your own riff on it.

Zimmer: One way I devised of restraining myself when I was making Zimmer poems was to imagine what it would be like if my favorite poets had made Zimmer poems.

Any poet writing in English is interested in Emily Dickinson. I've always thought a lot about her, and I've read a good deal about her. She is an awesome person to me in many ways, and I wanted to get that into the poem—a kind of uneasiness one would have being around that extraordinary kind of person.

Rubin: I don't think there really is anything that I know of in our poetry comparable to Wanda. It's so thorough in its attempt to deal with all the strains of a man's understanding of women.

Zimmer: Bless your heart, I'm going to give you some money.

Rubin: I'll take it, but after we're done.

But there's also in the book a pure lyric strain. I wonder if you'd read "Wanda Being Beautiful." That poem seems to catch a voice that is really sincere in its praise of beauty. Maybe you could say something about it.

Zimmer: I'd be happy to read it. I've often wondered what it would be like to be beautiful. I've never had that problem, but I think it would be difficult to be an extraordinarily beautiful person. Also, this is a Wanda poem that's not spoken by another man; it's spoken by me, the poet . . . or perhaps by Wanda herself.

Wanda Being Beautiful

To be beautiful is to somehow keep
A dozen fires burning at night,
To know that all eyes shining
Out of the trees are afraid of you.
It is to know that every crackle of
A twig, every footfall is a threat,
That desire is greatest from a distance.
To be beautiful is to stay on the move

> Through every season, to watch sharply
> As you take what you want; but mostly
> It is knowing how to choose dry wood,
> How to bank your fires against cold.

Rubin: That's quite a lovely poem and in some sense more sincere, if that's the right word.

Zimmer: I guess it is. It's a strange thing, but when I finished it I wasn't sure I liked it or that it was successful. I kept showing it to people, and they kept saying that they liked it. Usually I know when I've done something good. People had to tell me repeatedly that they liked this one before I believed that it was good.

Rubin: There is this edge of risk in all of these encounters with male and female archetypes, and with beauty. Your other poem ends with the speaker asking her not to come into his dreams again. This one has the marvelous lines that "to be beautiful is . . . to watch sharply as you take what you want." And both sides of that are dark—taking what you want and constantly being on guard because you're beautiful. The urban poem, "Gus Sees Wanda Drinking" is very dark. It ends with her promising, as she has fallen into the gutter, to never bother him again if he'll give her money to buy coffee. And she's one of these wandering, derelict types. The last line is she promises to "wash her face and never frighten me again." Would you say something about this fear element, this nervousness in these poems?

Zimmer: I've always been frightened of drunken women.

Rubin: Yeah, that's all right. That explains it.

Zimmer: When I worked in San Francisco many years ago, I ran a book warehouse in the middle of the wino district, and I used to have to walk through it every day. Whenever a man approached me and asked for a handout, I was an easy touch. When a woman would come up, I remember being frightened, scared because it just seemed unreal to me that a woman would be in this condition. The old woman-on-a-pedestal syndrome. At any rate, that's how I got into doing that poem. There's a couple of them, actually, about that.

Rubin: So you really didn't go through a lot of difficulties in speaking so directly and using your Zimmer, your own life. It wasn't a major struggle. It sort of came naturally for you.

Zimmer: It was a big struggle to make the break.

Rubin: What break do you mean?

Zimmer: From doing persona work and working through other people's voices, feeling comfortable with that and purposely avoiding doing autobiographical poems. It was the time of confessional poetry; Lowell,

Sexton, Plath, and people like that were in the forefront, and I didn't want to do that. I'm not a confessional poet and I was trying to do something different with the voices. But then when it occurred to me that I should really do some autobiographical things, it was just a shift of gears, and I seemed to go into it rather naturally. But I resisted it a long time. I'm not sorry I did.

Rubin: Why?

Zimmer: Because I think when I finally got around to doing it, I had practiced, practiced, practiced, you know. I knew something about how to do it, how to make poems and how they go together.

Rubin: What are your own working methods? Is there a particular set of conditions you require to do that kind of focusing? You must not get much time in your rather busy professional life.

Zimmer: No. I have a very busy professional life. I work eight hours a day in my office, and then I go home and read manuscripts at night for the press. I get up very early in the morning, about five-thirty, six o'clock in the morning, and get an hour or so of writing in before I go to work; then at noon at work I shut my door and wolf down a sandwich and work on a poem. I've always done this. These are the hours that I have, and this is the way I operate.

Rubin: You did mention revising a lot. You normally boil these poems down? Do you sweat over individual words, or do you write large amounts and find yourself cutting it down?

Zimmer: I take them any way I can get them. Yes, I do sweat and strain, and they're usually boiled down from random notes and ideas. I never start with a preconceived idea that I'm going to make a sonnet about a woman sitting under an apple tree and she's got a beautiful hat on and bang-bang-boppity-bop. I end up with a mess if I try that. So I begin with some kind of sensory writing or trying to describe something, a memory, or something that I'm holding in my hand—a stick or something I see out the window, something very simple which reminds me of something else. I try to get into it that way.

I have a lot of stuff just scribbled on pieces of paper. This is where the practice comes in. You begin to know better and better how to bring these things together. But I have to relearn the process every time I do it. I'm very impatient about it. It's a hard process, and when I've finished with one poem, and that deep void of the blank paper is in front of me, I hate it because I know I've got to start all over again—and I forget how to do it. Sometimes it is exasperating.

Rubin: That answers the question, in part; it's a struggle and it's a kind of love / hate. Have you had cold periods where for months perhaps you didn't find poems coming? You seem so prolific.

Zimmer: It doesn't seem to me that I am very prolific. Yes, I've had a few patches where I've not written very much. Right now I'm having probably the coldest period I've ever had. It's worrisome to me. But I always sit down and try. If I walk away from it and say, "O.K., I'm not going to do anything for three or four months and then I'll see what happens," I fear that I would lose the gift. It's important to keep trying, giving the Muse her due—at least it is for me.

Rubin: Do you read a lot of contemporary poetry?

Zimmer: Over the years, I have. I've been the editor of the Pitt Poetry Series and the Georgia Series, and I've read a lot of poetry in my work.

Rubin: Some of the poetry you read might be inhibiting because it's not all inspiring.

Zimmer: Yes. There was one time at the University of Pittsburgh Press, during the first years of that series, when we called for first manuscripts and received sixteen hundred first manuscripts of poetry. That's fifty pages or more per manuscript. They all were sitting in my office. That was an awesome sight. I swear I could hear the Muses groaning under the strain.

Rubin: But, of course, you read every word.

Zimmer: Oh, every word! I did read *something* of each manuscript; that's all you can do in a situation like that. You begin to sift and work the piles down. I read the first poem, the last poem, and the middle poem of every manuscript, and if I didn't see something that really grabbed me it was gone. But if I saw something in one of those poems that really caught my eye, I'd set it aside and work the piles down to a more manageable group, then work those down, and so on.

Editing is a very subjective business. That's what I'm paid for—to be subjective and to bring what I know to the task—and it's impossible to be objective.

Rubin: How did you come to this profession?

Zimmer: Oh, by a long, circuitous route. I started out working as a warehouse man for a book wholesaler. I got to be the manager of the place and from there I went on to manage bookstores. One time I managed the UCLA bookstore—a three-million-dollar operation; I had seventy people working for me, but I felt more like a referee than a human being. So I decided I wanted to get into book publishing. I didn't want to go to New York or Boston and get into trade publishing and that three-piece madness. I love scholarly books so I decided I would go into university press publishing. There was an opening at Pitt for a marketing director, and I got the job. After about a year I began to work my way into editing and eventually became the associate director of the Press. Fred Hetzel, the director at Pitt, is a very cordial man, a wonderful man to work with. I worked with him for twelve years. He taught me most of what I know about directing a scholarly press. He allowed the poetry series to begin. It started with the U.S. Awards of the International Poetry

Forum, and when the award stopped we went on without it. Over the eleven, twelve years I was at Pitt, we did about seventy books of poetry.

Rubin: You then went to Georgia where you continued to publish poetry and also established, among other things, a fiction series.

Zimmer: Yes, the Flannery O'Connor Award Series, which I'm very proud of. It has done very well. In addition to the literary publishing, mostly I am scholarly book publisher. That is the main part of my work.

Rubin: How does any of this business have impact on your own writing? Were you writing when you began editing?

Zimmer: I have been writing since I was about twenty-one or twenty-two. The publishing business is my work, and the editing of poetry has nothing to do with my writing of poetry. It is part of my work, and I perform it as my work. On my lunch hour and early in the morning, I'm a poet. In fact, I'm a poet all the time. But I do this work so I can be a poet. I made a decision a long time ago that I wanted to be a father and a husband. I fell in love when I was twenty-four, and I wanted to have a family. I had to make a living, and they don't pay poets by the hour in America.

Rubin: So they're really separate realms? You don't apply some withering, critical eye to your own work? You're able to be creative about it?

You have, certainly, a very fine career as an editor. What does going to Iowa mean to you? You just took over this position a month or so ago.

Zimmer: It's a challenge that I was very anxious to take up. The Iowa University Press has been minimal for a number of years, doing four to six books a year, and the university is anxious to build it up to a much larger volume, maybe twenty or twenty-five books a year. I did that when I went to Georgia. Georgia was doing ten or fifteen books a year; last year they did fifty. That's one of the reasons Iowa hired me. So, I'm excited about it. It's nice to be in proximity to the famous Workshop. I don't really have much to do with it, except that I have good friends there. I'm not going to teach any workshops. I don't have time. The Workshop brings in a lot of excitement—writers coming through town all the time.

Rubin: What do you think of the state of publishing today? We know the problems, and there's been a lot of press for years about the shrinking list of the commercial big houses, the importance of small publishers in poetry. In fact, your poetry, your publishing career, indicates that— Dryad and other small presses. What do you see as the role of the university press?

Zimmer: I think we have a responsibility, which the commercial publishers have essentially forsaken, to publish fine writing. There are still some trade houses that do it, but because of the conglomerating that's been going on and the pressures from the mega-corporations on editors to publish profitable works, it's fallen to university presses, more than ever before, to publish strong, intellectual books that are going to have limited appeal but are going to be of great importance.

Rubin: You're talking about scholarly works now.

Zimmer: Yes, and literary things too.

Rubin: Is there a competition there? The presses you've been associated with have had very notable poetry and fiction series. Are there resources there, or were you in danger of having a lot of work just not get published?

Zimmer: I think plenty of good work is being published and the resources are there. The National Endowment for the Arts—I don't care what other people think—has been a tremendous blessing because of the money that they have given to publishers and to writers. A lot of things have happened that are very, very good. When I think about the sixteen hundred poetry manuscripts I had in my office, I think there are too many poets in the world. But then I think, God, people could be doing a lot worse things than making poems. It is kind of wonderful that so many are worrying about the holy words and trying to do something important with them. It is good that so many people are trying to use words well. It can't be bad.

Rubin: Let's go back to your own poetry. We spoke before about how you moved to speaking in a Zimmer voice directly. You just read "Wanda Being Beautiful" a few minutes ago. Here's another love poem called "An Enzyme Poem for Suzanne." It's in a Zimmer voice. You might or might not tell us who Suzanne is.

Zimmer: Suzanne is my wife. The poem was first called "Suzie's Enzyme Poem." I thought, I'm going to have a *Selected Poems* and it's going to be a more dignified thing, so I changed the title to "An Enzyme Poem for Suzanne." She liked that. It's an odd kind of love poem. I've been in love for twenty-six years now, but I've resisted making love poems because I don't like romantic imagery in love poetry. How can you improve on what's been done? So I wanted to make an unusual love poem. I suppose that's what this is, but it is a very *loving* poem.

An Enzyme Poem for Suzanne

What a hulking bore it must be for you!
I slog along, ignoring you like my heart beat.
I gurgle and mold like an old fruit cellar,
Then suddenly you'll walk through a door
And foam me up like ancient cider in heat.
Then I'll fall all about you, blathering
With lost time, making you numb with words,

Wanting to mix our molecules, trying
To tell you of weeks in fifteen minutes.
Sometimes you must wonder what the hell
It is with Zimmer.
                 This is to tell you
That you are my enzymes, my yeast,
All the things that make my cork go pop.

Rubin: I think it's just wonderful.

Zimmer: I've always wanted to end a poem with the word "pop."

Rubin: I don't know how your wife could have failed to appreciate it. I'd like to proceed with the Zimmer voice and ask you to read one more Zimmer poem—maybe "Zimmer Warns Himself With Vivid Images Against Old Age." We're taking about the darker side of self-knowledge here. In fact, let's put the reading off. I want to ask you something.

Looking at your work with all its many voices, one might get the impression that here is somebody that really has access to the inner life. Similarly, looking at your parodies and the kind of formal things you do from the earliest English forms, Skeltonics, up through really more contemporary things—you parody Robert Frost, "Death of the Hired Zimmer"—it would seem that here is somebody who really knows form and really has been trained in school. What is it a poet needs to know?

Zimmer: Needs to know?

Rubin: Yeah, what should a poet know? You didn't go to workshop yourself.

Zimmer: That's a hard question to answer. Poets should know patience. Poems are not made in a hurry. I think that's one of the things that young people have most difficulty realizing, when they make a very important decision, a life decision, to be a poet. There are not going to be great hordes of people interested in what they're trying to do at first—and maybe never. The important thing is to work at the poems, to work with the holy words, to *try* things. So poets should know patience. They must learn it very quickly, or they're sunk.

Rubin: You say, "the holy words," showing your reverence for language. Is that just born in you, or do you acquire that from teachers or models or what?

Zimmer: I've always liked words and been interested in them. There were a few teachers who taught me that I should love words too, more by their example than anything else. I had a teacher in high school—an old football coach who would read from Shakespeare and actually weep. It just knocked me out. Here was this incredible, tough man who was crying over these words. That's one thing I remember.

Rubin: Well, you didn't find yourself drifting towards, for whatever reasons, creative writing programs or writing workshops.

Zimmer: There weren't many in the 1950s, and I didn't have the academic record for it anyway. I was an English major and took a creative writing course once, but there weren't any workshops I could attend.

Rubin: Would you say that the real-world experience is more valuable than the purely academic experience?

Zimmer: It was for me. Let me answer it that way.

Rubin: Your work makes clear that you've used it. When did you first know you were a poet? Was it first publication?

Zimmer: No. It was that time I made the poem about the witch. That was the day when I really realized what it meant to be a poet. I felt so good about that.

Rubin: Did you study forms?

Zimmer: Oh yeah, I practiced them for years and I still practice.

Rubin: Would you say someone should do that, or is that just your way?

Zimmer: Oh yeah, I think so definitely. And you should not only read the contemporary poets, but the old poets too, the old English and European poets.

Rubin: We're near the end and I guess it's appropriate—probably even a better time—to ask you to read the poem "Zimmer Warns Himself With Vivid Images Against Old Age." And that will probably be the end of our discussion so you might want to briefly introduce it if you have something to say about it.

Zimmer: I made this poem about fifteen years ago, and I'm fifty now. As an older middle-aged person, I'm beginning to realize that there's prophesy here.

Zimmer Warns Himself With Vivid Images Against Old Age

Well, Zimmer, old reeking cricket,
There you go sliding your galoshes
Along cement as dismal and
Hard as your petrified bowels,
Your hands like frayed moths
Raising a yellow snot rag
To your swampy nostrils.
With your eyes unplugged now
Behind the fly-speckled spectacles,
Your knees squawking, elbows flaring,

Joints burning, penis trickling,
Feet dead and teeth long gone,
You pay now with mumbling for
All the money you never saved
And all the poems you ever wrote.

Notes on the Editors and Interviewers

Editors

EARL G. INGERSOLL, born in Spencerport, New York, is an Associate Professor of English at SUNY College at Brockport, where he has taught since 1964. He was educated at the University of Rochester, received his M.A. from Syracuse University, and holds a Ph.D. from the University of Wisconsin at Madison. Although his primary research interest is D. H. Lawrence—his articles have appeared in *The D. H. Lawrence Review, Studies in the Humanities*, and *Bulletin of Research in the Humanities*—he has published numerous interviews with contemporary writers, including a collection, *SF Talk: Conversations with Writers of Fantasy and Science Fiction* (Penkevill), 1988.

JUDITH KITCHEN grew up in Painted Post, New York, was educated at Middlebury College, and holds an M.F.A. from the Warren Wilson College Program for Writers. She has been active in the poets-in-the-schools programs for years and is currently an adjunct professor for SUNY College at Brockport. She has recently received an individual artist's award from the New York Foundation for the Arts. Her book of poems, *Perennials*, won the 1985 Anhinga Prize, chosen by Hayden Carruth. In addition to poetry, she writes fiction and critical essays. She is currently writing a book on the work of William Stafford, to be published by the University of South Carolina Press.

STAN SANVEL RUBIN was born in Philadelphia, educated at Temple University, and was a Danforth and Woodrow Wilson fellow at Harvard, where he received his Ph.D. He is Associate Professor of English at SUNY College at Brockport, where he teaches film studies and writing. Currently serving his fourth term as Director of The Brockport Writers Forum and Videotape Library, Dr. Rubin was also founding director of The Brockport Summer Writing Workshops. He is a recipient of the SUNY Chancellor's Award for Excellence in Teaching. He has published a chapbook of poems, *Lost*, and a full-length book of poetry, *Midnight* (State Street Press), in addition to co-editing numerous published interviews from the Forum collection. His articles have appeared in *Film Criticism, The Journal of Narrative Technique, Reader,* and elsewhere.

Other Interviewers

GREGORY FITZ GERALD was born in New York City, lived in various New England states, and was educated at Boston University. He received his Ph.D. from the University of Iowa, where he studied with Paul Engle, Donald Justice, and Vance Bourjailly. Fitz Gerald was the founding director of The Brockport Writers Forum in 1967 and has interviewed over sixty-five writers for the Videotape Archives. His stories and poems have appeared in numerous periodicals. His books include *Hunting the Yahoos, Neutron Stars, Modern Satiric Stories: The Impropriety Principle, Past, Present, and Future Perfect,* and *The Late, Great Future. The Druze Document,* a novel, is forthcoming from Cliffhanger Press. A science fiction novel is currently in progress.

WILLIAM HEYEN was born in Brooklyn, holds a Ph.D. from Ohio University, and is currently Professor of English and Poet in Residence at SUNY College at Brockport. His books of poetry include *Long Island Light, Lord Dragonfly,* and *Erika: Poems of the Holocaust.* A romance, *Vic Holyfield and the Class of 1957,* was published by the Available Press. The editor of several volumes including *The Generation of 2000: Contemporary American Poets,* William Heyen has won a John Simon Guggenheim Memorial Foundation Fellowship, the Eunice Tietjens Memorial Prize from *Poetry* Magazine, two fellowships from the National Endowment for the Arts, and the Witter Bynner Prize for poetry from the American Academy of Arts and Letters.

A. POULIN, JR. was born in Lisbon, Maine. He was educated at St. Francis College, Loyola University, and holds an M.F.A. from the University of Iowa. Since 1971, Poulin has taught at SUNY College at Brockport, where he is Professor of English (on leave) and a past director of The Writers Forum. Mr. Poulin has been the recipient of a fellowship from the National Endowment for the Arts, a translation award from Columbia University's Translation Center, and many other awards. A poet, translator, and editor, he is founding editor and publisher of BOA Editions, and has translated Rilke from both the German and the French. His anthology, *Contemporary American Poetry* (Houghton Mifflin), is now in its fourth edition. In addition, he has published several volumes of his own poetry, including *In Advent, The Slaughter of Pigs,* and, most recently, *A Momentary Order* (Graywolf, 1987).

Acknowledgments

Some of these interviews first appeared in the following journals:

Arizona Quarterly: A Conversation with Michael S. Harper.

Ball State University Forum: A Conversation with Paul Zimmer

Black American Literature Forum 20, no. 3 (Fall 1986): A Conversation with Rita Dove.

Indiana Review 10, no. 3 (Spring 1987): A Conversation with Gregory Orr.

The Literary Review 30, no. 4 (Summer 1987): A Conversation with Stephen Dunn.

Tar River Poetry 26, no. 1 (Fall 1986): A Conversation with Jonathan Holden.

Tar River Poetry 26, no. 2 (Spring 1987): A Conversation with Charles Wright.

Webster Review: A Conversation with Stanley Plumly; A Conversation with Katha Pollitt.

Poems in these interviews were reprinted from:

Bruce Bennett: "The Storyteller" and "Straw Into Gold" were published in *Straw Into Gold* (Cleveland, Ohio: Cleveland State University Press, 1984); "Sort of a Sestina" appeared in *Not Wanting to Write Like Everyone Else* (Brockport, N.Y.: State Street Press, 1987).

Carl Dennis: "Charity," "Letter from John," and "More Music" were published in *The Near World* (New York: William Morrow and Co., 1985).

Rita Dove: "Anti-Father," "Delft," "Dusting," and "Parsley" were published in *Museum* (Pittsburgh, Pa.: Carnegie-Mellon University Press, 1983).

Stephen Dunn: "Corners," "Desire," and "Essay on the Personal" were published in *Not Dancing* (Pittsburgh, Pa.: Carnegie-Mellon University Press, 1984); "The Substitute" appeared in *Local Time* (New York: William Morrow/Quill, 1986).

Michael S. Harper: "'It Takes a Helleva Nerve to Sell Water'" was published in *Healing Song for the Inner Ear* (Urbana: University of Illinois Press, 1985).

Edward Hirsch: "I Need Help," "Omen," and "The Skokie Theatre" were published in *Wild Gratitude* (New York: Alfred A. Knopf, 1986).

Jonathan Holden: "An American Boyhood" and "Seventeen" appeared in *Leverage* (Charlottesville: University Press of Virginia, 1983); "The Edge," "Falling from Stardom," and "Junk" were published in *Falling from Stardom* (Pittsburgh, Pa.: Carnegie-Mellon University Press, 1984).

William Matthews: "Whiplash" was published in A *Happy Childhood* (Boston: Little, Brown and Company, 1984); "*Lucky* and *Unlucky*" and "Self-knowledge" are from *Foreseeable Futures* (Boston: Houghton Mifflin, 1987), copyright © 1987 by William Matthews. Reprinted by permission of Houghton Mifflin Co.

Robert Morgan: "Mountain Bride" by Robert Morgan is taken from his book of poems, *Groundwork* (Frankfort, Ky.: Gnomon Press, 1979), published by Gnomon Press, P.O. Box 106, Frankfort, KY 40602-0106. Permission to reprint "Mountain Bride" courtesy of Gnomon Press. "Buffalo Trace" and "The Gift of Tongues," copyright © 1987 by Robert Morgan, reprinted from *At the Edge of the Orchard Country* (Middletown, Conn.: Wesleyan University Press, 1987) by permission of Wesleyan University Press.

Lisel Mueller: "My Grandmother's Gold Pin" was published in *The Private Life* (Baton Rouge: Louisiana State University Press, 1976); "The Story" appeared in *The Need to Hold Still* (Baton Rouge: Louisiana State University Press, 1980); "After Whistler" was published in *Second Language* (Baton Rouge: Louisiana State University Press, 1986).

Gregory Orr: "The Lost Children" appeared in *The Red House* (New York: Harper & Row, 1980); "After Botticelli's 'Birth of Venus,'" copyright © 1986 by Gregory Orr reprinted from *We Must Make a Kingdom of It* (Middletown, Conn.: Wesleyan University Press, 1986) by permission of Wesleyan University Press.

Linda Pastan: "Eclipse," "Go Gentle," "Short Story," "To A Daughter," and "You are Odysseus" reprinted from *Aspects of Eve* (New York: Liveright, 1975), poems by Linda Pastan, by permission of Liveright Publishing Corporation. Copyright © 1970, 1971, 1972, 1973, 1974, 1975 by Linda Pastan.

Stanley Plumly: "Valentine" was published in *Summer Celestial* (New York: Ecco Press, 1983); "Say Summer/For My Mother" and "This Poem" were published in *Out-of-the-Body Travel* (New York: Ecco Press, 1976).

Katha Pollitt: "Archaeology" and "In Memory" appeared in *Antarctic Traveller* (New York: Alfred A. Knopf, 1981).

Philip Schultz: "Laughter" was published in *Like Wings* (New York: Viking Press, 1978); "Anemone," "Ode," and "Ode to Desire" appeared in *Deep Within the Ravine* (New York: Viking Press, 1984).

Michael Waters: "Apples" and "In Memory of Smoke" were published in *Not Just Any Death* (Brockport, N.Y.: BOA Editions, 1979); "Lipstick" appeared in *The Ohio Review*; "The Mystery of the Caves" and "Singles" appeared in *Anniversary of the Air* (Pittsburgh, Pa.: Carnegie-Mellon University Press, 1985).

Nancy Willard: "The Graffiti Poet" and "The Poet Invites the Moon for Supper" were printed in *Carpenter of the Sun* (New York: Liveright, 1974); "When We Come Home, Blake Calls for Fire" was published in *A Visit to William Blake's Inn* (New York: Harcourt Brace Jovanovich, 1981); "Questions My Son Asked Me, Answers I Never Gave Him" appeared in *Household Tales of Moon and Water* (New York: Harcourt Brace Jovanovich, 1987).

Charles Wright: "Ars Poetica" was printed in *The Southern Cross* (New York: Random House, 1981); "Dog Creek Mainline," copyright © 1972 by Charles Wright reprinted from *Country Music: Selected Early Poems* (Middletown, Conn.: Wesleyan University Press, 1982) by permission of Wesleyan University Press. This poem first appeared in *Poetry* magazine. "The New Poem," copyright © 1971 by Charles Wright reprinted from *Country Music* (Middletown, Conn.: Wesleyan University Press, 1982) by permission of Wesleyan University Press. This poem first appeared in *The Venice Notebook* (Barn Dream Press).

Paul Zimmer: "Dear Wanda" appeared in *With Wanda: Town and Country Poems* (Washington, D.C.: Dryad Press, 1980); "The Eisenhower Years," "An Enzyme Poem for Suzanne," "Wanda Being Beautiful," and "Zimmer Warns Himself With Vivid Images Against Old Age" were published in *Family Reunion: Selected and New Poems* (Pittsburgh, Pa.: University of Pittsburgh Press, 1983).

Photo Credits

Bruce Bennett by Jim Keller; Carl Dennis by Heidi Cretien; Rita Dove by Fred Viebahn; Stephen Dunn by Donna Connor; Michael S. Harper by Chip Cooper; Edward Hirsch by Janet Landay; Jonathan Holden by Steve Briggs; William Matthews by Star Black; Robert Morgan by Hank DeLeo; Lisel Mueller by *Libertyville Independent Register*; Gregory Orr by Tom Cogill; Linda Pastan by George Murphy; Stanley Plumly by Brigitta Shroyer; Katha Pollitt by Helen Ganly; Philip Schultz by Thomas Victor; Michael Waters by Rick Maloof; Nancy Willard by Eric Lindbloom; Charles Wright by William Stafford.

DATE DUE